IMAGES
of America

ELK COUNTY

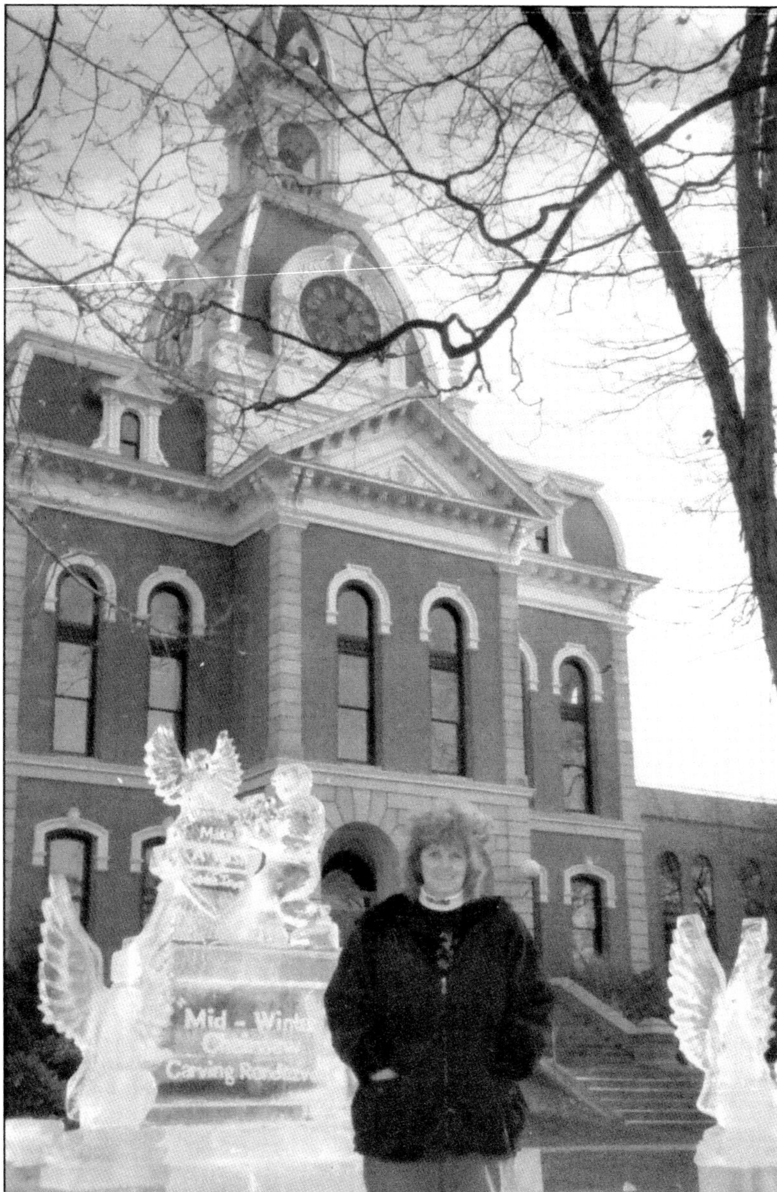

Elk County pays homage to its lumbering and logging heritage today with an annual Chainsaw Carvers Rendezvous in mid-February. Chainsaw carvers from around the world are drawn to Ridgway, the county seat, to compete in carving both ice and wood with chainsaws to benefit charity. Note the life-size ice sculpture of a chainsaw carver in front of the Elk County Courthouse. (Dennis McGeehan.)

On the cover: Here is a scene of Main Street in Kersey, located in Fox Township. Kersey was located on the Milesburg-Smethport Turnpike and was an early community in Elk County. The road was unpaved and there was little traffic, so residents could pose in the middle of the road. A photographer must have been a novelty at the time. (St. Marys and Benzinger Township Historical Society.)

IMAGES
of America

ELK COUNTY

Dennis McGeehan

ARCADIA
PUBLISHING

ISBN 978-0-7385-5479-2

Published by Arcadia Publishing
Charleston, South Carolina

Printed in the United States of America

Library of Congress Control Number: 2007926054

For all general information contact Arcadia Publishing at:
Telephone 843-853-2070
Fax 843-853-0044
E-mail sales@arcadiapublishing.com
For customer service and orders:
Toll-Free 1-888-313-2665

Visit us on the Internet at www.arcadiapublishing.com

Dedicated to Deb, my constant companion, who always waits for me

Contents

Acknowledgments 6

Introduction 7

1. Town and Village 9

2. Business and Industry 53

3. Social and Sporting Life 87

ACKNOWLEDGMENTS

I would like to thank all the people who helped me in the preparation of this book: Debra McGeehan for her tireless work at every stage of the process, without whom this book would not have been possible; Mark Wendel and Dave Woods for allowing me to use their collections; Bill Bauer for his extensive knowledge of railroad history; Bill and Paul Krellner for sharing their knowledge of mining; Mary Miller and Jeanne Dostal, proofreaders; Dick Dornisch, critic; Ray Beimel; John Imhoff; Mark and Bekki Titchner; Melna Simbeck; John Dill; Bob Beimel; James O. Auman; Michael J. DeStefano; Pete Winklbauer; Frances Hack; John T. and Elizabeth D. McGeehan; the late Charles J. Schaut; and the late Edwin Grotzinger.

I would also like to thank all fellow directors of the St. Marys and Benzinger Township Historical Society for their support.

All photographs, unless otherwise noted, are courtesy of the St. Marys and Benzinger Township Historical Society.

INTRODUCTION

Elk County is a mountainous region located in north-central Pennsylvania. The area sits atop the eastern continental divide with half of the county draining toward the Atlantic Ocean and half toward the Mississippi River. Because of its remote location and inaccessibility, the region was settled relatively late. Pioneers had already reached the Mississippi River before venturing into the wilds of north-central Pennsylvania in the late 18th century. Another reason this region was settled so late was Native American control of the area. The Cornplanter Branch, Seneca tribe of the Iroquois Confederation used this region as hunting grounds and defended it with fierce determination long after the frontier had moved west. Ruins of several Native American fortifications have been excavated in Elk County and a branch of the Iroquois Main Road Native American trail is known to have traversed the county. Early maps label this section of the state as the "Great Buffalo Swamp" or the "Great Wildcat Swamp."

The first white pioneers to Elk County were John Bennett and his father, who came up the Bennetts Branch of Sinnemahoning Creek in 1787 to the present village of Caledonia, to trap beavers. In 1798, a General Wade and Lieutenant Slade penetrated to the headwaters of Toby Creek on a mission to remove Native Americans.

The first permanent settlers in Elk County arrived at the headwaters of Toby Creek in 1810 to found Centreville (later Kersey) where William Kersey built a gristmill.

Also in 1810, David Johnson settled at the junction of the East and West Branches of the Clarion River. Johnson was associated with Benjamin F. Cooper, who had purchased the land around the forks of the Clarion. Johnson shortly moved on, but the town that would grow at the site would be named Johnsonburg. Johnsonburg's survival would be ensured in 1888 when the Clarion Pulp and Paper Company was founded by Meylert M. Armstong Sr. The Johnsonburg paper mill has been a prosperous concern ever since.

Jacob Ridgway, a wealthy Philadelphia Quaker, purchased a large tract of land in the area and sent his agent James L. Gillis to manage his holdings. In 1821, Gillis and his family settled the area of Montmorenci but soon moved down to the better-located site on the Clarion River to found the town of Ridgway. The town of Ridgway became an important lumbering center and the source of log drives and timber rafting to markets down the Clarion River. Allied industries of timber sprang up such as tanning and wood chemical plants. In 1843, Elk County was created from surrounding counties with Ridgway as the county seat.

In 1842, a group of German Catholic settlers from Philadelphia and Baltimore founded the settlement of St. Marys on the banks of Elk Creek. St. Marys would eventually become the largest city in the county and the industrial center. Lumber, coal, and clay products fueled

St. Marys's early development. However, looking to the future when extractive industries would be depleted, lumber baron Andrew Kaul in 1899 brought in John Speer, and together they founded Speer Carbon Company. St. Marys would become the leader in the world in carbon products. Kaul's son-in-law H. C. Stackpole founded the Stackpole Carbon Company, which for many years was the leading employer in the county. Today the allied industries of powdered metal and tool and die making provide Elk County with a solid industrial base.

In 1858, the settlement called Buena Vista (beautiful view) was renamed Wilcox, after Alonzo I. Wilcox, a prominent lumberman of the area on the West Branch of the Clarion River. Wood and its by-products insured the town's growth. At one time Wilcox boasted of the world's largest tannery, but the town quickly declined after the timber was harvested.

Bennetts Valley's prosperity was based on coal. Strip-mining made many fortunes in the valley, and this occupation is still being carried on today.

The entire region's economy declined after the era of the big timber. However, the second-growth forest and the area's remote location have made Elk County today a sportsmen's paradise. Fishing, hunting, and camping draw many visitors to this land of natural beauty. A wild elk herd is one of the few such populations in the east. The large numbers of elk that used to abound in the area have given Elk County its name, and the herd is today a major tourist attraction.

Elk County is known far and wide for the small, privately owned Straub Brewery that attracts beer connoisseurs from around the country and the world.

Elk County has associations with several well-known people. Thomas L. Kane started the famous Civil War regiment the "Bucktails," whose members were drawn from Elk County and the surrounding region. Kane stayed in northern Elk County before founding the town that bears his name just north of the county. Kane often fished the waters of Elk County, several times with his friend Pres. Ulysses S. Grant. The famous cowboy movie star Tom Mix was born in Mix Run on the Cameron/Elk County border. In 1979, St. Marys native Edward C. Meyer was named U.S. army chief of staff. Hall of fame baseball pitcher George "Rube" Waddell was a St. Marys resident.

A local legend holds that "Mad Anthony" Wayne haunts the area of Highland since one of his bones was lost in the area as his body was being transported from Erie to Philadelphia for reburial. There is also a fortune in gold bars lost in the Dents Run area from a Civil War shipment that has never been recovered. Another tale is of the marriage of Lieutenant Slade and the Native American maid of Blue Rock after a Native American skirmish with pioneers on Toby Creek. Legendary woodsmen, mythical animals, ghosts, bad men, and good men all inhabit the Elk County of lore and song. Fires, floods, tornadoes, and hard times have failed to drive away the people who love Elk County.

Elk County's primeval forest, which nurtured the Native Americans for so many years, was rugged and remote. Its wilderness character was a barrier to European pioneers. However, eventually trails, roads, and railroads snaked into the region and carried away the big timber. Millionaires were made in the blanket of green that covered the summit between the Clarion and Sinnemahoning drainages. Logs flowed down the mighty rivers of the Allegheny and Susquehanna until the woodhick camps, the sawmills, and the tanneries went silent one by one. Some Elk County towns evolved into new enterprises. Others became ghost towns that live on in the memories of one-room schoolhouses of remote fastness. However, the empty green carpet harbored the seed that would bloom anew. As the new forest grew, one by one the lovers of wild places would return. Today hunters and fishermen, hikers and canoeists, bird-watchers and photographers are drawn back up the rivers and streams from Pittsburgh and Philadelphia and all corners to celebrate the land. Old ghost towns reverberate with the sounds they once knew. Wilderness camp crossroads come alive for another fishing or hunting season. The people who stayed and endured find their roots in the sense of this place. Visitors to Elk County come to enjoy its history and legends, its wilderness scenery, and its mountain music.

One

TOWN AND VILLAGE

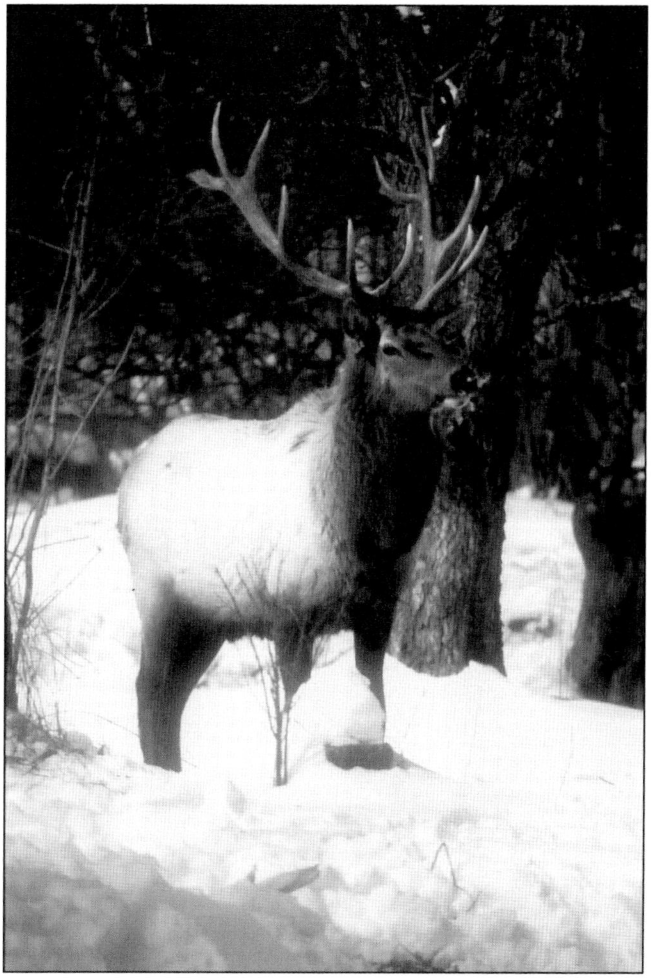

The majestic elk is the namesake and symbol of Elk County. After the original herd was all killed off, elk from the Rocky Mountains were reintroduced into Pennsylvania in 1913. For a time the herd dwindled to a precious few, but today the elk herd is thriving, and a limited hunt now brings much tourist revenue into the area. (Dennis McGeehan Wildlife Photography.)

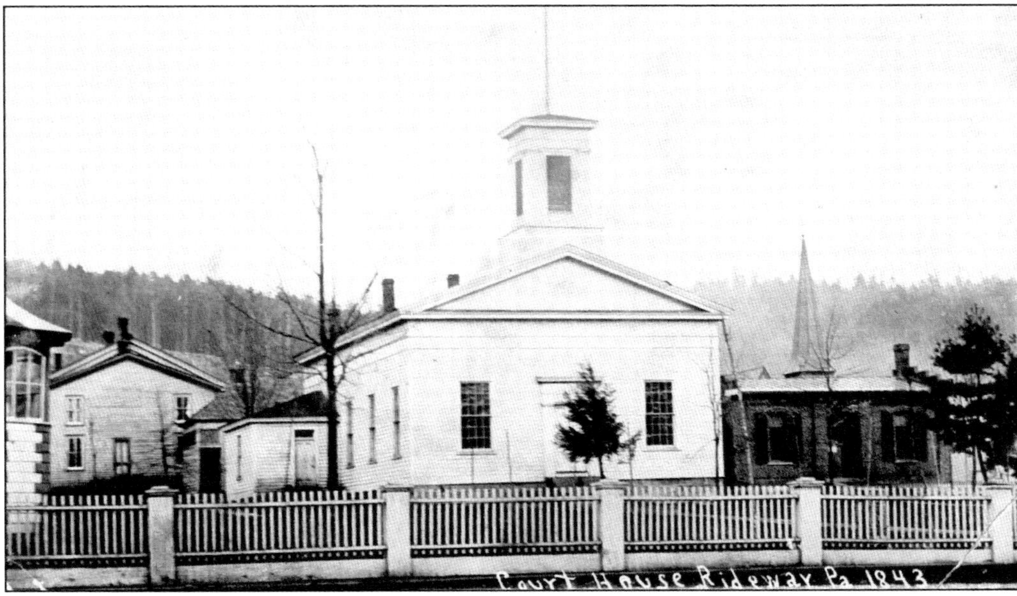

The first Elk County Courthouse in Ridgway was built in 1845 of wood frame construction by Edward H. Derby. He had also built the Clarion County Courthouse. The building served as a courthouse for 34 years before being condemned. In 1879, a new courthouse was built of red brick and dressed local sandstone. The architect and builder was J. P. Marston, who had recently completed the Warren County Courthouse. (Dave Woods.)

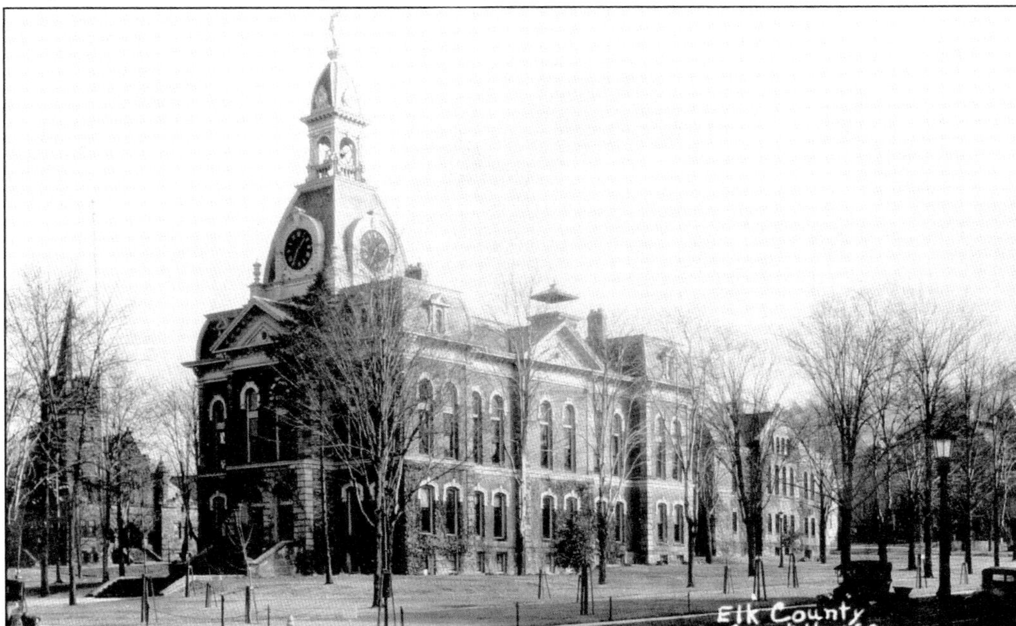

The present Elk County Courthouse has three stories with a mansard roof surmounted by an elegant, slate-covered tower. The tower included a nine-foot diameter clock, a 1,000-pound steel bell, and a nine-and-a-half-foot zinc statue of the Goddess of Justice that was struck by lightning and removed. The courthouse is approached by a grand staircase. Today the grounds are accented with lampposts, cannons, and stately trees.

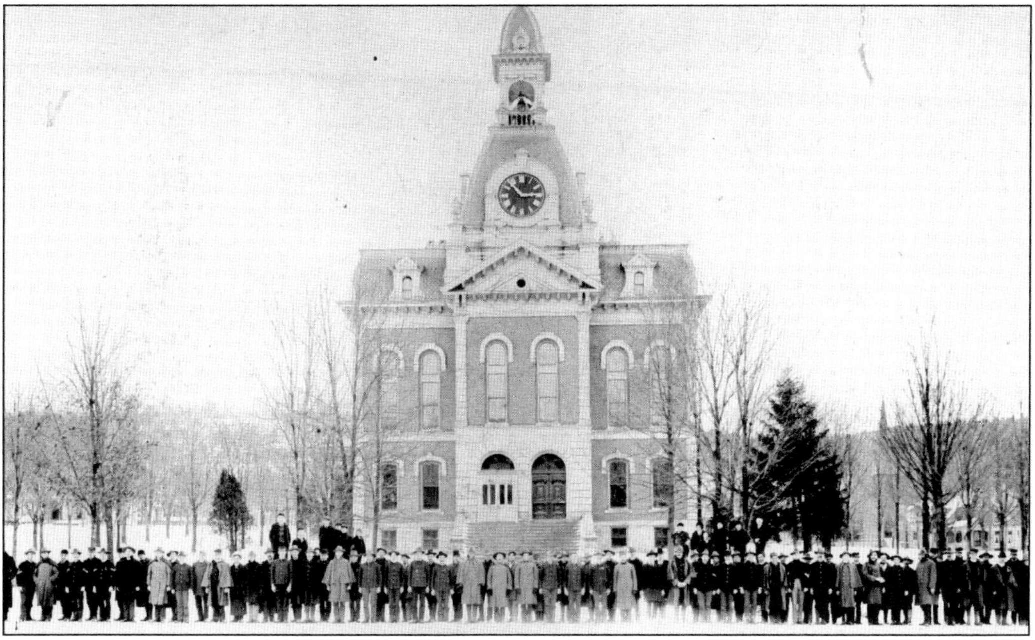

Elk County has a long tradition of military service to the nation. Memorial Day and Veterans Day services are always well attended. One Revolutionary War veteran is buried in Elk County. The famous Bucktail Regiment included a company of Elk County Rifles. In this photograph, Company H veterans of the Spanish-American War pose at a reunion in front of the courthouse.

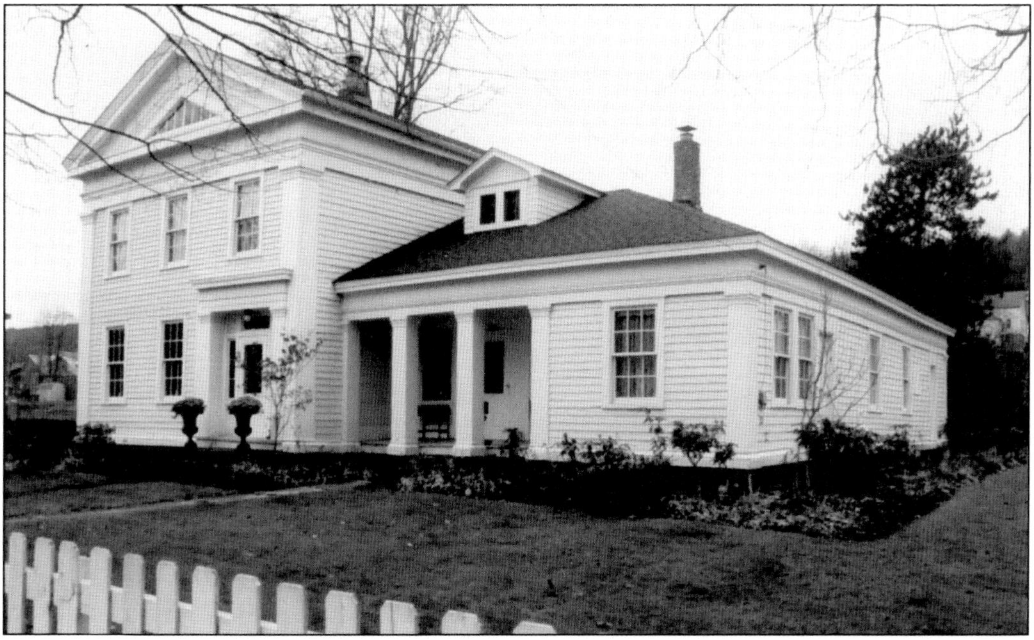

The George Dickinson House on West Main Street is the oldest residence in Ridgway Borough. George Dickinson came to Ridgway from New York State in 1832. He erected a water-powered sawmill and developed the area of west Ridgway. He also built a store in west Ridgway and was involved in many other businesses. (Dennis McGeehan.)

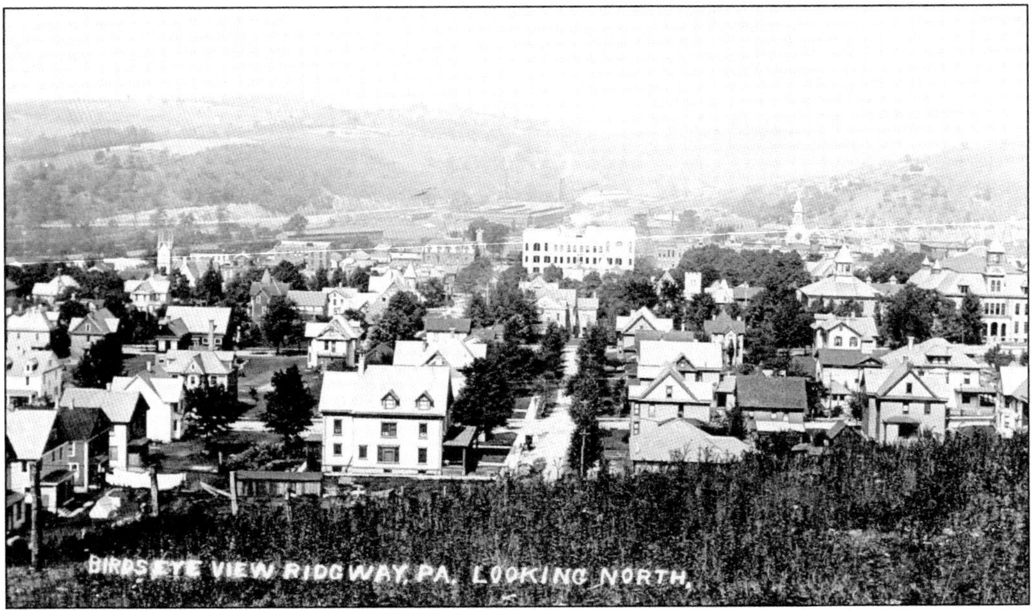

This photograph shows Ridgway looking north. The view is up the valley of the Clarion River. The industrial section of Ridgway is apparent in the smokestacks along the river at the top. The Elk County Courthouse tower is visible at right center, and the old public school buildings are at middle left. The large white building in the center is the Masonic temple. (Mark Wendel.)

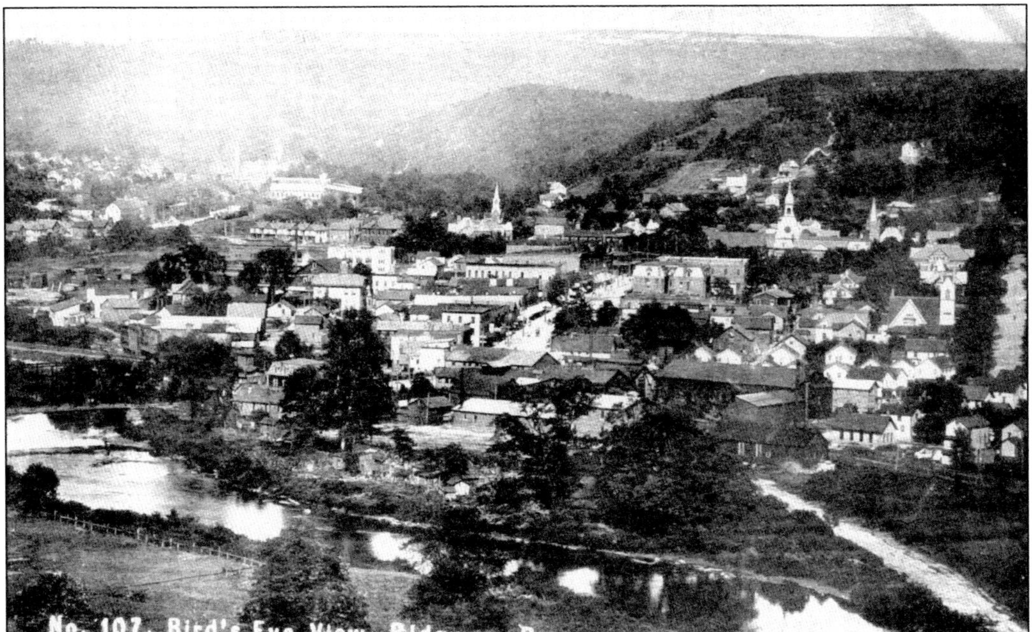

Ridgway is shown looking east. The Clarion River is visible at the bottom of the scene. The Elk County Courthouse is in the middle right with Main Street in front of it. The valley of the Clarion River flows toward the top left of the view on to Johnsonburg, and the Elk Creek valley, top right, continues on to St. Marys. (Dave Woods.)

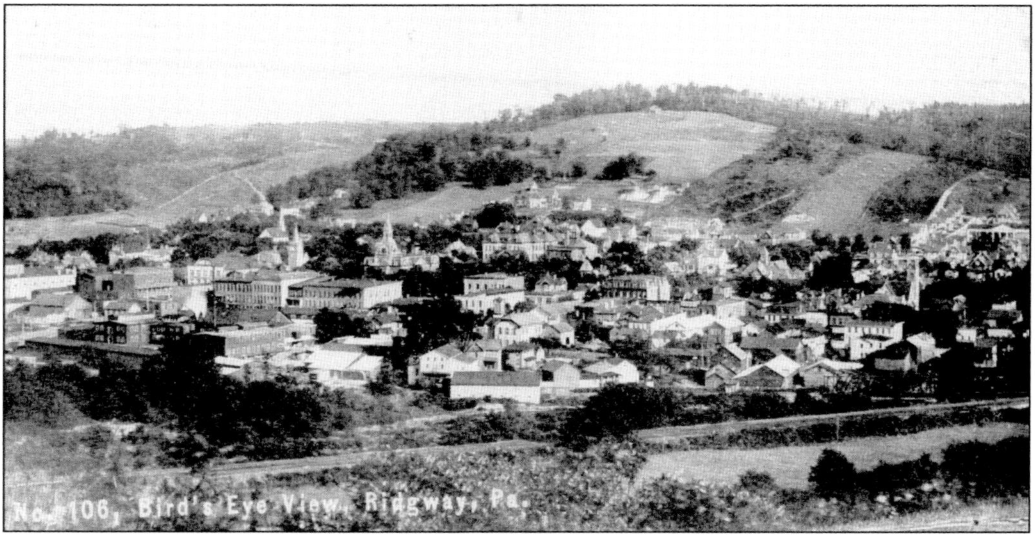

Here is a view of Ridgway looking south. The Elk County Courthouse is just left of center with the Trinity United Methodist Church to the left of the courthouse. The Clarion River is in the foreground. The Elk County General Hospital is on the right edge of the photograph. Note the cleared area on the hill above the town, which is forested today. (Mark Wendel.)

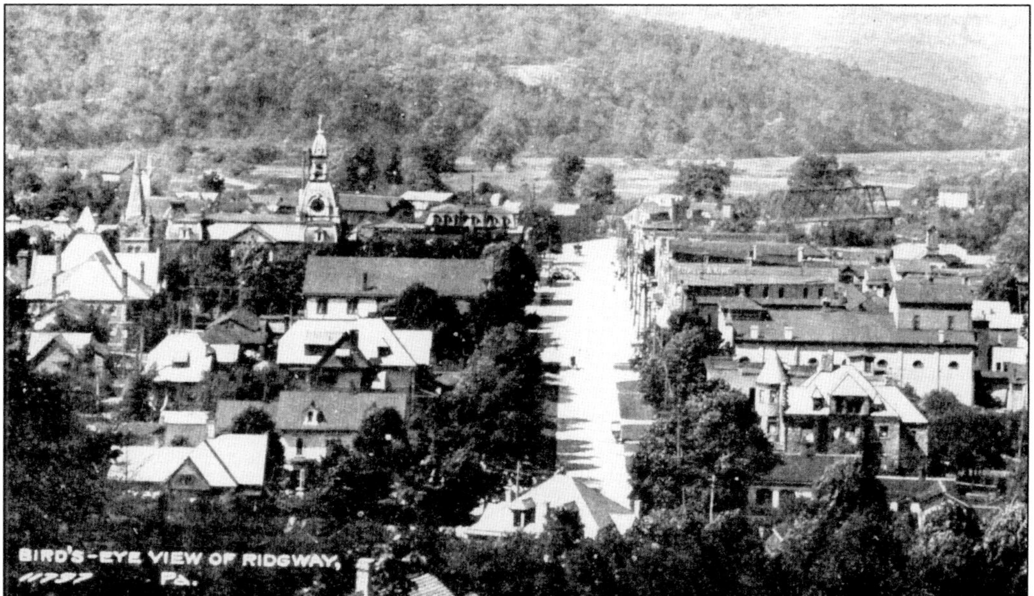

This photograph shows Ridgway looking west. The view is looking down Main Street. The end of Main Street curves to the right, and the bridge over the Clarion River is visible. In the left center of the photograph, the tower of the Elk County Courthouse can be seen. To the left of the courthouse, the Trinity United Methodist Church steeple rises.

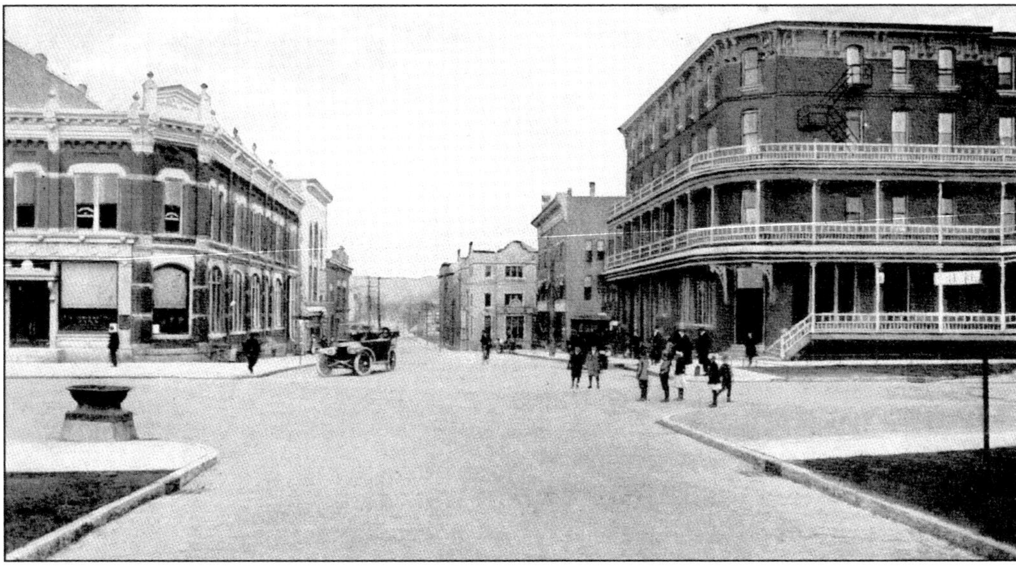

This is the intersection of Broad and Main Streets in Ridgway. On the right is the Hyde Hotel, built in 1858 by Joseph Smith Hyde. In 1890, an addition, much larger than the original, was added. The original section burned in 1891. The hotel was demolished in 1965. National City Bank now occupies the site. The building on the left was formerly the Elk County National Bank. (Mark Wendel.)

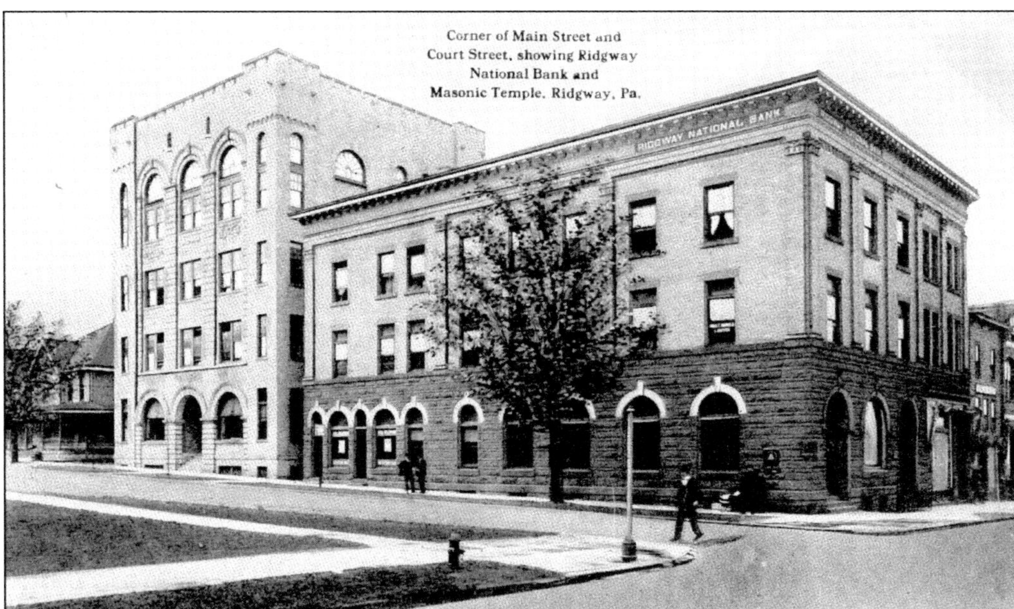

In 1903, the Ridgway National Bank moved into its new building at the corner of Main and Court Streets, across from the Elk County Courthouse. The building was constructed by M. V. Van Etten of Warren, who also built the Elk County Jail. In 1967, the bank moved into new quarters at the corner of Court and Center Streets. The building on the left here is the Masonic temple. (Mark Wendel.)

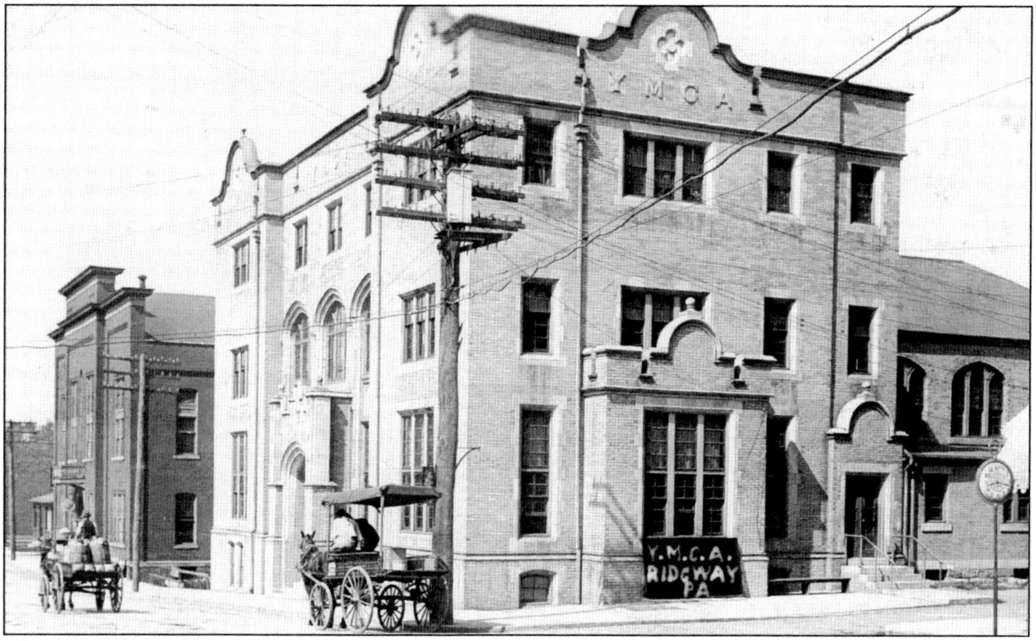

The Young Men's Christian Association (YMCA) in Ridgway was realized largely through the efforts of Dr. W. M. Pierce, superintendent of the Ridgway Borough Schools. When the new building was constructed on North Broad Street, it included a gymnasium and eventually a swimming pool. The YMCA was used for classes, lectures, and theatrical and musical performances. At the left of the YMCA in this view is the Ridgway Armory building. (Dave Woods.)

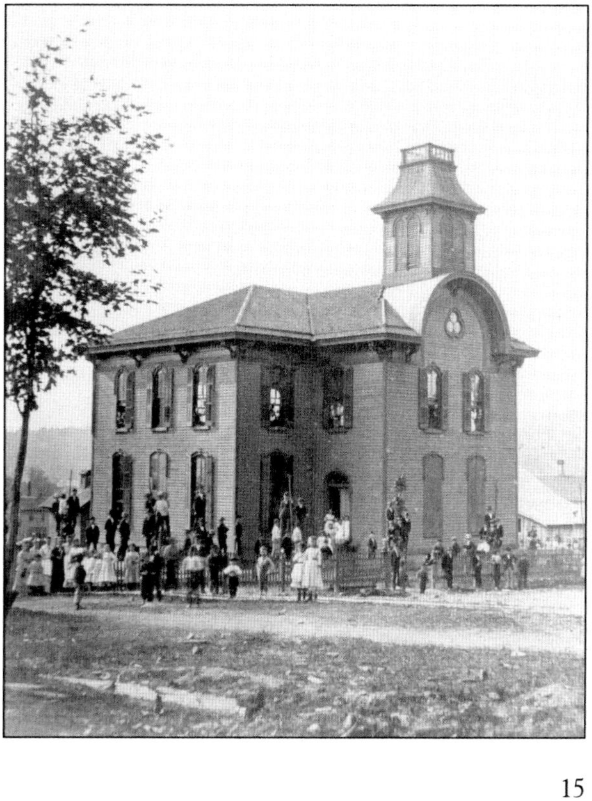
In 1870, when Ridgway needed a larger school, this two-story frame building was built at the corner of South Broad and South Streets. At the time it was the largest school building in Elk County. This building was torn down to make way for an even larger school in 1899. This photograph appears to have been taken during recess. (Dave Woods.)

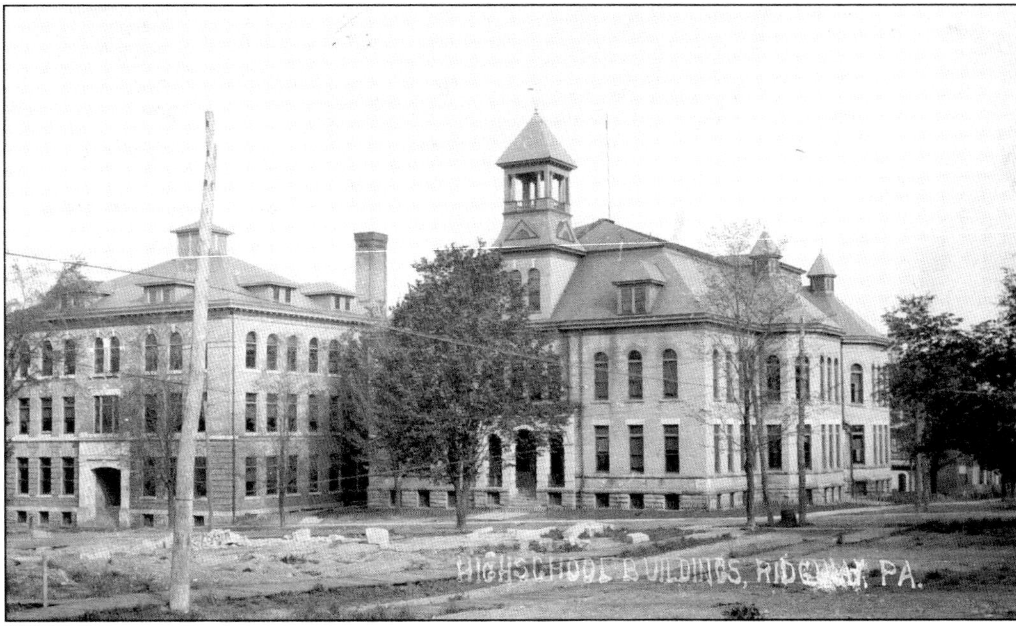

On the right is the 1899 school, known as Central, and on the left is the 1909 high school building. The 1909 building was torn down in the early 1960s, and the lot was turned into a playground. The Central school was refurbished, had the tower removed, and today is the Udarbe Complex, which houses medical offices. (Dave Woods.)

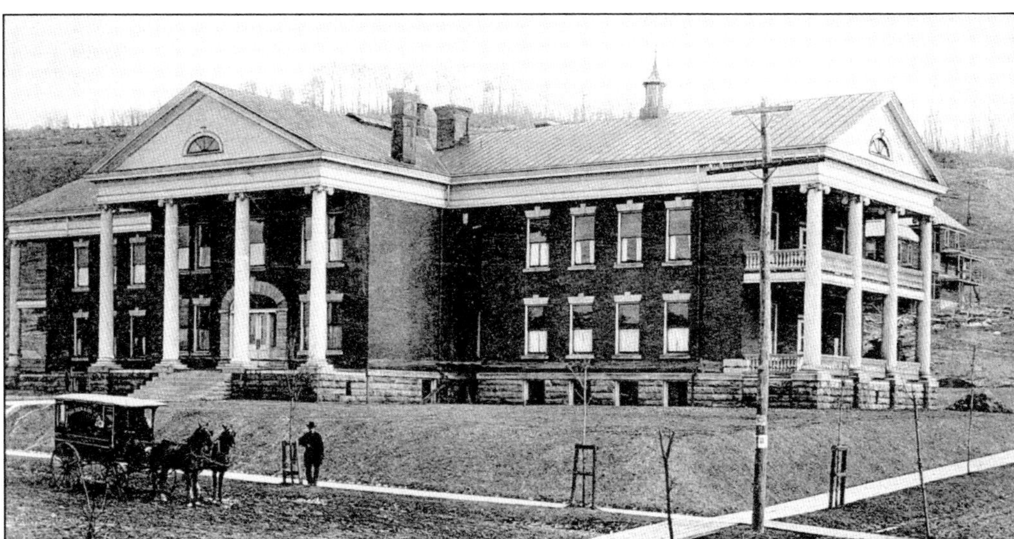

The first Elk County General Hospital was built in Ridgway in 1901 by local architect H. C. Park. An adjacent nurses' home was built in 1907. Additions to the hospital were built in 1925 and 1959. In 1980, the 1959 building was renovated, with the 1901 and 1925 buildings removed for parking. Today the complex is part of the Elk Regional Health Center. (Dave Woods.)

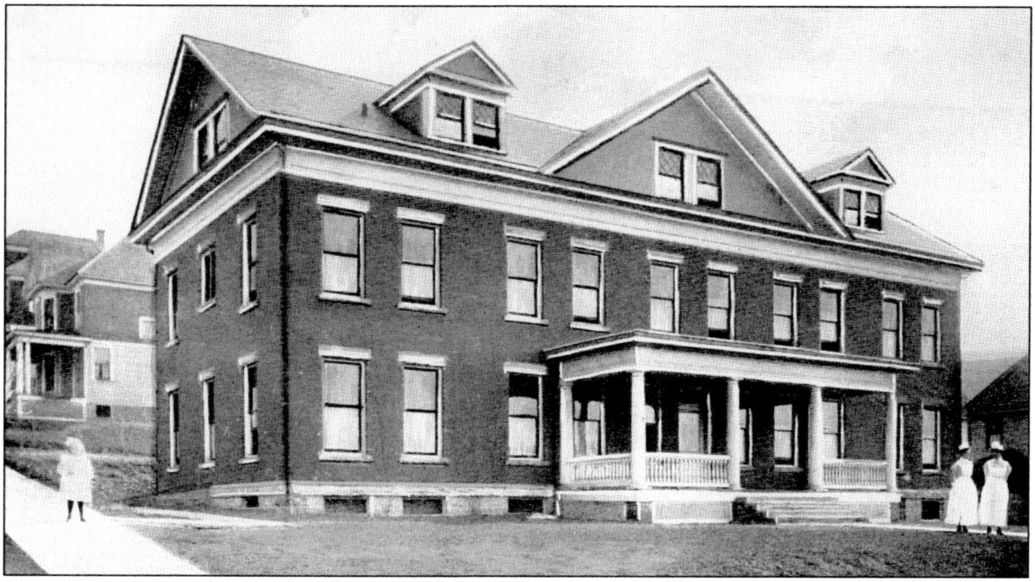

The former Elk County General Hospital nurses' home in Ridgway became the first outpatient psychiatric clinic to operate in a rural area in Pennsylvania, in 1958. Under the guidance of Dr. Robert J. Dickinson, the facility served a six-county area. It was associated with the Elk County General Hospital until 1960, when it became an independent corporation. (Mark Wendel.)

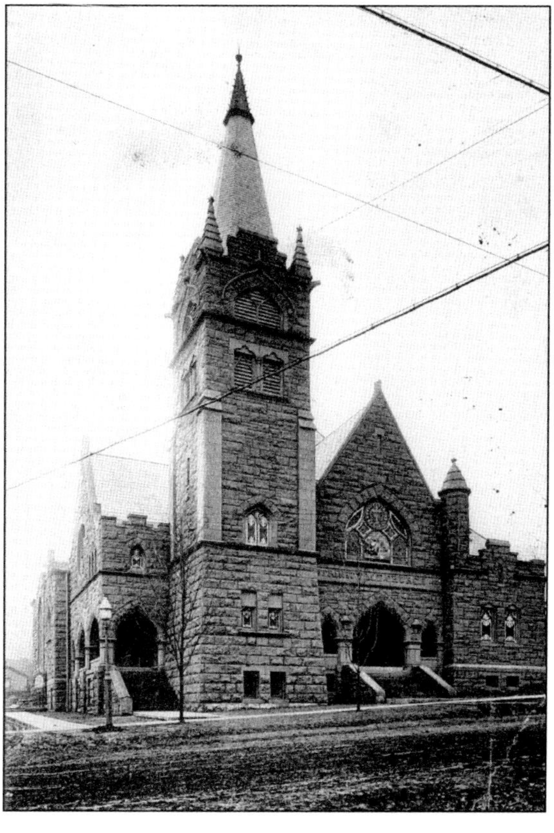

The Trinity United Methodist Church was built on South Broad Street in Ridgway in 1903. This handsome structure was built of Hummelstown brownstone and is located across the street from the Elk County Courthouse. Reuben Aylesworth is credited with bringing Methodism to Ridgway in 1833. This is the congregation's second building. (Dave Woods.)

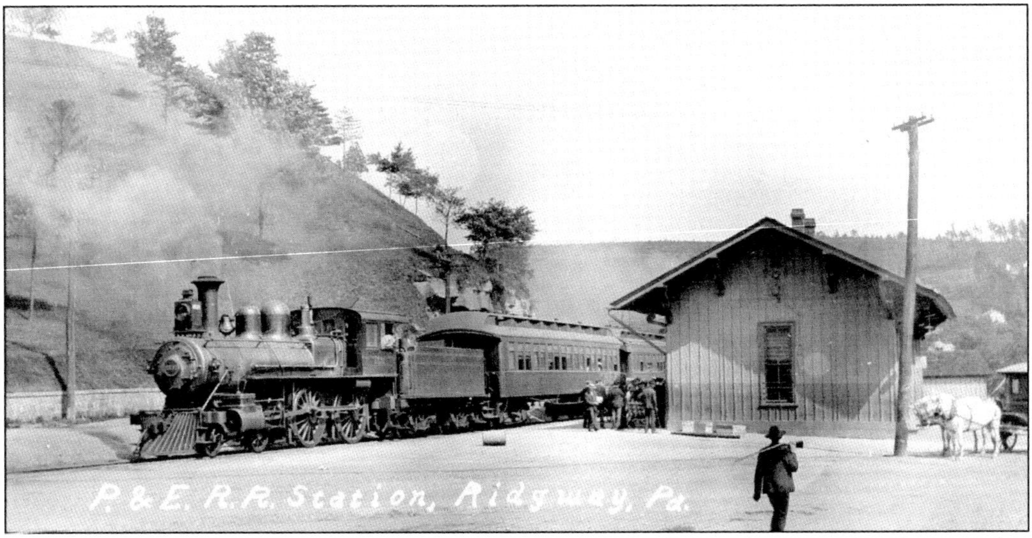

The Sunbury and Erie Railroad was renamed the Philadelphia and Erie Railroad. Later this line became part of the giant Pennsylvania Railroad. This is its passenger station in Ridgway at North Broad and Osterhout Streets. The coming of the railroad in 1864 brought Elk County out of the wilderness and connected it to the outside world, guaranteeing the county's economic survival. (Dave Woods.)

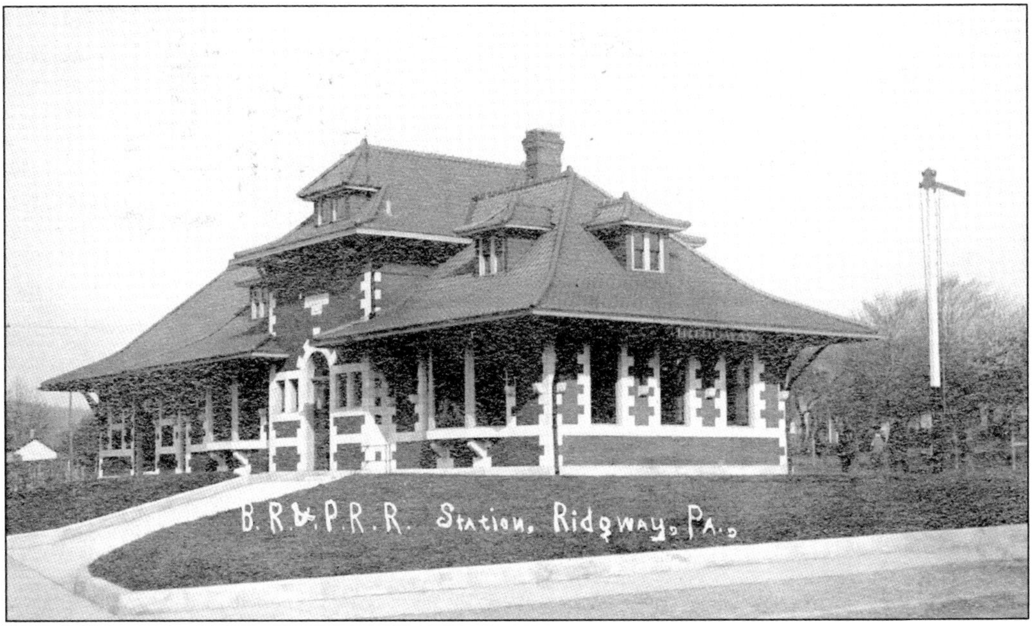

The Buffalo, Rochester and Pittsburgh Railroad traversed Elk County and built this beautiful passenger station in 1903. The major freight of the Buffalo, Rochester and Pittsburgh Railroad was coal and coke to the Great Lakes. In 1932, the Baltimore and Ohio Railroad purchased the Buffalo, Rochester and Pittsburgh Railroad and took over its trackage and stations. (Mark Wendel.)

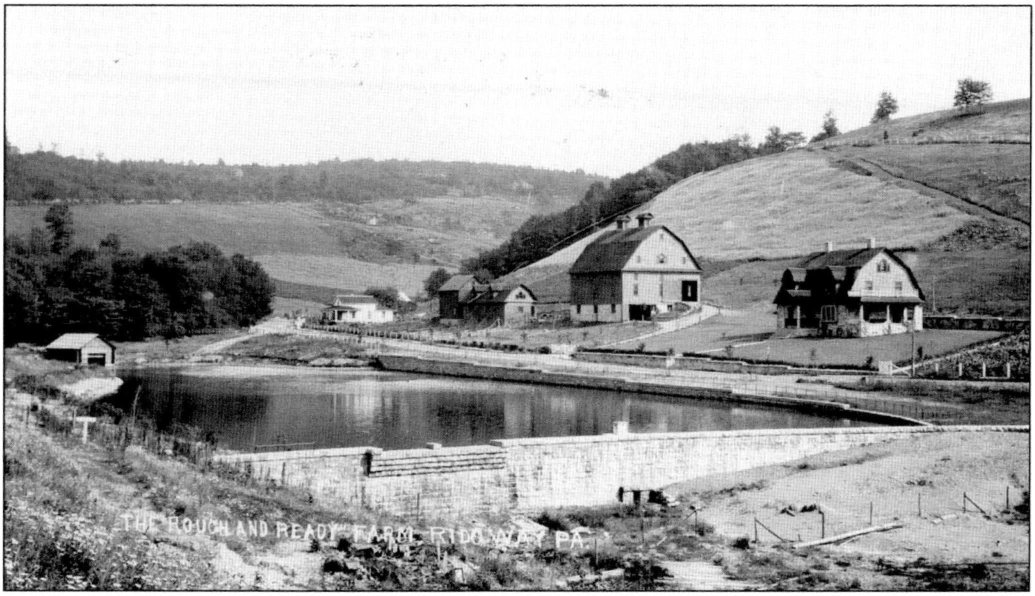

The Rough and Ready Farm in Ridgway was where James Knox Polk (J. K. P.) Hall started his numerous activities in Elk County. Eventually Hall became involved in lumbering, mining, manufacturing, real estate, railroads, law, politics, and philanthropy. He partnered with Andrew Kaul in many activities throughout the Elk County region. (Dave Woods.)

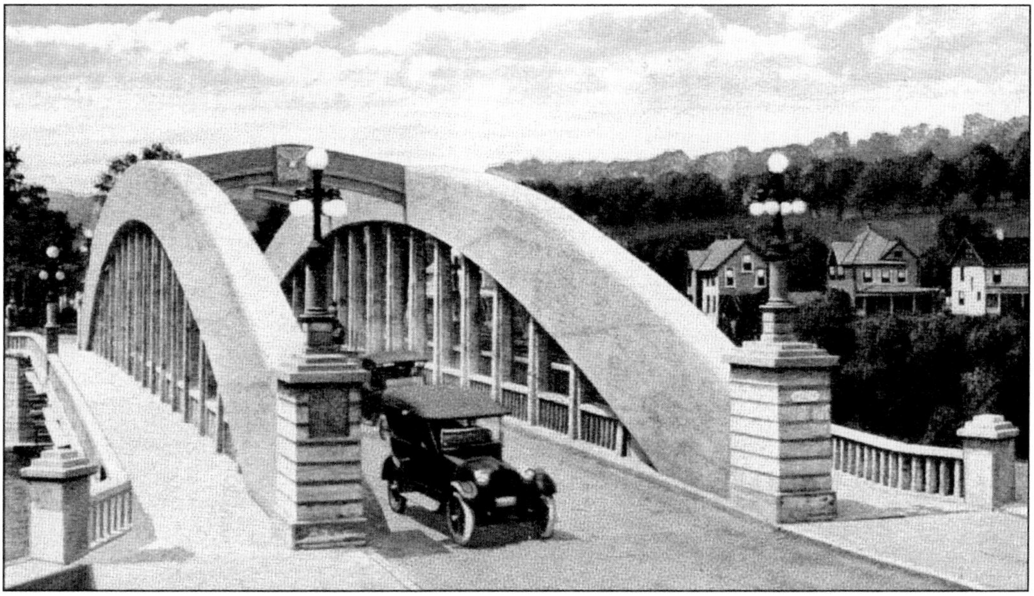

Ridgway is situated on the Clarion River and has had six bridges spanning the river. The first bridge crossing was a toll bridge and had a toll collector's house nearby. The most well-remembered bridge at this site is probably the Will Dickinson Bridge, pictured here, which was built in 1915. Dickinson was the son of pioneer settler George Dickinson.

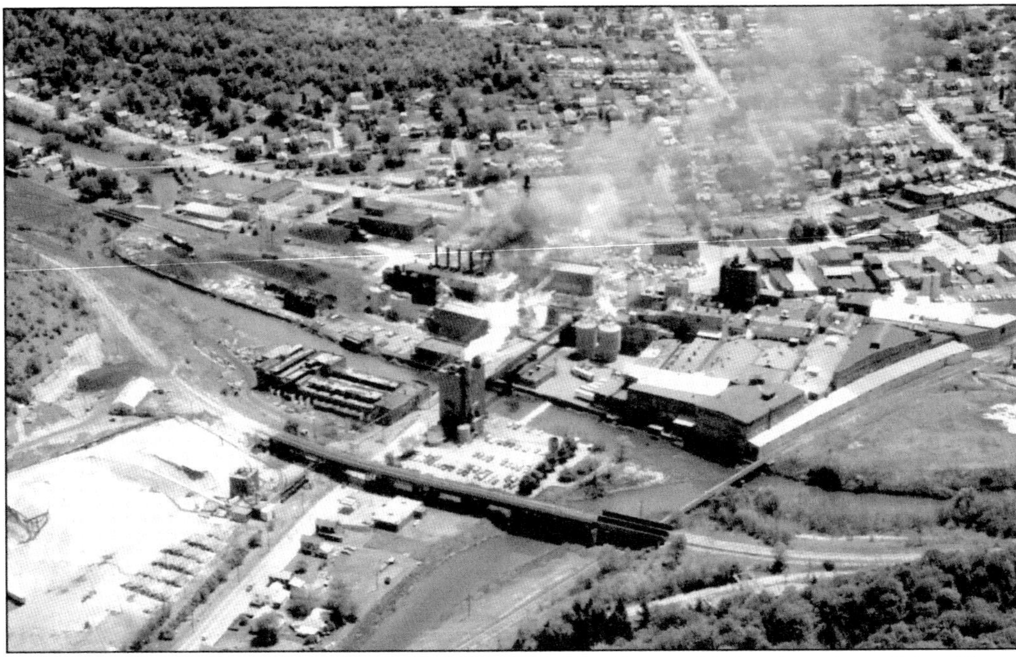

Johnsonburg Borough is located at the confluence of the East and West Branches of the Clarion River. The town is dominated by a paper mill. The mill has been known as the Clarion Pulp and Paper Company, New York and Pennsylvania Company, Penntech, Weyerhauser, Willamette, and Domtar. The large white area in the lower left of this aerial photograph is a huge mound of sawdust. (Photograph by James O. Auman.)

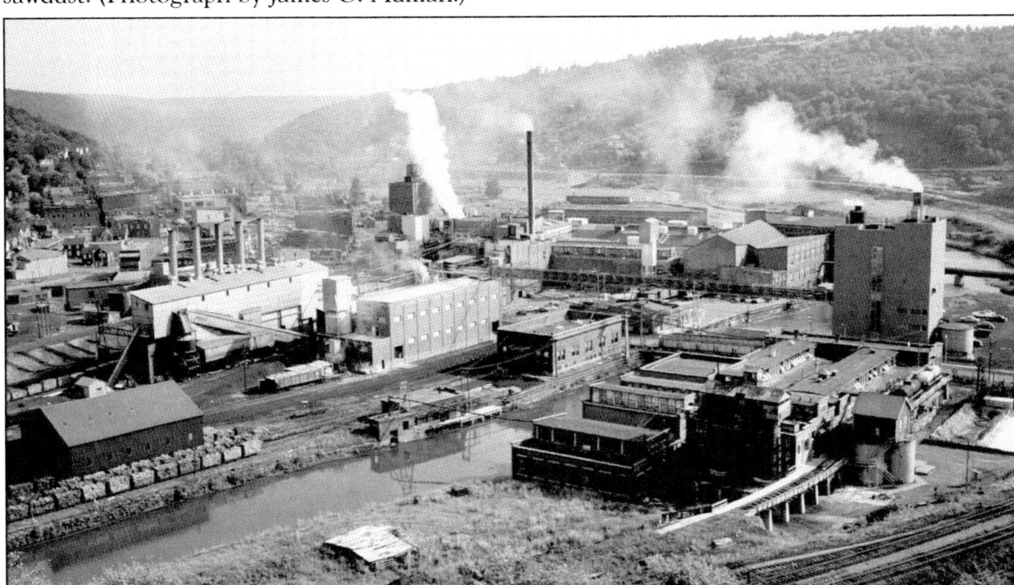

The Johnsonburg paper mill is shown here with the East Branch of the Clarion River flowing through the mill to join the West Branch in the background. Note the long lines of pulpwood cars along the river waiting to be processed. The Philadelphia and Erie (later Pennsylvania) Railroad went through Johnsonburg, giving it access to raw materials and markets. (Grotzinger Collection, St. Marys and Benzinger Township Historical Society.)

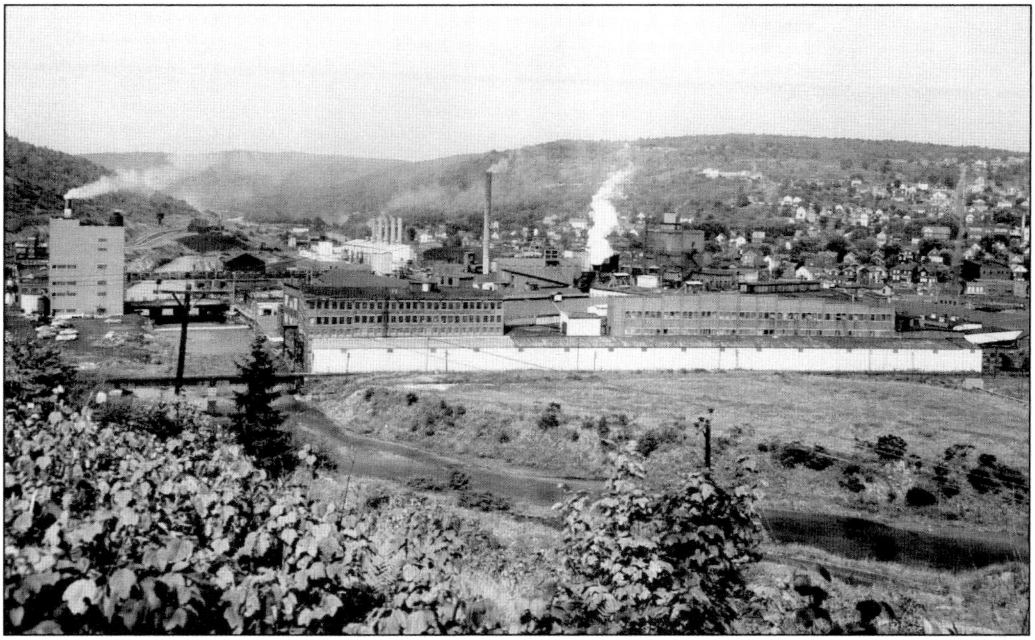

This is a view of the Johnsonburg paper mill looking up the East Branch of the Clarion River valley. The West Branch flows in from the left of this photograph (the juncture is at the large pine tree). Johnsonburg's access to timber, water, and natural gas made it a natural location to manufacture paper. (Grotzinger Collection, St. Marys and Benzinger Township Historical Society.)

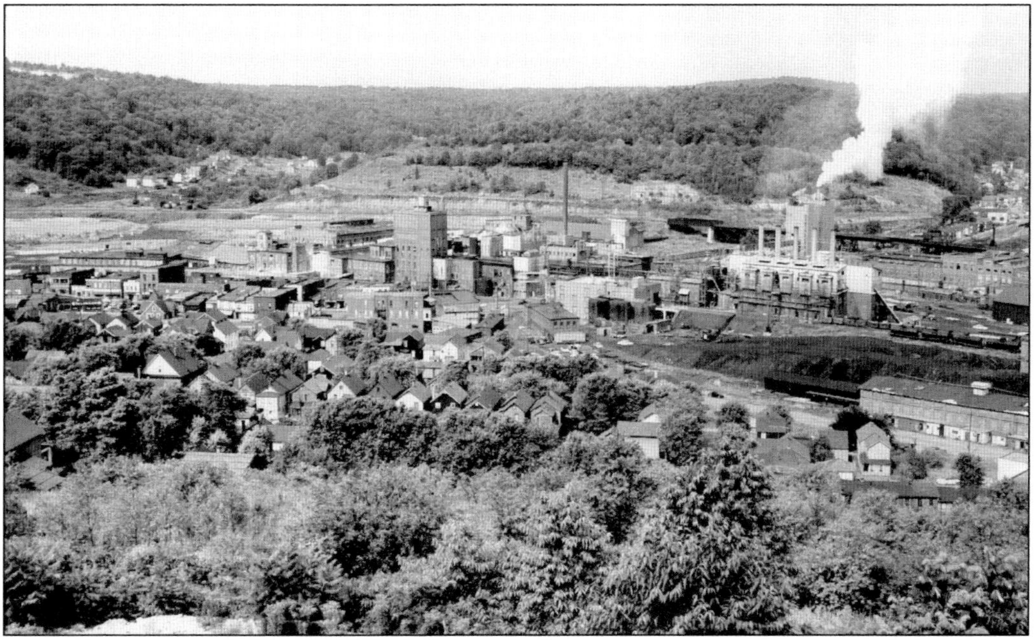

Shown here is the Johnsonburg paper mill in the 1960s. Many of the buildings in this photograph have been remodeled or removed. The mill has been completely renovated and is today a state-of-the-art paper processing facility. Part of Johnsonburg today is Rolfe, founded by a direct descendant of John Rolfe, governor of the Virginia colony. (Grotzinger Collection, St. Marys and Benzinger Township Historical Society.)

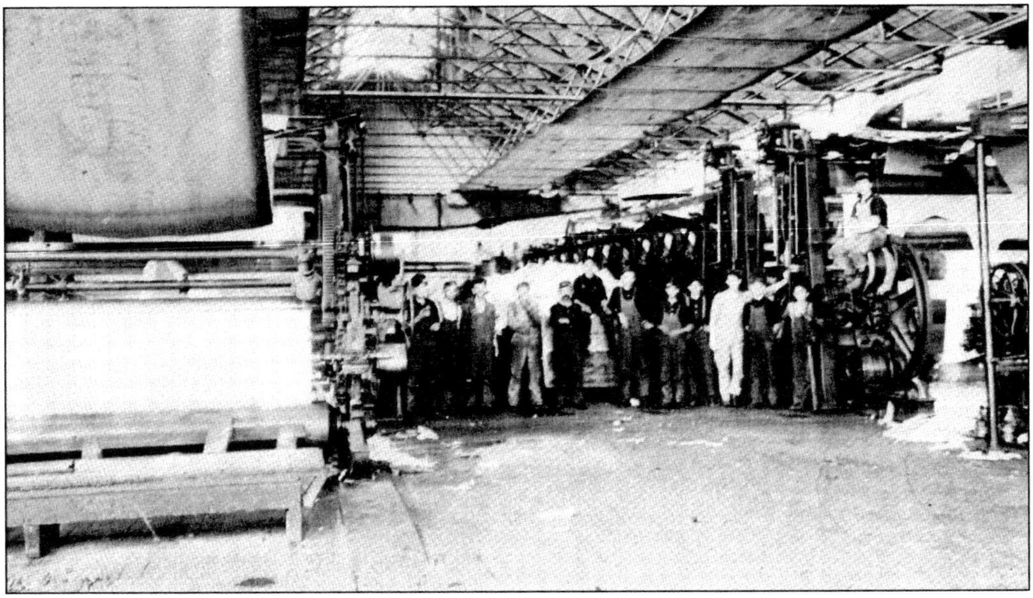

The Johnsonburg paper mill made more coated paper for magazine printing than any other mill in the world. At one time the Curtis Publishing Company controlled the mill and printed paper for its publications, the *Saturday Evening Post* and the *Ladies Home Journal*. The Johnsonburg mill is one of the leading employers in the county. (Mark Wendel.)

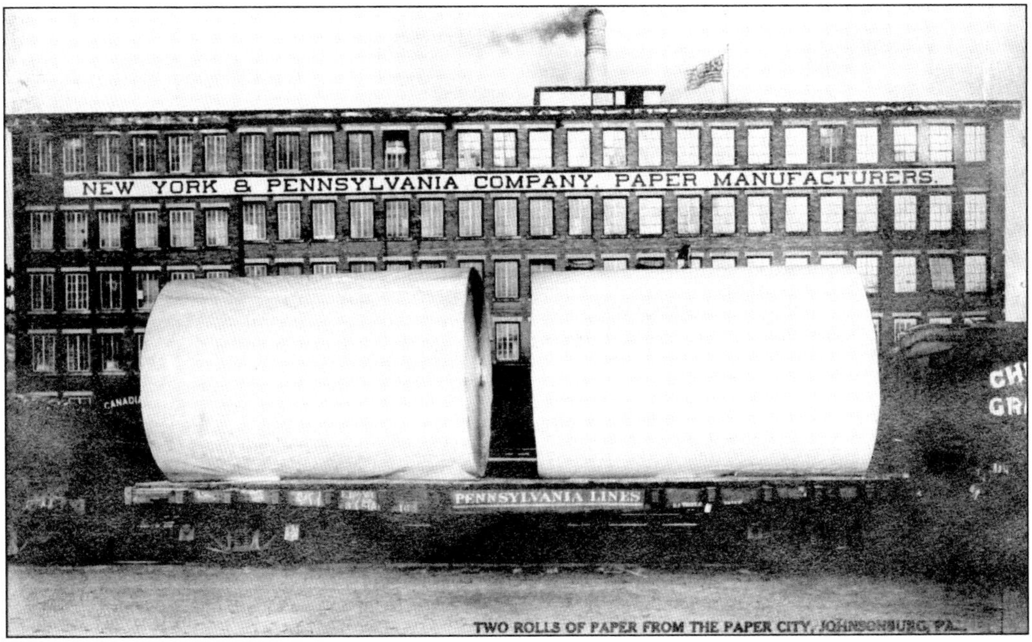

Here is a photograph of the output of the Johnsonburg paper mill when the facility was known as the New York and Pennsylvania Company. These two huge rolls of paper take up an entire railroad flatbed car. The mill itself is its own little city of buildings and storage yards connected by railroads and overhead pipes and wires. (Mark Wendel.)

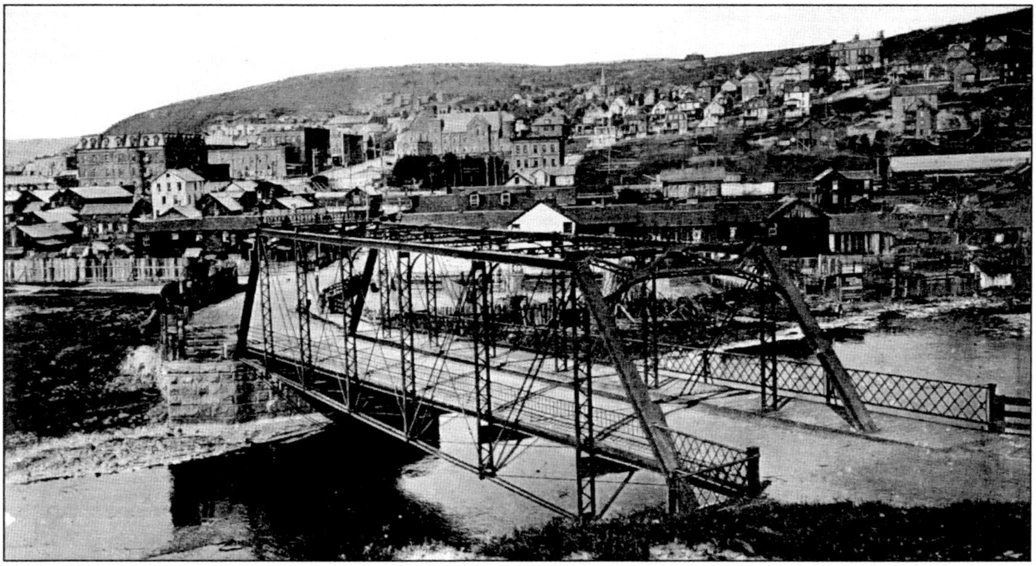

Shown here is the bridge across the Clarion River in Johnsonburg, just below where the East and West Branches join. The river then flows on to Ridgway, the county seat. On the far side of the bridge is the main part of Johnsonburg Borough. The paper mill is just out of the scene to the left. The photograph was taken from the Clarion Heights section of town. (Mark Wendel.)

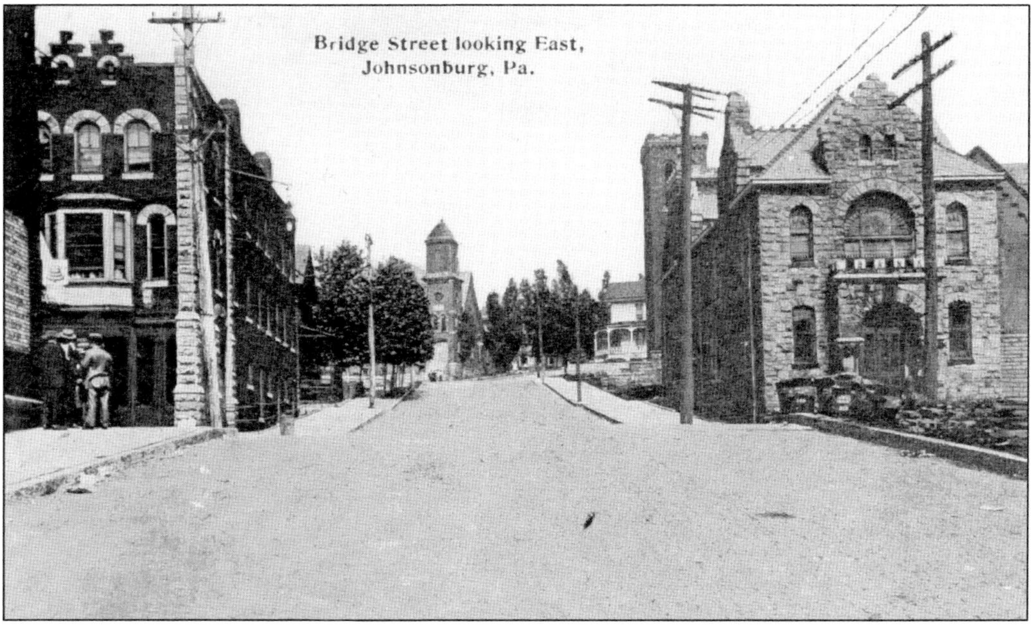

This is the intersection of Bridge and Market Streets in Johnsonburg. Buildings are (from left to right) the Brick Block, the Johnsonburg Methodist Church, the Holy Rosary Church, and the Johnsonburg National Bank. The bank building has operated under many different corporate names but is still being used as a bank. (Mark Wendel.)

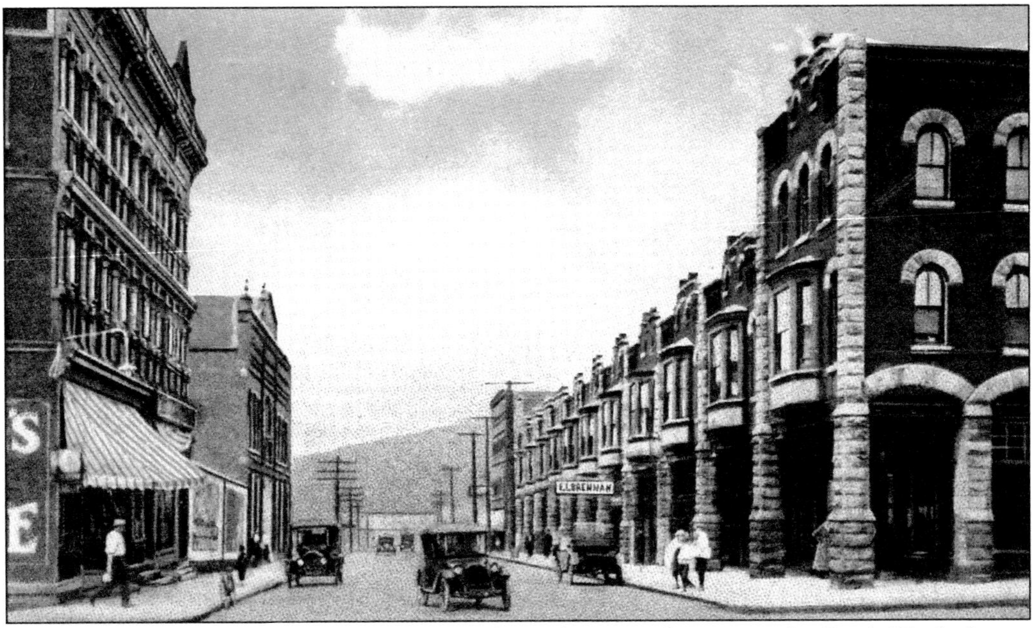

The north side of Market Street (right) in Johnsonburg was known as the Brick Block. It was the first shopping plaza in Elk County. The block was developed by Meylert M. Armstrong Sr. The block featured a long brick and stone structure that had businesses on the ground floor with residential apartments above. The Johnsonburg Post Office was formerly on the right end of the block (Mark Wendel.)

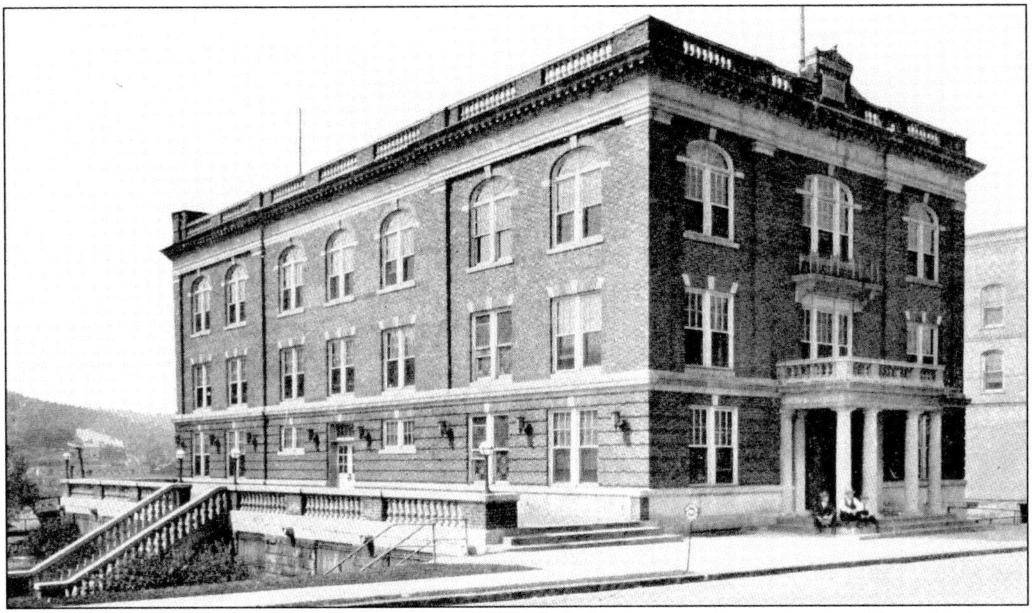

The Johnsonburg Community Building on Market Street was built by the New York and Pennsylvania Company (paper mill) and was presented to the people of Johnsonburg for social and recreational uses. The building even included a swimming pool. The stairs at the left in the photograph lead down to a playground. The building at one time also housed the public library and Johnsonburg borough offices. (Mark Wendel.)

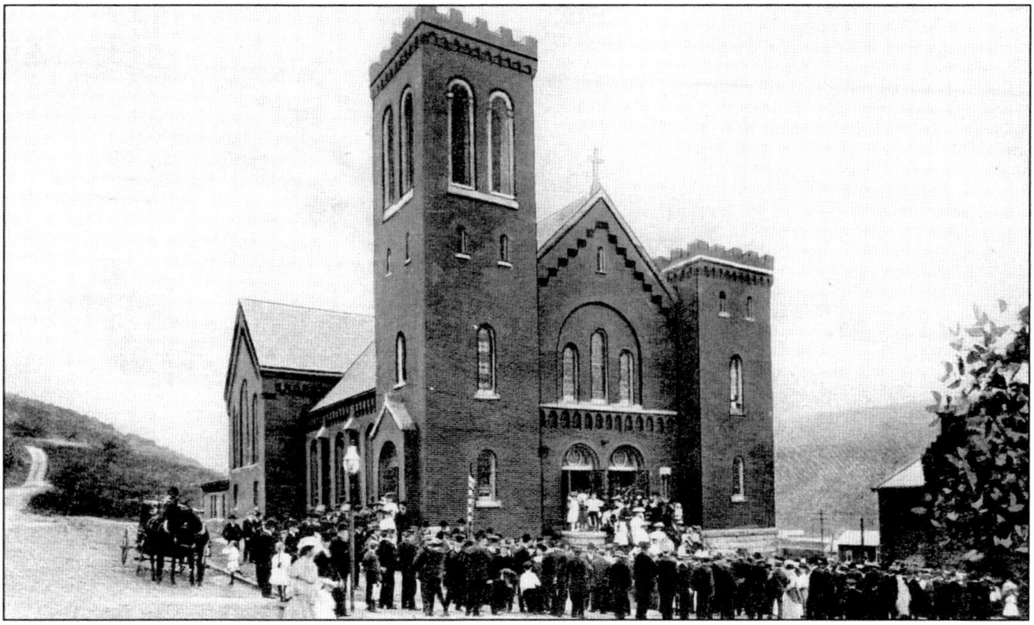

Here is a scene from the dedication of the Holy Rosary Church in Johnsonburg in 1906. This brick structure replaced an earlier wood frame church built in 1889. The Holy Rosary Parish would eventually add a rectory, school, and cemetery. Before 1876, Johnsonburg Catholics traveled to Kane for services until residents organized a local parish. (Mark Wendel.)

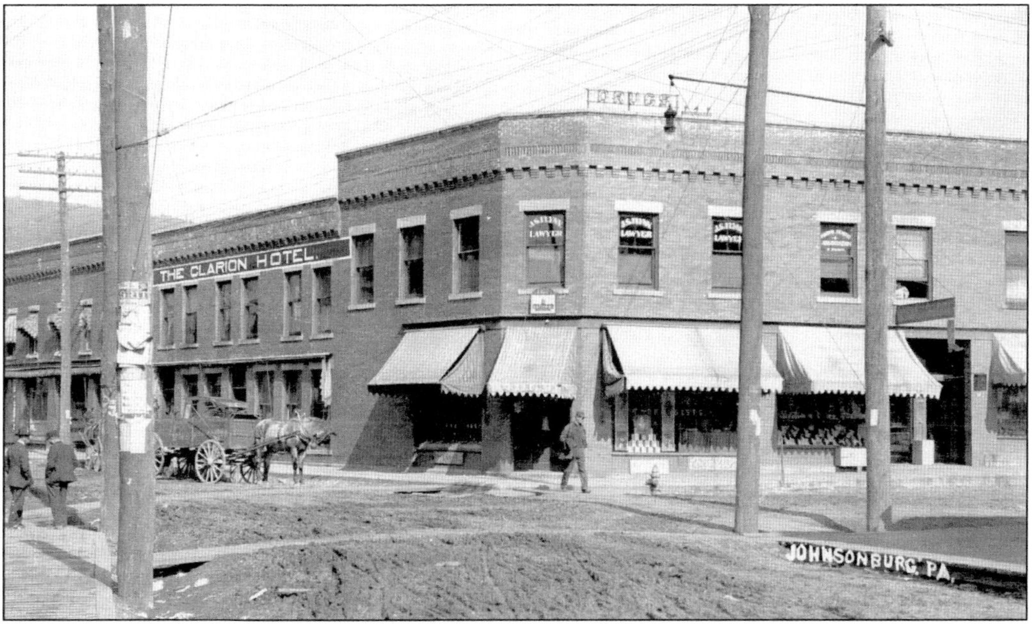

The Florin and Johnson Block, in Johnsonburg, was at the intersection of Center and Cobb Streets. On the corner are a drugstore and market with lawyers' offices on the second floor. To the left is the Clarion Hotel. The Clarion Hotel was a modern establishment when built, stocking the finest imported and domestic beverages and the best cigars. (Mark Wendel.)

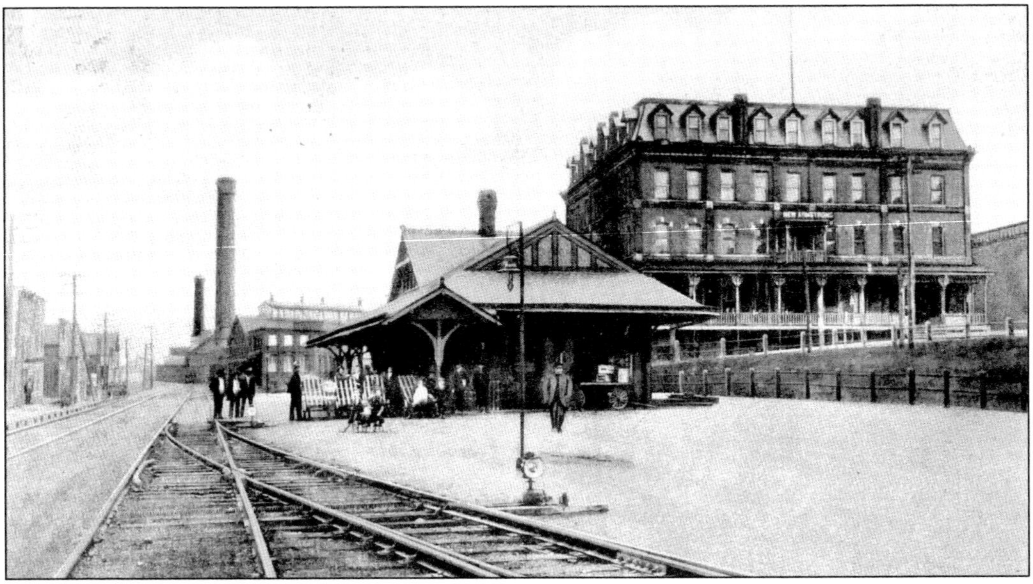

The Armstrong Hotel and the Pennsylvania Railroad station are shown here on Bridge Street in Johnsonburg. The Armstrong Hotel was a world-class establishment at one time, featuring 60 rooms. The large dining room served the finest cuisine, and the hotel offered many other amenities. In 1908, the business became the Straessley Hotel and in the 1930s suffered a fire and was torn down. (Mark Wendel.)

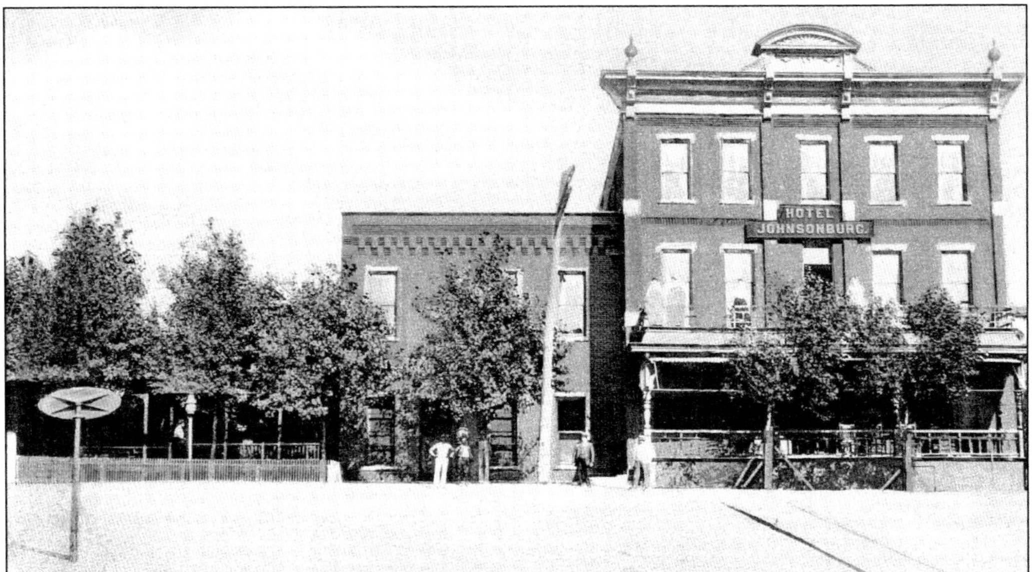

The Hotel Johnsonburg was a four-story structure that offered 30 rooms for $2 per day. It had an elegant dining room and handsome bar. The hotel was built around a mineral well that served the guests, some claiming with beneficial results. The famous heavyweight boxing champion John L. Sullivan lived here while training for fights. (Mark Wendel.)

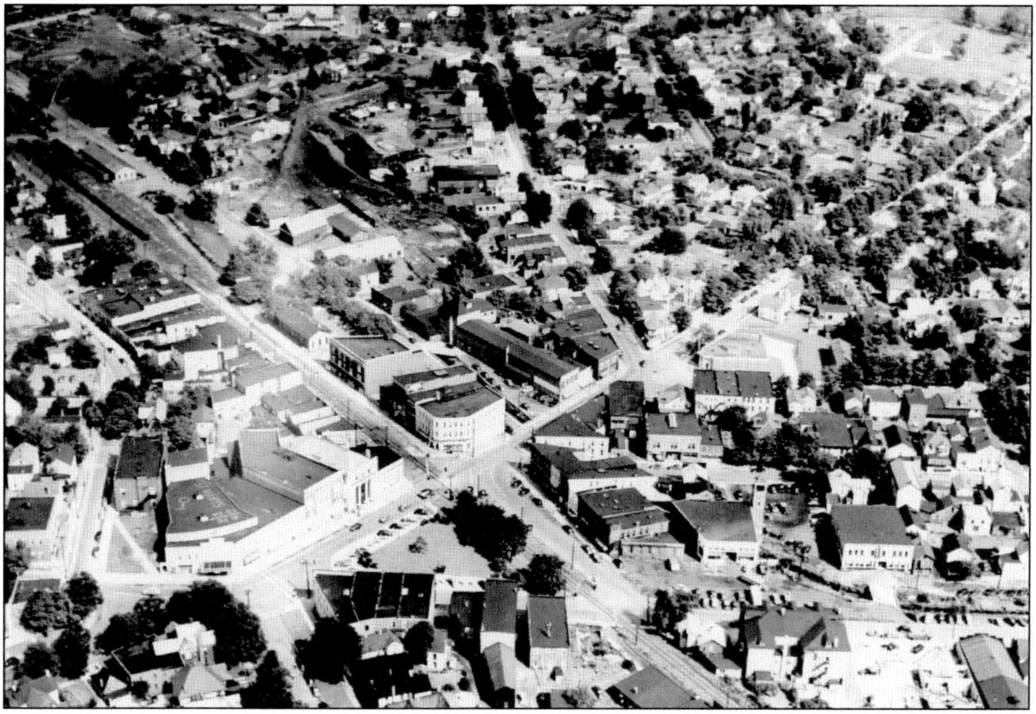

This is an aerial view of St. Marys looking southeast, taken in 1951. In the center of the photograph is the diamond, which is the center of the downtown area. The large building across from the southeast corner of the diamond is Kantar's Department Store, which today is the Marienstadt Center. Note the aviation markings on the large building, lower left, which is the St. Marys Movie Theater.

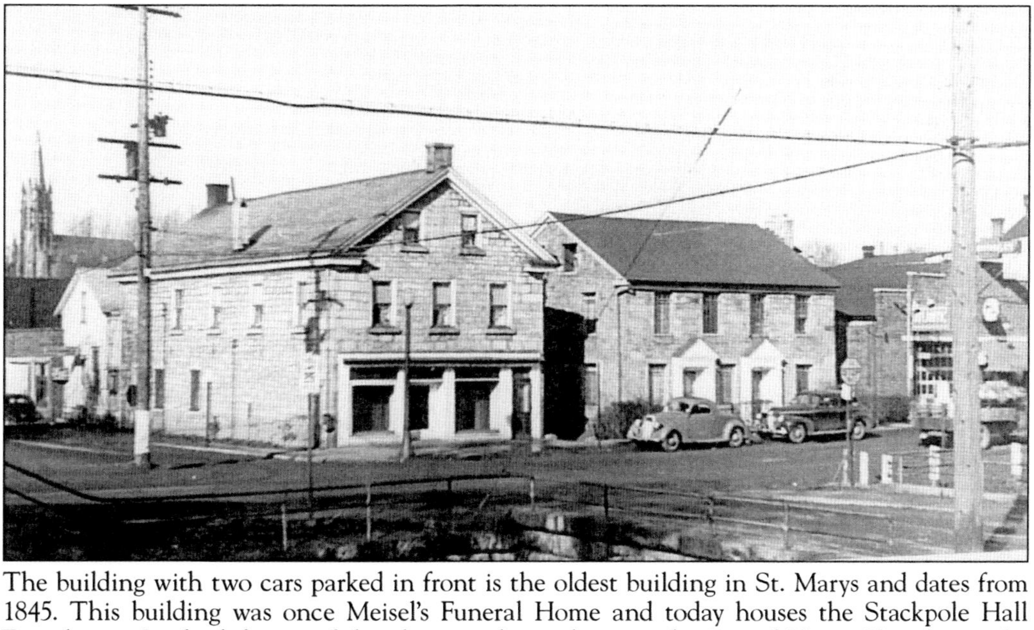

The building with two cars parked in front is the oldest building in St. Marys and dates from 1845. This building was once Meisel's Funeral Home and today houses the Stackpole Hall Foundation. In the left rear of the photograph can be seen the Sacred Heart Church steeple. Note the bridge carrying Mill Street over Elk Creek in the foreground.

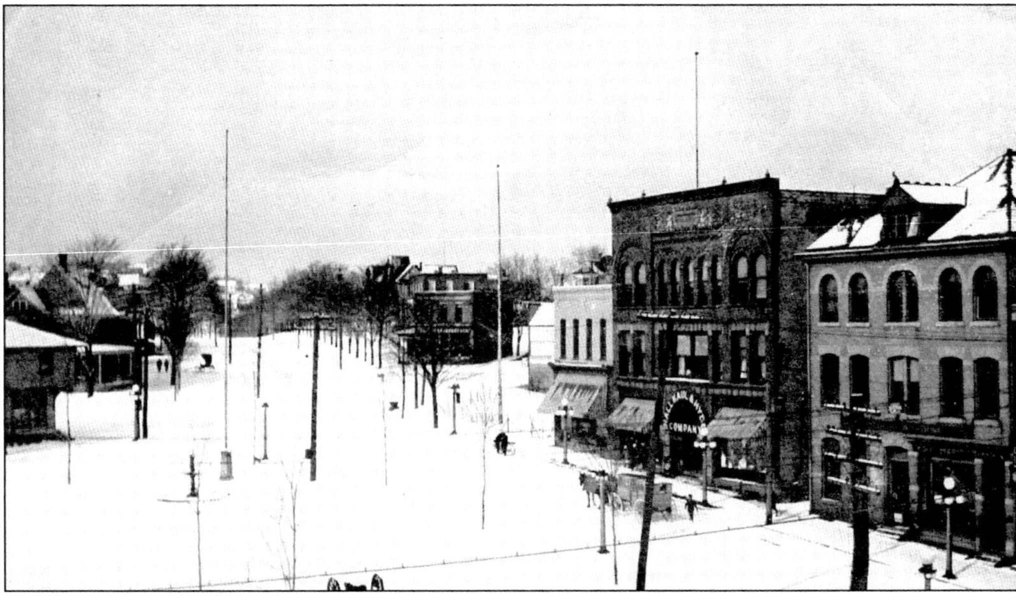

Here is a view of the north end of the diamond in St. Marys. The building at the top center of the photograph is John Weidenboerner's store, which was the first brick building in town. The largest of the buildings on the east side of the diamond is the Hall and Kaul Department Store. Note the horse-drawn carriage moving up North Michael Street.

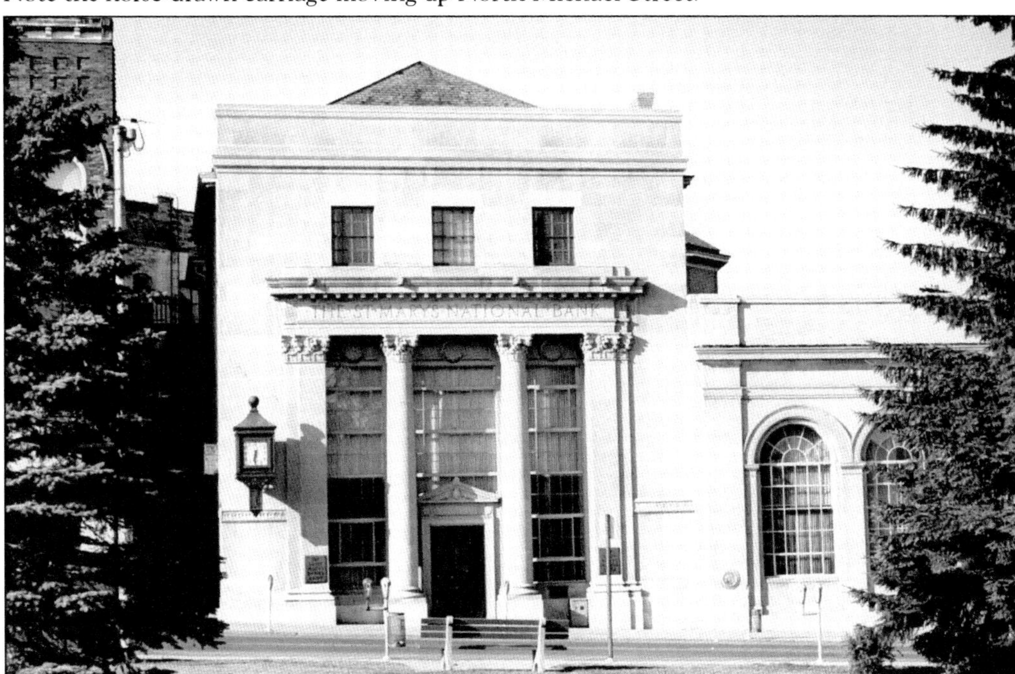

The St. Marys National Bank stood on the east side of the diamond. The facade was adorned with fancy Corinthian columns. It originally had a clock that stood on a post on the sidewalk. Later this clock was remounted on the wall of the bank. Eventually the St. Marys National Bank merged with the St. Marys Trust Company, partially visible in this view to the right. (Grotzinger Collection, St. Marys and Benzinger Township Historical Society.)

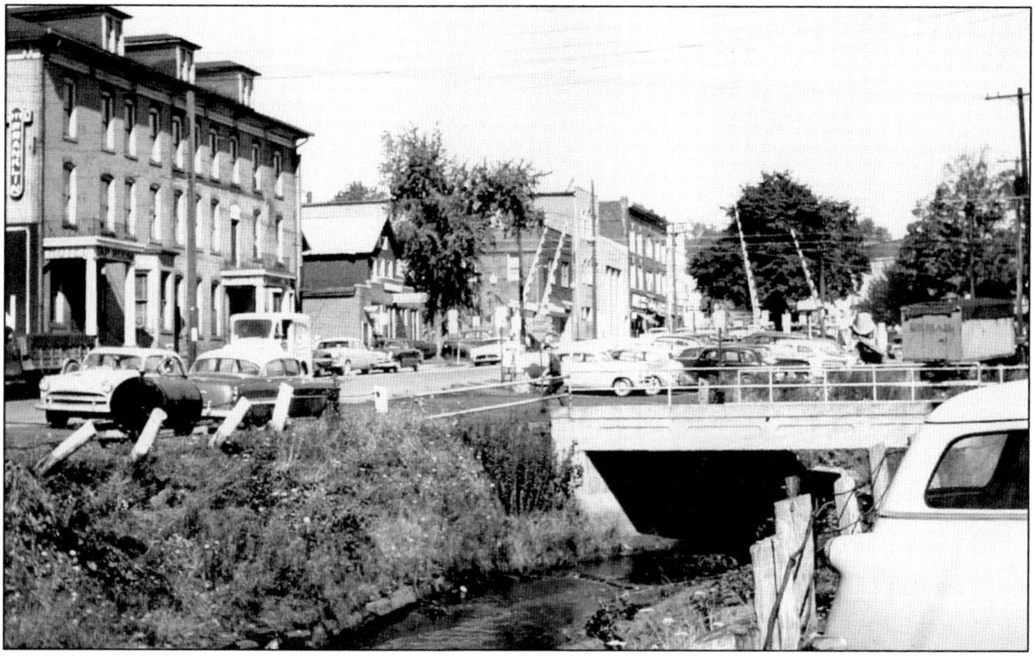

Here is a view of Elk Creek flowing along South St. Marys Street. The creek was covered in 1957 and the street renamed the Boulevard. Traffic flowed in both directions on South St. Marys Street. The large building on the left side of the photograph is the Franklin Hotel, which burned in 2000. Note the railroad crossing gates on the south side of the diamond.

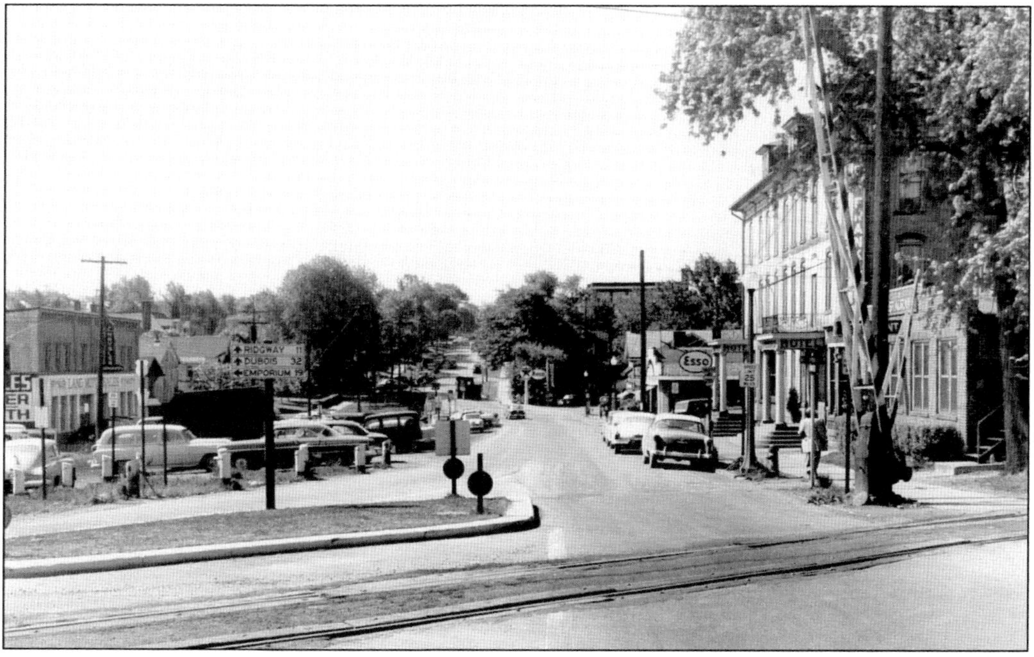

Here is another view of South St. Marys Street before Elk Creek was covered. The east side of the divided roadway was an access road for businesses on that side of the creek, including Lang Motor Sales. The Franklin Hotel is visible on the right of the photograph, and beside it is Cook's Restaurant. Farther up the street, just the square top of the St. Marys High School is visible.

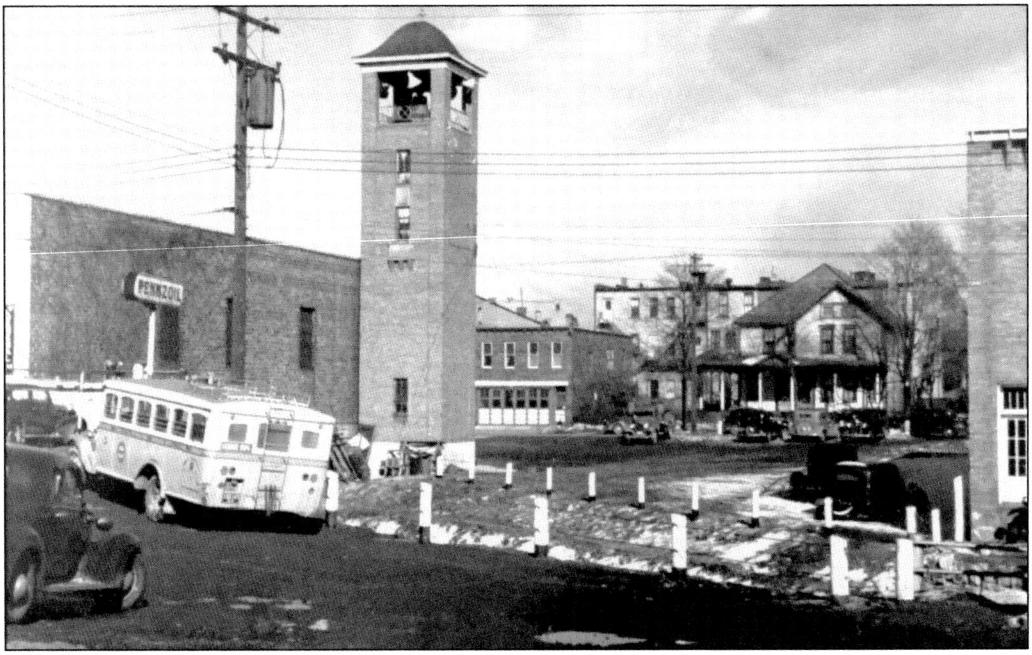

The brick St. Marys Memorial Bell Tower replaced an earlier wooden structure. It was used to hang fire hoses to dry. The original St. Marys Town Hall stood adjacent to this tower and was not replaced after it burned. This vacant lot is today the municipal parking lot. The Schaut Bus Lines service was housed in the building on the left.

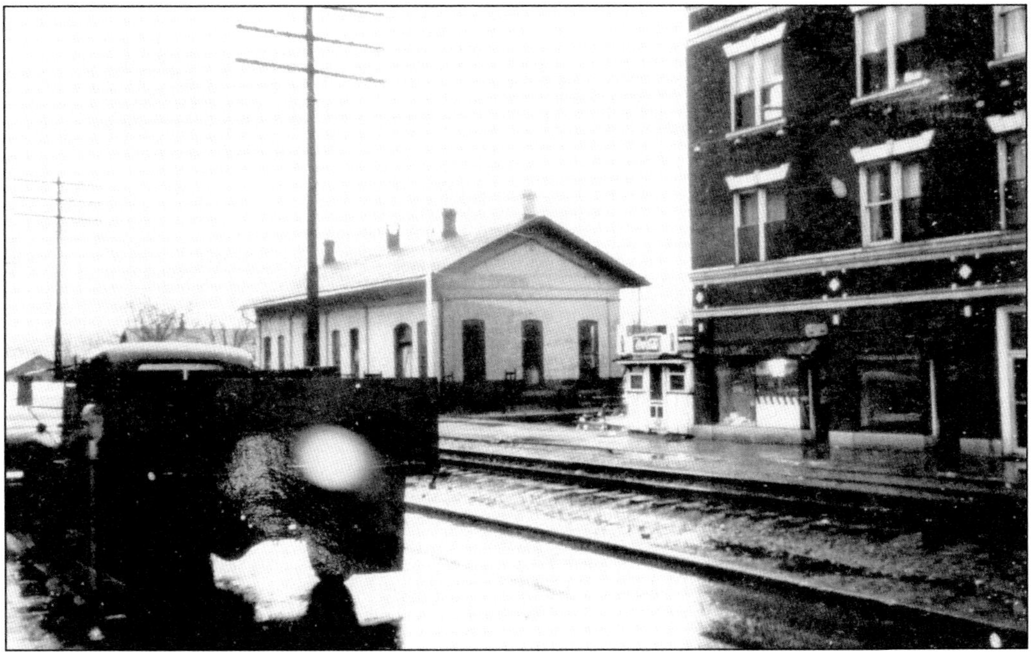

This is a view along Erie Avenue in St. Marys showing the south side of the street along the railroad tracks. The buildings are (from left to right) the Pennsylvania Railroad passenger station, which was torn down; a small diner, which operated in two different sites on the avenue; and the Moose building, which burned on a frigid winter night in 1989.

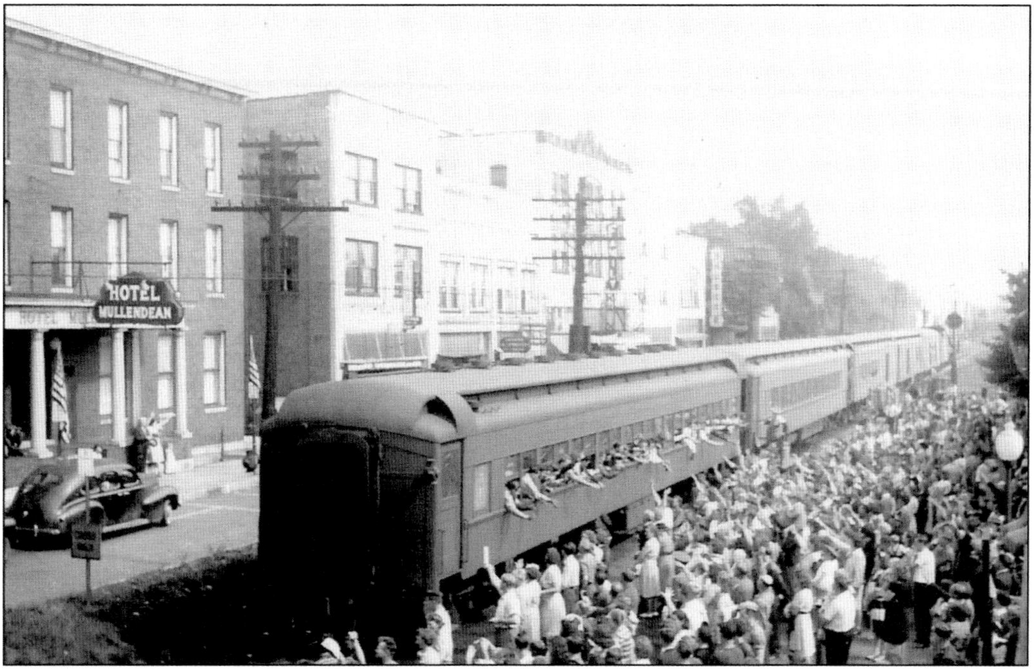

When St. Marys men enlisted in the army in 1942, they were sent to Erie for their physicals. The men who passed were then sent for induction into the service. Ironically they had to pass through St. Marys again on their way to induction. The men were not allowed to get off the train in their hometown, but well-wishers greeted the train.

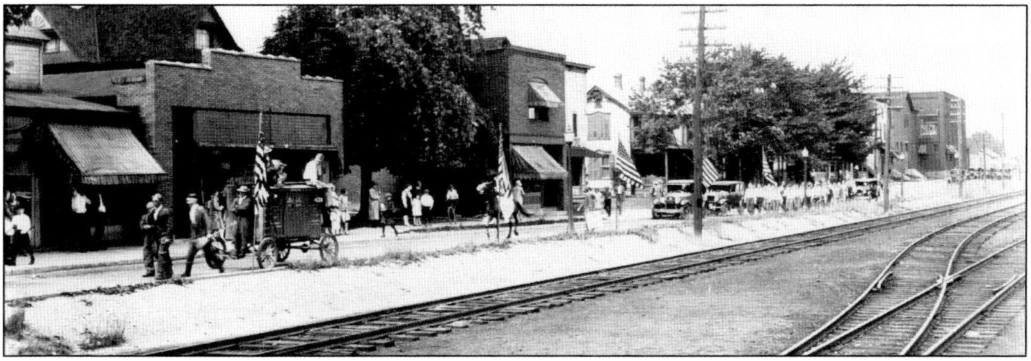

A parade moves down Erie Avenue in St. Marys. The building on the far right is the Novelty Incandescent Light Company, the forerunner of the Sylvania Corporation. The building later became St. Marys Municipal Building before being torn down. The site today houses the combined fire and police departments.

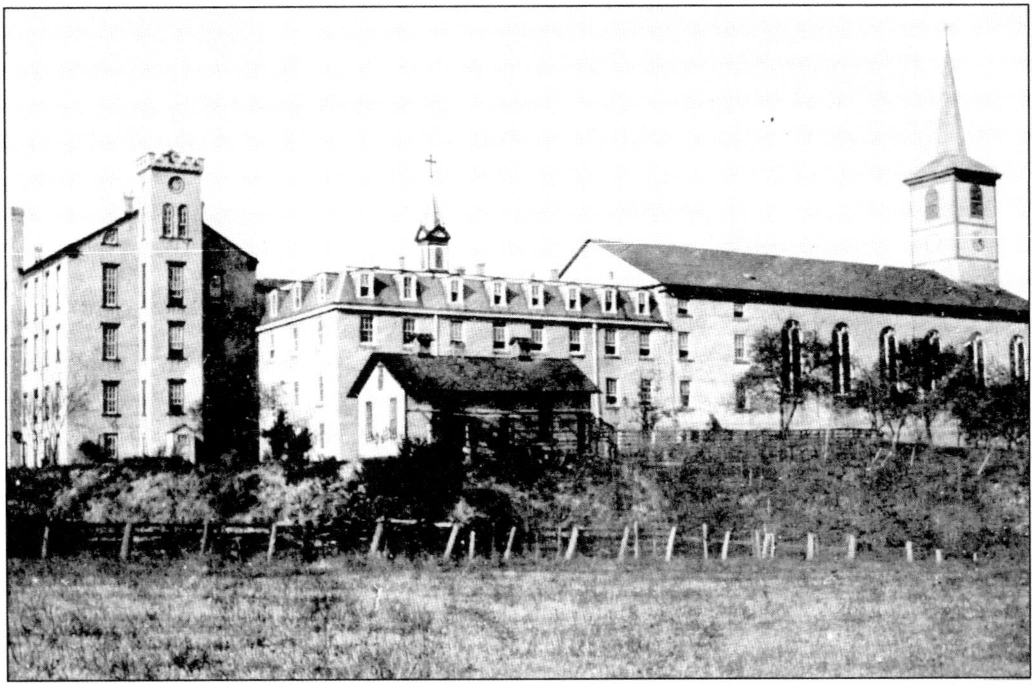

This photograph illustrates how the St. Joseph's Convent was built directly onto the back of the St. Marys Church, which was constructed in 1853. The smaller steeple in the center is the convent's chapel. The convent had extensive gardens and farm acreage. More buildings were eventually added to the convent complex.

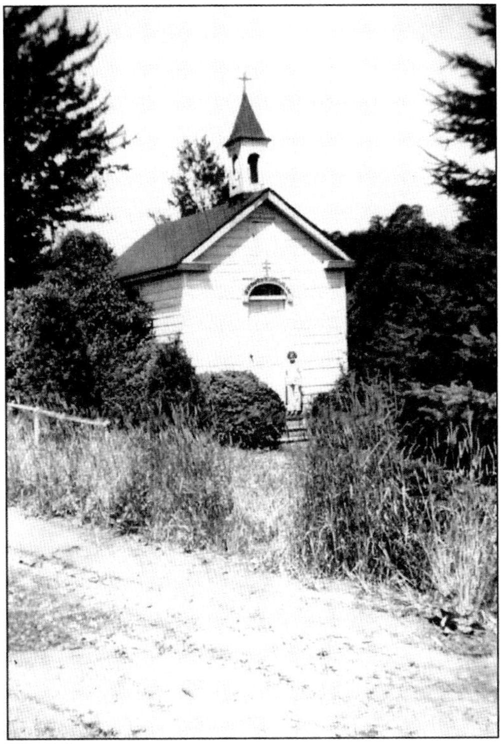

Deckers Chapel in St. Marys is reputed to be one of the smallest churches in the United States and is one of the county's tourist attractions. It was built in 1856 by George Decker after a fall from a tree. He vowed to build the chapel if he recovered. His son Michael became a priest and often said mass in the little church.

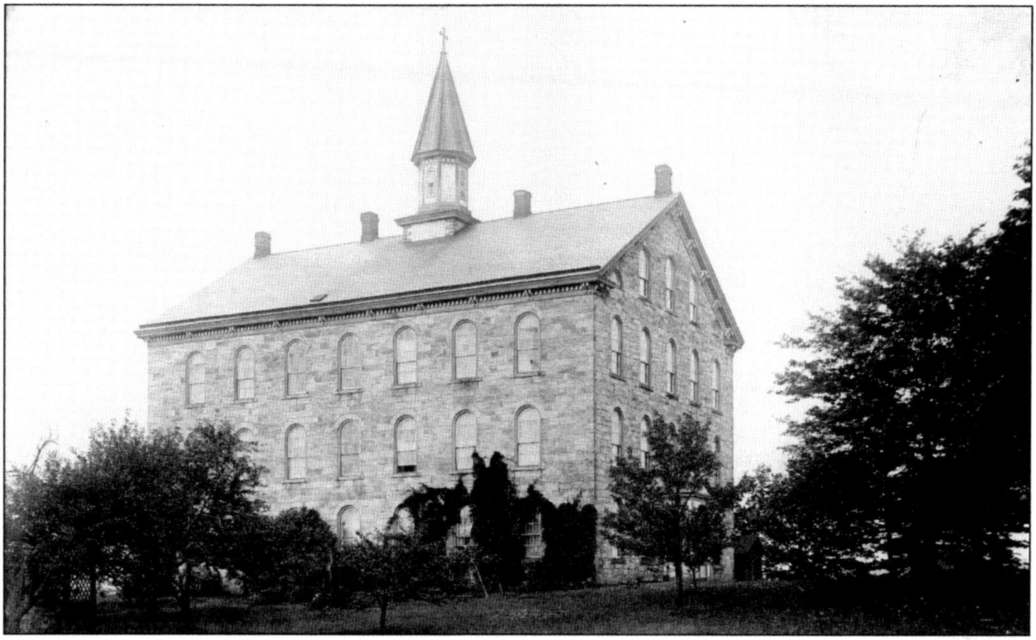

This structure was originally constructed to be a college in St. Marys but was never used for that purpose. It became a monastery for local priests before being turned into a hospital by the daughters of Andrew Kaul. It eventually grew into the Elk Regional Health Center with many additional wings and new buildings.

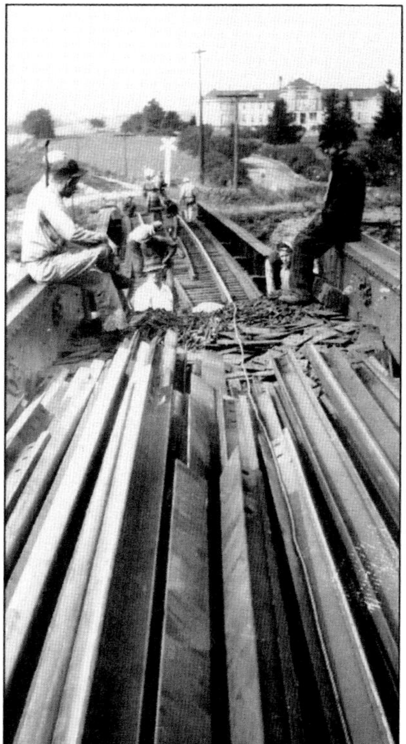

The Pittsburg, Shawmut and Northern Railroad operated between Brockway, Pennsylvania, and Wayland, New York, during the years 1899 to 1947. It carried coal, passengers, and freight. The principal shops were located in Angelica, New York, and St. Marys. In this photograph, the tracks are being pulled up at the end of its existence. In the background the Elk County Home is visible. (Bauer collection.)

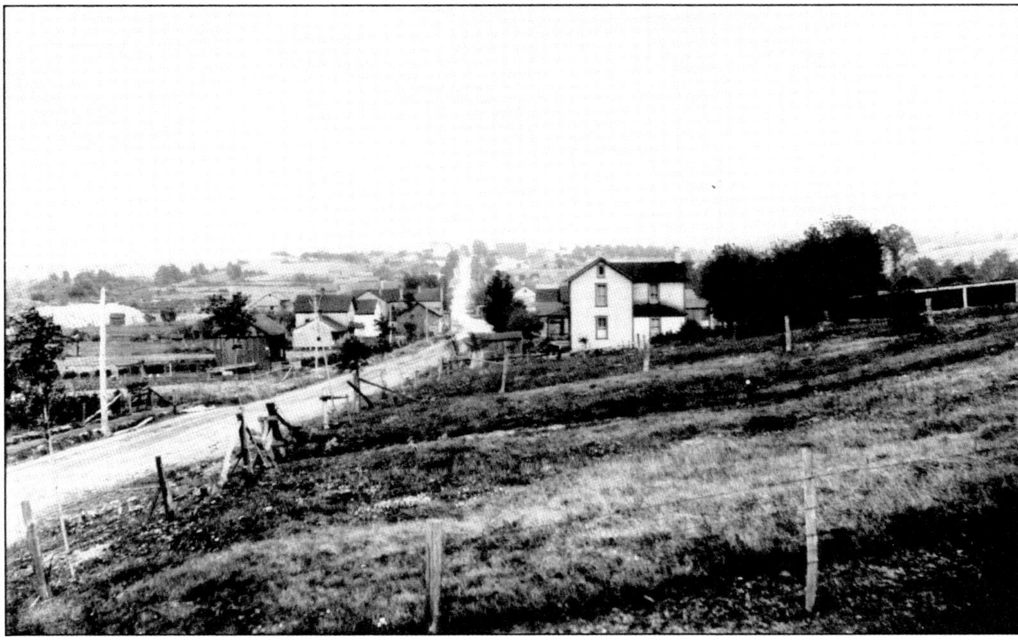

This is a view of Kersey from the west. Originally known as Centreville, Kersey predates Elk County. It had previously been part of Clearfield County. In 1810, when William Kersey erected a sawmill, the site was renamed for him. Timber and coal were the original industries. Kersey is located at a high elevation on Red Hill Summit.

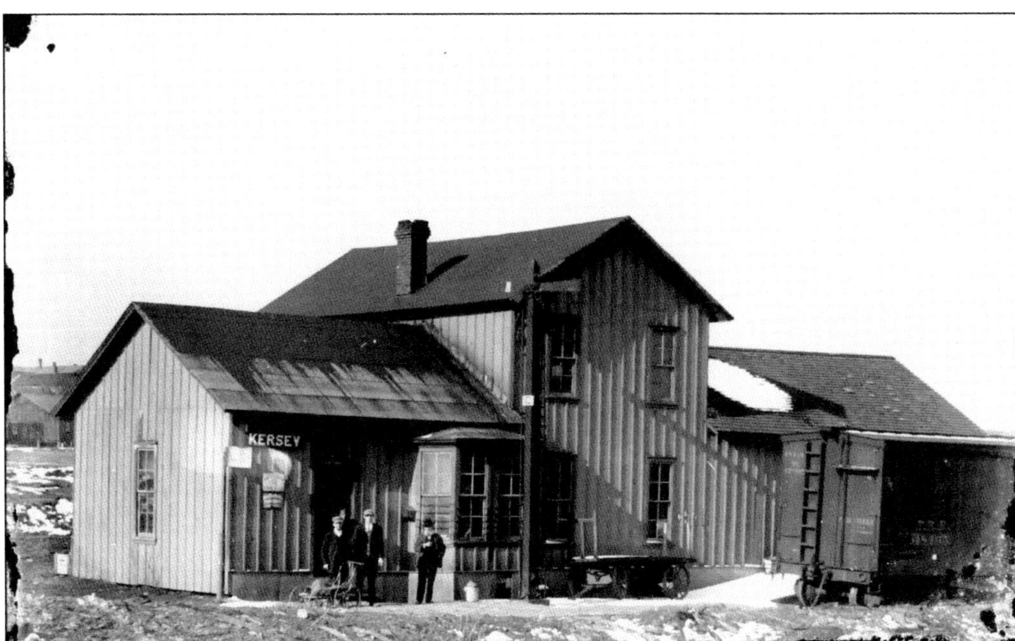

Here is a view of the railroad depot in Kersey. The Pittsburg, Shawmut and Northern Railroad ran through Kersey. The railroad was a coal carrier, but it also had a Brill motor car called the "Hoodlebug" that carried passengers and went between Kersey and Olean, New York. There is also a Pennsylvania Railroad boxcar in this photograph.

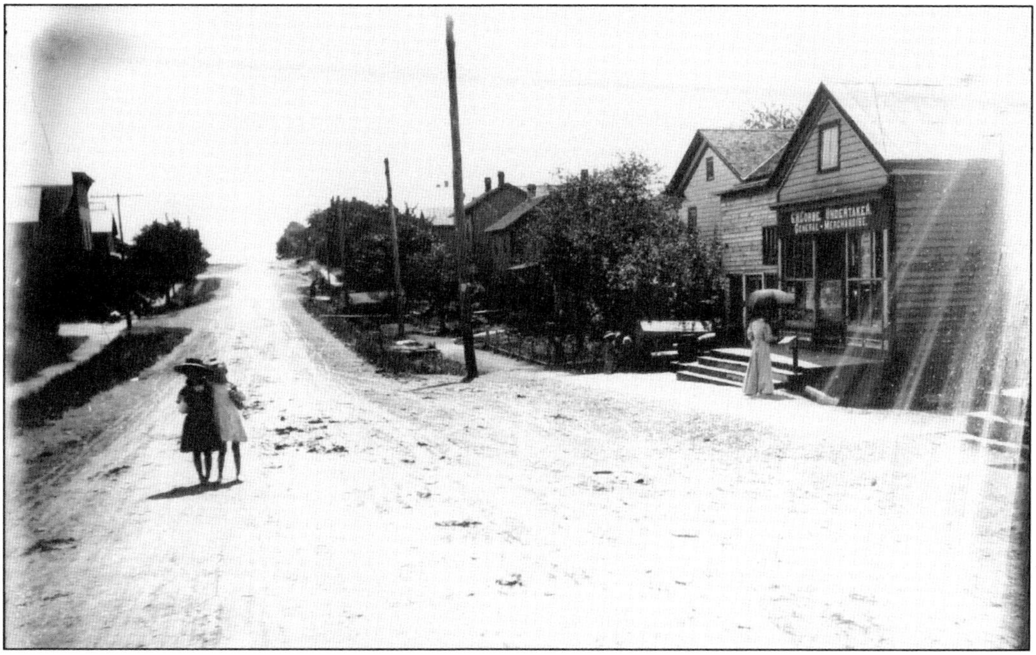

Main Street in Kersey seems to have been the local residents' outdoor photography studio. Here are two girls, all dressed up and wearing their best bonnets, posing for a photographer while their mother, using a parasol on this sunny day, window shops at the G. H. Corbe, Undertaker and General Merchandise emporium.

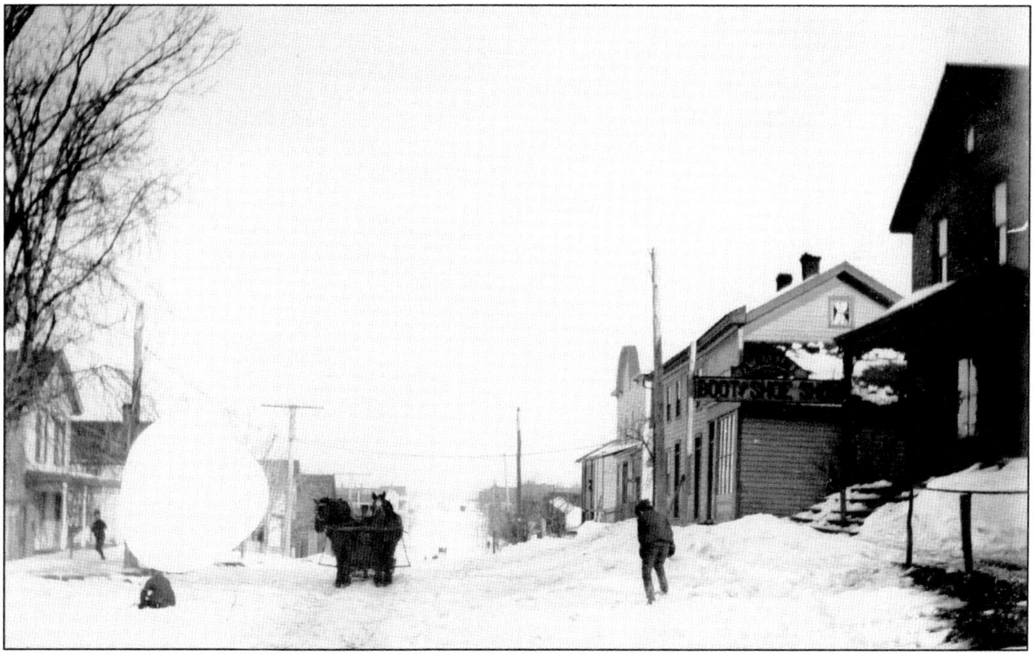

This winter scene of Kersey illustrates the unhurried pace of times past. Although a horse team is trudging up Main Street, there is a group of the people in the background who appear to be using the street as a sledding hill. A sled rider has just moved out of the way of the horses. Another pedestrian slogs home through the snow past the Fashionable Boot and Shoe Shop.

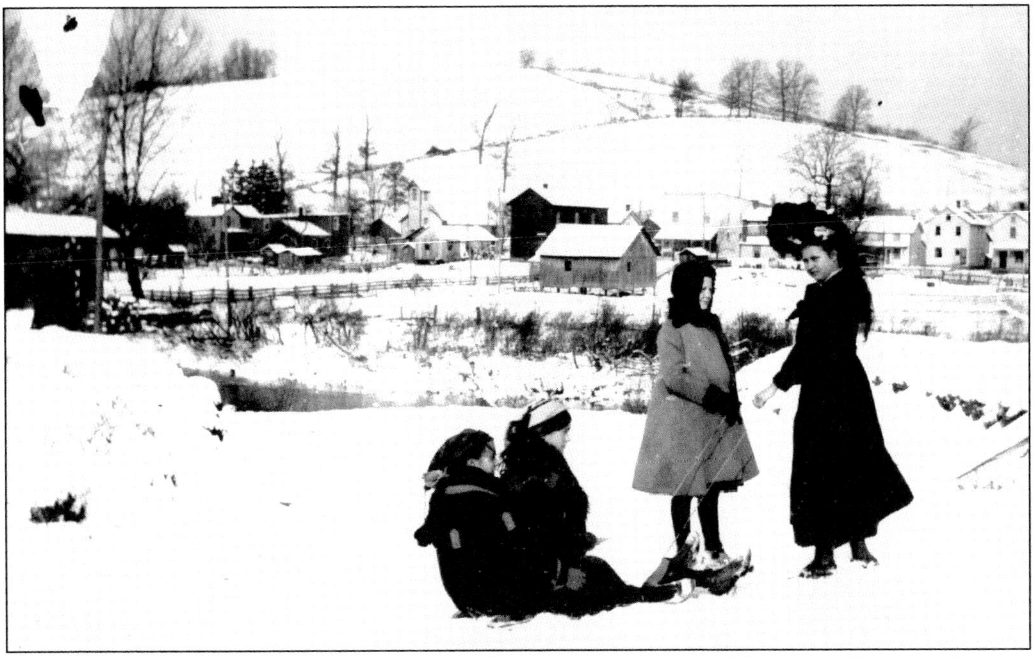

The community of Kersey is located on Red Hill Summit between the Clarion and Sinnemahoning drainages. It receives plenty of snowfall every winter for the residents to enjoy. Sledding was a popular pastime in the village. Pictured are several girls enjoying a winter outing on their sled among the snow-covered hills. They seem well bundled up against the cold.

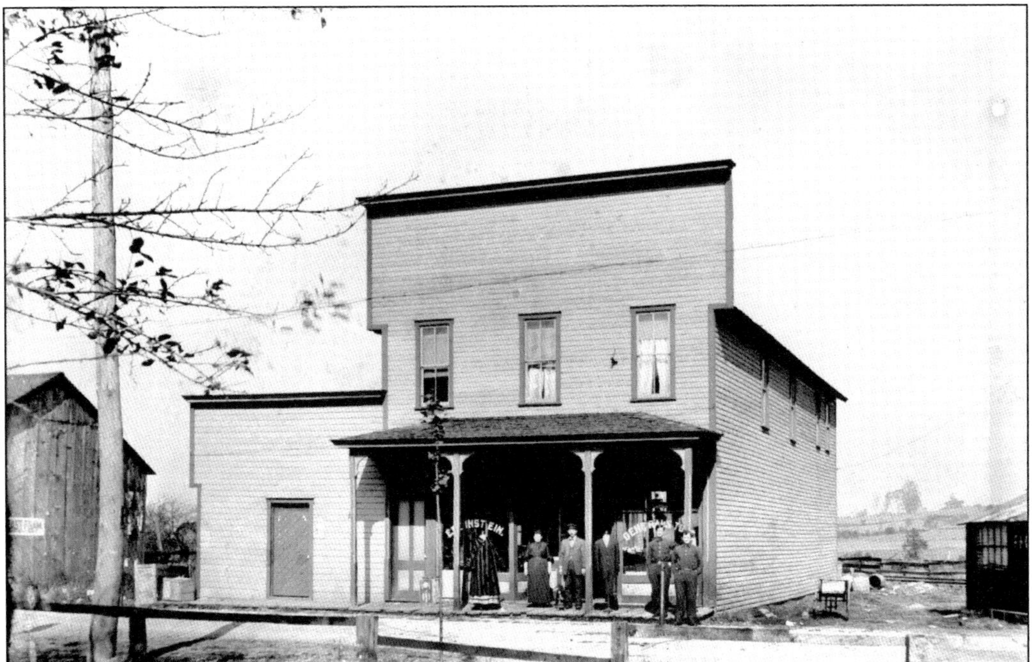

The E. Weinstein General Store was located in Kersey. In this photograph it appears to be having a sidewalk sale as it has suits and dresses displayed out on the street. It must have done a brisk business, as it seems to have at least two clerks ready to serve any customers who walk up.

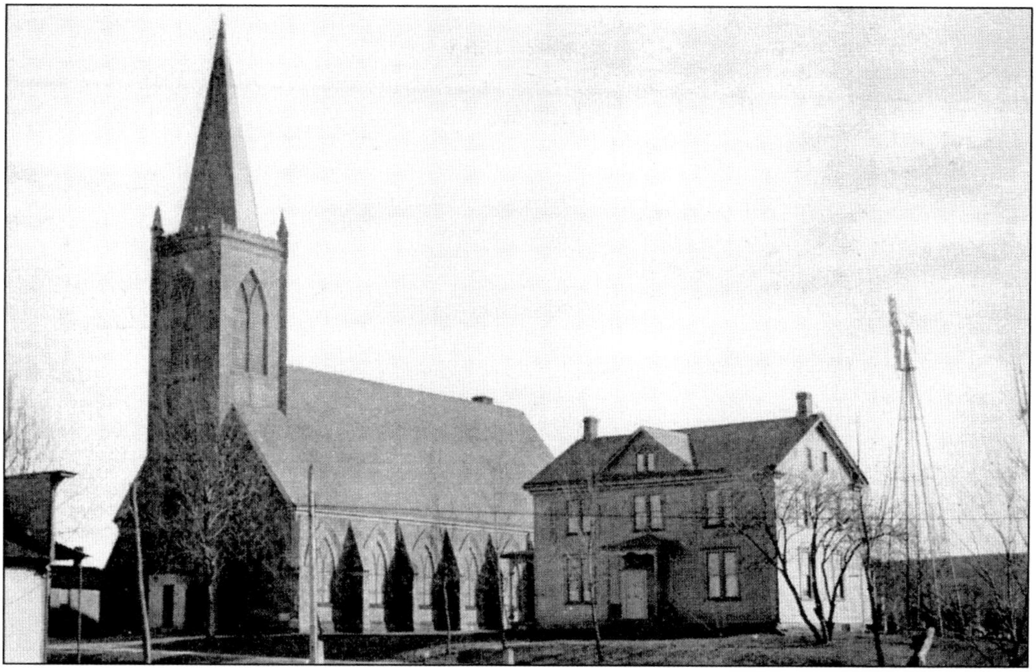

St. Boniface Catholic Church in Kersey is a brick structure that was built in 1893. This church replaced an earlier church built in 1854 and named St. Ann. The old frame school building, shown in this photograph, has been replaced by a modern brick school. There is a cemetery behind the church/school complex. Note the windmill in the yard.

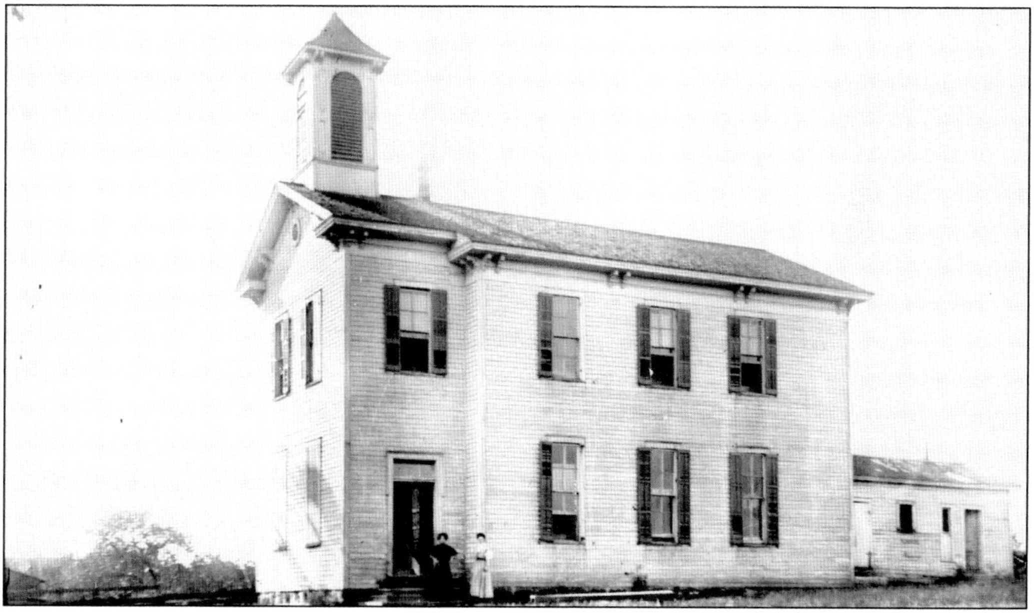

An early settler's education was homeschooling or work training. One-room schools came along only to be replaced by township schools, which had all grades in the same building. Older students usually left to go to work. Eventually schools were consolidated when townships could not afford the costs of higher education. This building was a convent before being used as the first St. Boniface schoolhouse.

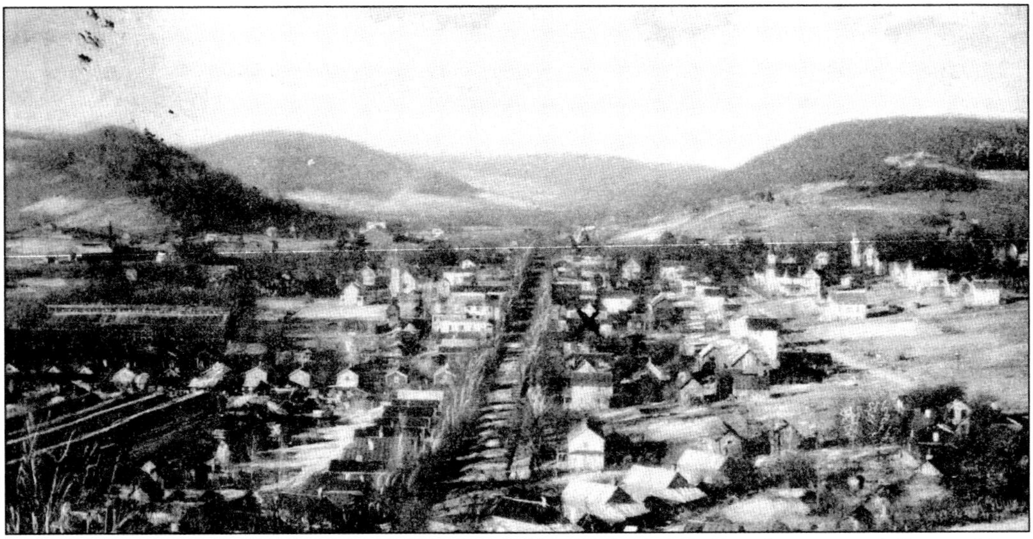

Wilcox is located on the West Branch of the Clarion River. It was first named Buena Vista (beautiful view), but the name was later changed to Wilcox in honor of Alonzo I. Wilcox. Wilcox was a local entrepreneur who had interests in timber, oil, and railroads. He built a beautiful home in Wilcox, which was later used as an American Legion clubhouse. (Mark Wendel.)

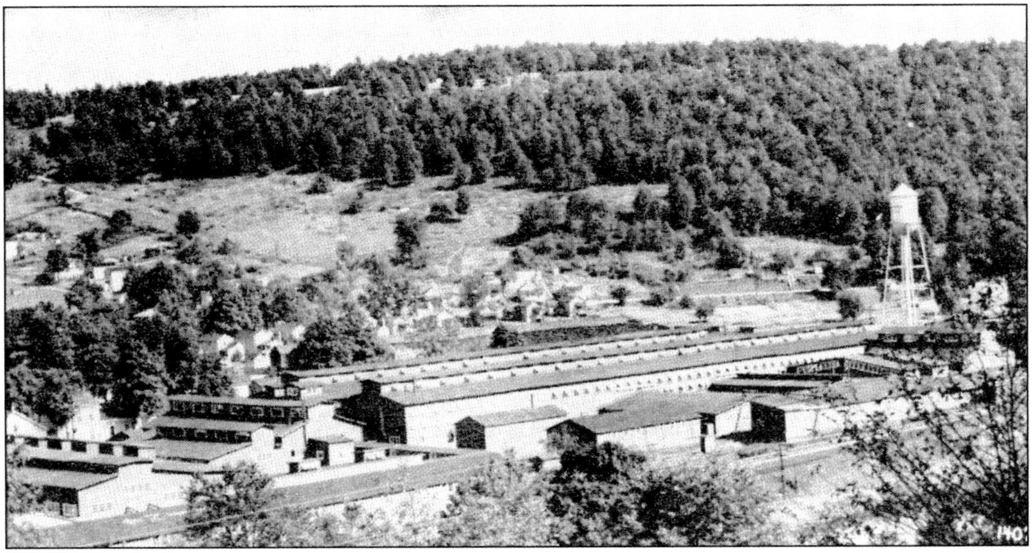

The Wilcox Tanning Company later became the Elk Tanning Company and then merged into the huge United States Leather Company. It employed many area residents and was reported to be the largest sole leather tannery in the world. Hemlock bark from a wide surrounding area was used by the mill. The huge mill burned in a spectacular fire in 1966. (Mark Wendel.)

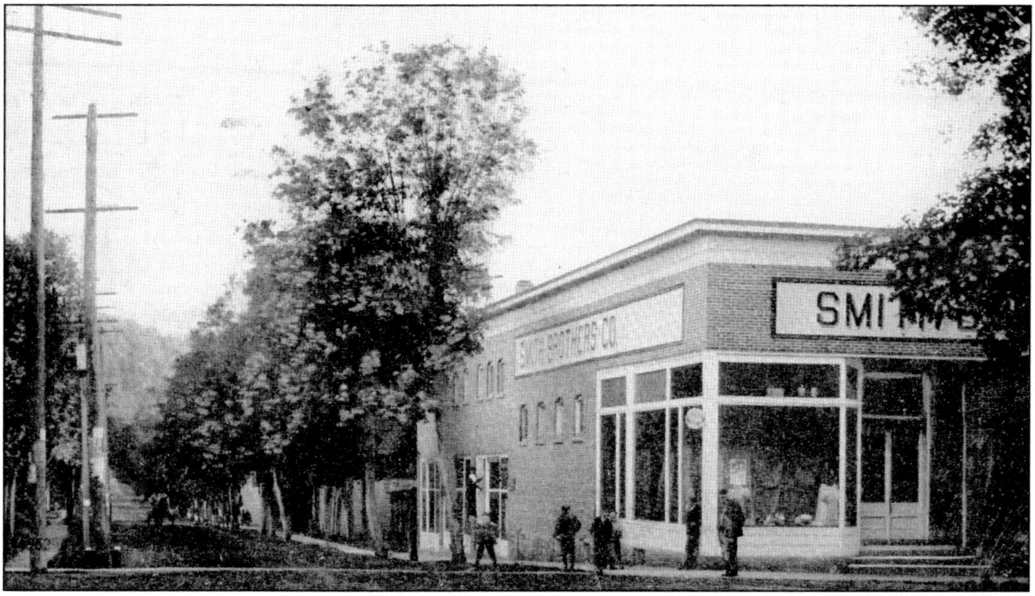

The Smith Brothers Company was a general merchandise store located on Marvin Street in Wilcox. The first store on the site, the Town and Country Store, was built by Alonzo I. and Lucius Wilcox. When that store burned, the Company Store was erected and was later purchased by the Smith Brothers Company of Ridgway. (Mark Wendel.)

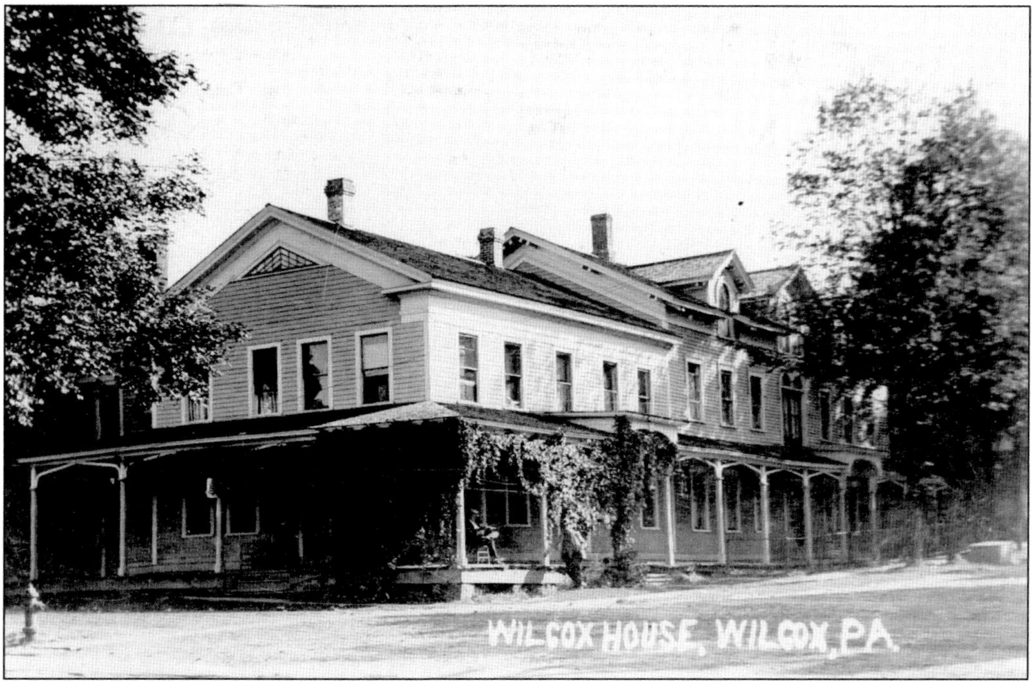

The Wilcox House was the first hotel in Wilcox and was opened by Thomas J. Goodwin. An interesting fact about this hotel is that one of the hotel's early registers reveals that Jefferson Davis, president of the Confederacy, was once registered there, and the hotel was the site where Gen. Thomas L. Kane registered volunteers for his famed Bucktail Regiment to fight against the Confederacy. (Mark Wendel.)

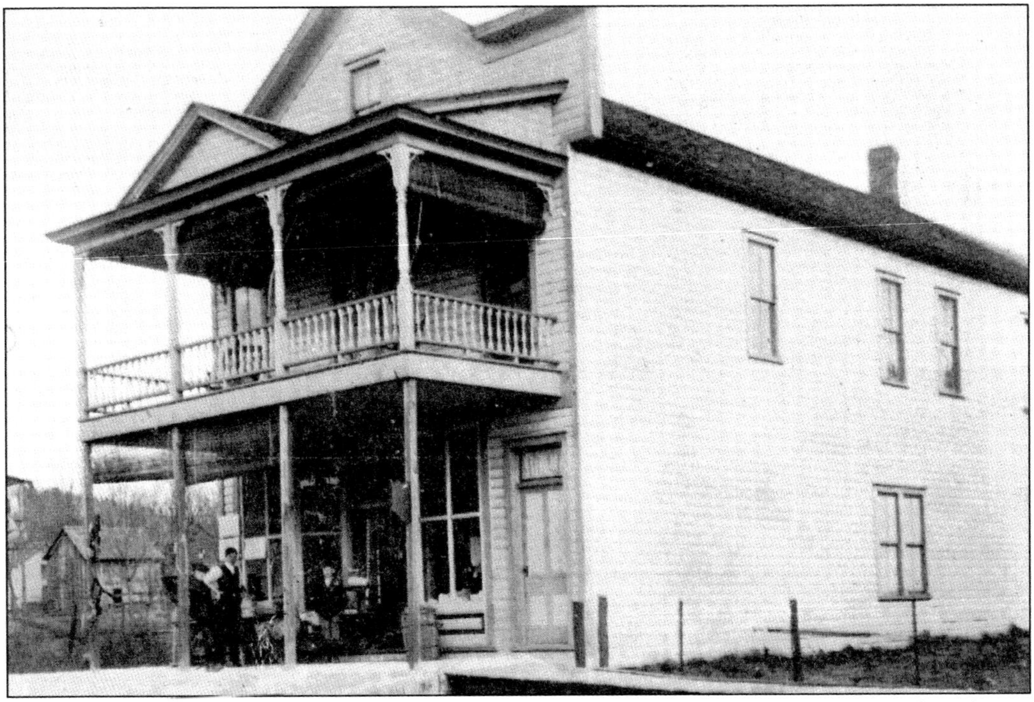

C. J. Anderson opened a general store in Wilcox in 1906. When V. C. Carlson bought an interest in the store, the establishment became known as the Anderson and Carlson Store. The large frame building was a landmark in downtown Wilcox for many years. It furnished many of the daily necessities to the village before regional superstores. (Mark Wendel.)

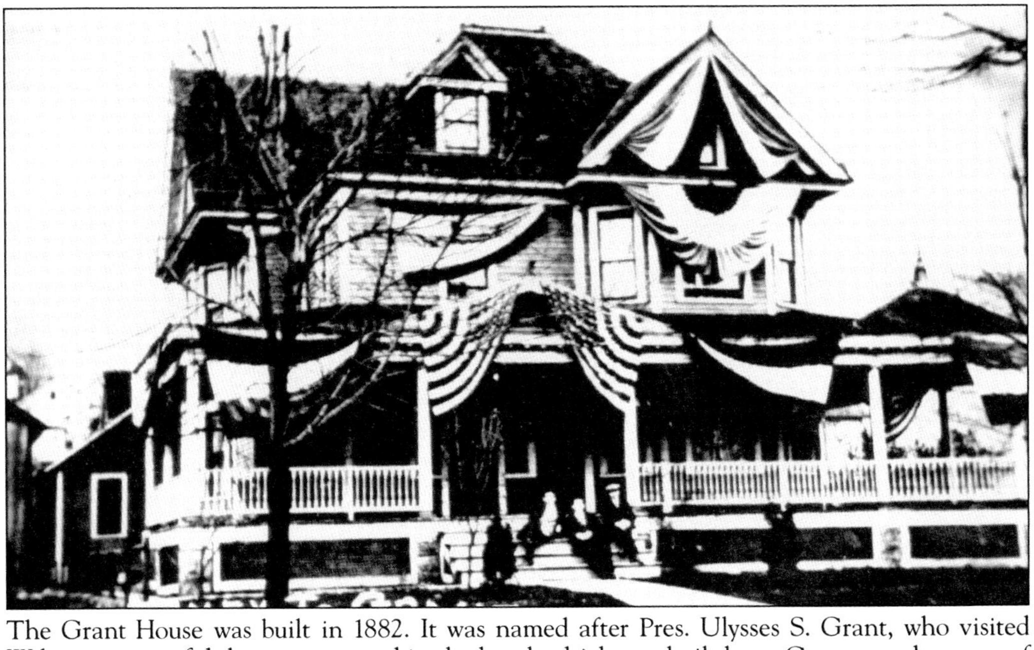

The Grant House was built in 1882. It was named after Pres. Ulysses S. Grant, who visited Wilcox twice to fish but never stayed in the hotel, which was built later. Grant was the guest of his friend Thomas L. Kane on a fishing trip. During the expedition, the president was charged with illegal fishing in what appears to have been a practical joke.

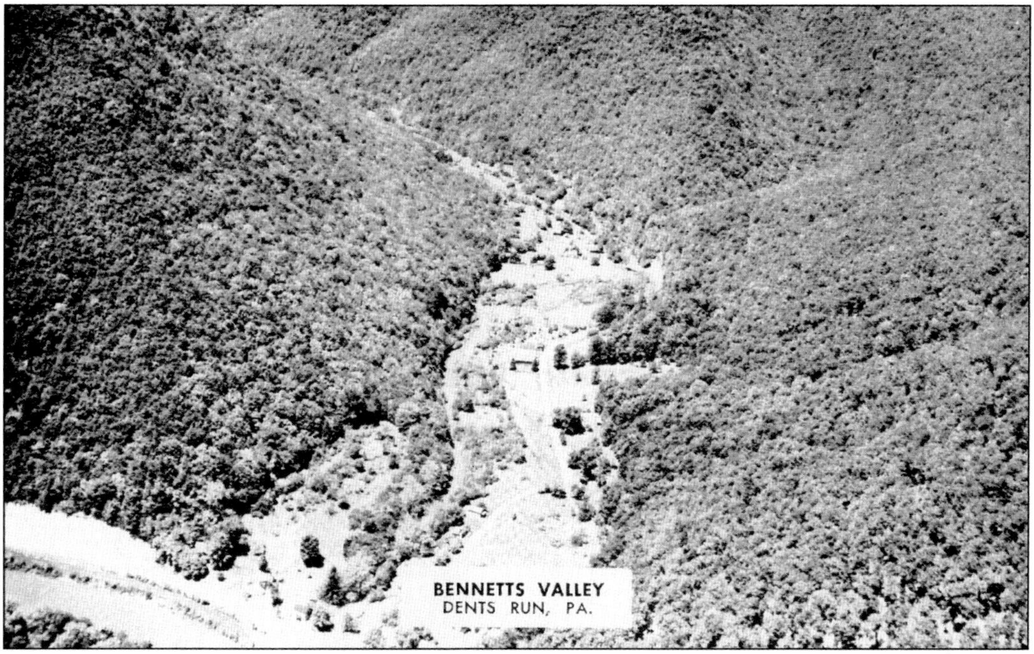

Dents Run is a narrow wooded valley that flows into the Bennetts Branch of the Sinnemahoning Creek. The village was a lumber patch that flourished until the timber was cut. Dents Run's claim to fame is that a Civil War shipment of gold bullion was lost in its wilderness and never found. Some area residents still search for it. (Mark Wendel.)

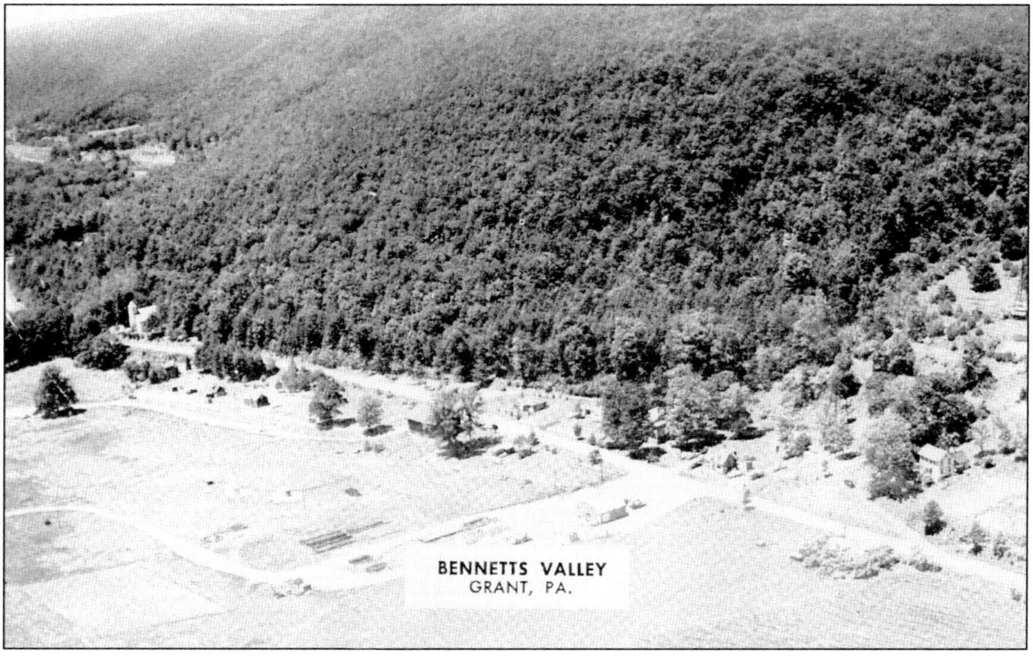

The village of Grant is located on the Bennetts Branch of the Sinnemahoning Creek. The town is named after Pres. Ulysses S. Grant, who vacationed here to fish during his first term in office. The president stayed in an elegant railroad car that transported him from the capital. Grant loved to fish and visited Elk County on three separate occasions. (Mark Wendel.)

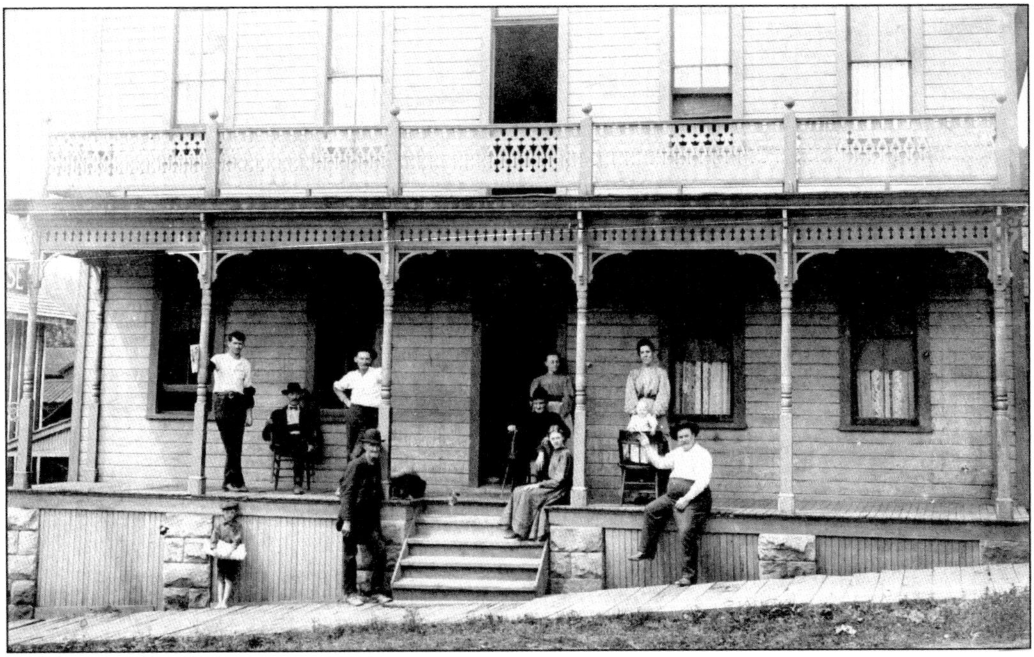

Benezette is the center of the elk tourism business today. On Winslow Hill, above Benezette, the game commission has developed elk-viewing areas. This photograph of the Benezette Hotel is from a quieter time when folks sat on the porch and waved at the passing photographer. Note the barefoot newsboy at lower left.

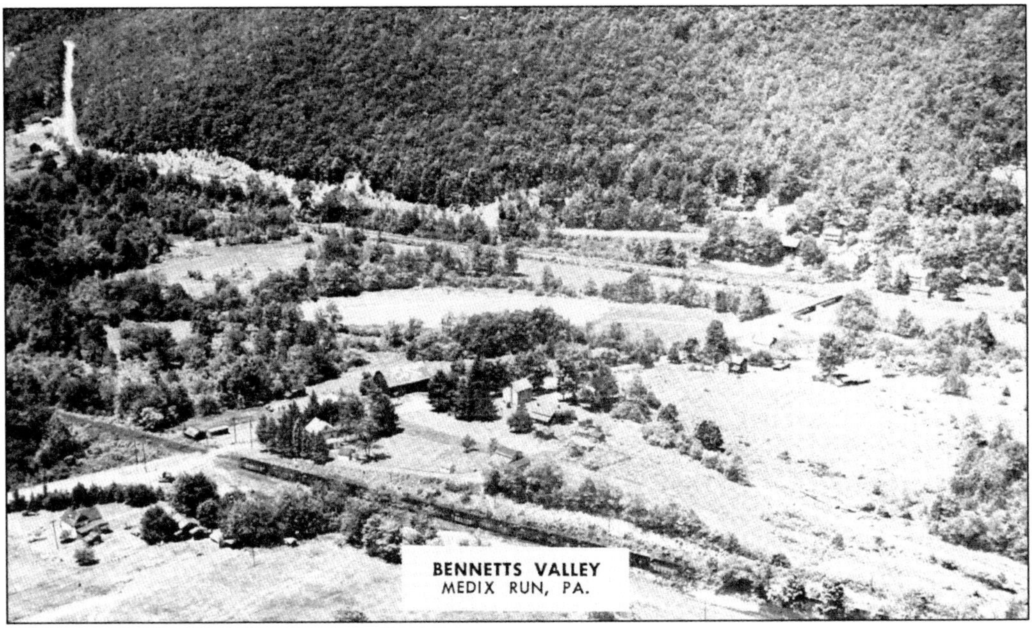

Medix Run flows into the Bennetts Branch of the Sinnemahoning Creek. Where the two join is an old establishment, the Medix Hotel, which today entertains visitors to the Quehanna Wild Area. The hotel has seen famous guests including U.S. presidents Ulysses S. Grant, Grover Cleveland (who had mining interests in the area), and silent-movie cowboy star Tom Mix (who was born nearby). (Mark Wendel.)

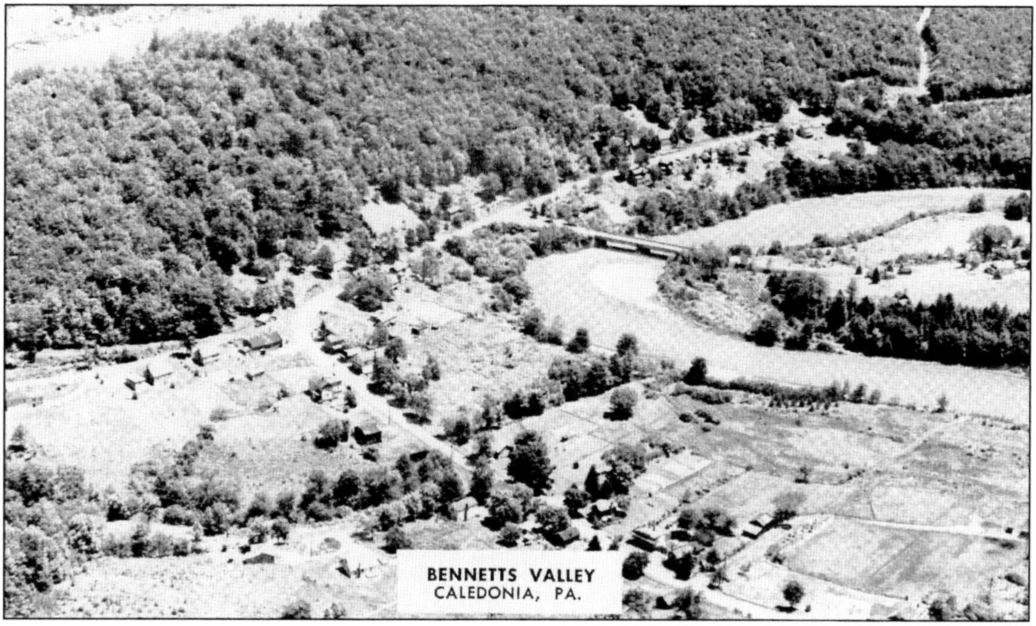

The first pioneers to Elk County, John Bennett and his father, arrived at the future site of Caledonia in 1787. They did not stay, but the Bennetts Branch of Sinnemahoning Creek is named after them. Caledonia, which dates from 1815, is one of the oldest settlements in Elk County and was located on the Milesburg-Smethport Turnpike. It had the first post office and county court in Elk County. (Mark Wendel.)

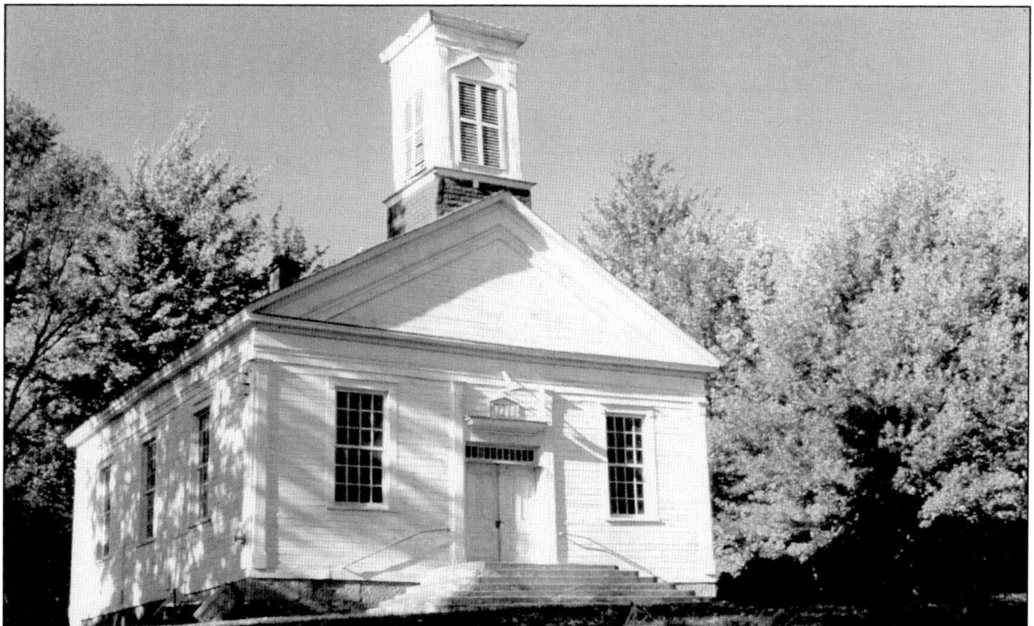

The Mount Zion Church in Jay Township was Elk County's oldest Protestant church. It was built between 1850 and 1856 by Alfred Pearsall, who was also a minister, to fulfill his father's dream. His father, early settler Peter Pearsall, was the first person to be interred in the Mount Zion Cemetery. The church burned in August 1976.

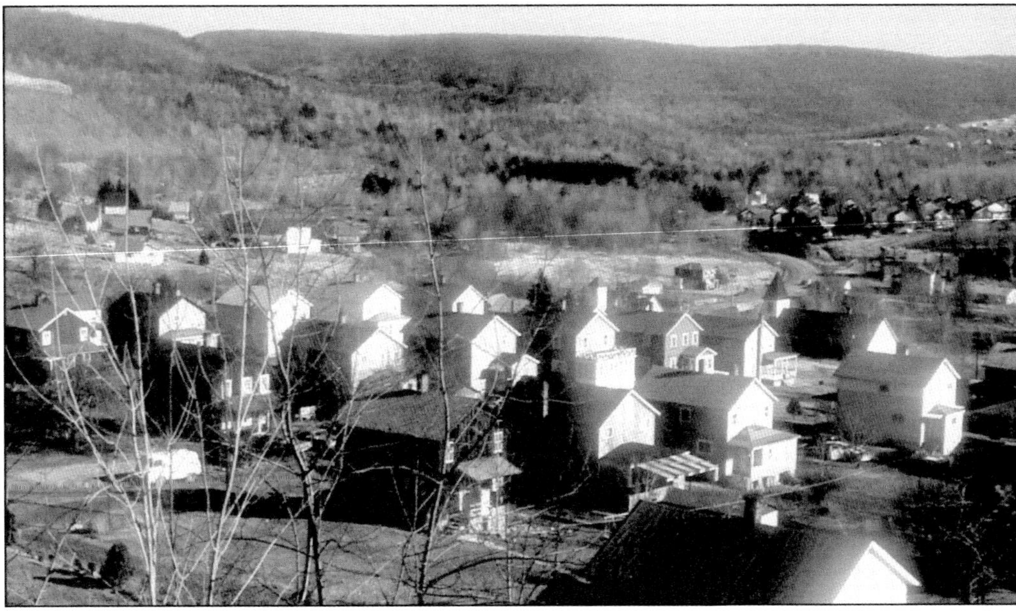

Byrnedale was founded in 1900 and was a coal-mining community. It was named after Mr. Byrne, the head of the coal company. In this view of the village on Byrnes Run, two church steeples are visible. The church on the left is the Byrnedale Union Protestant Church. The church on the right was the Byrnedale Catholic Church and is now the Bennetts Valley Senior Center. (Christopher Dill.)

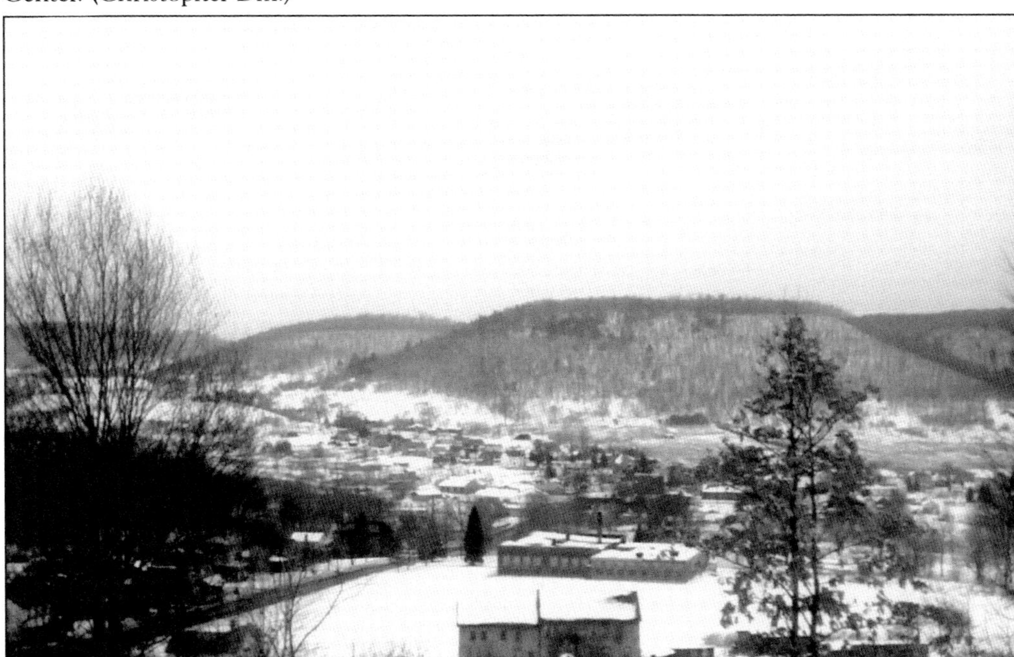

John Boyd built the first sawmill on the Bennetts Branch of the Sinnemahoning Creek in 1816 where Kersey Run joins the Bennetts Branch at Weedville. In 1820, Frederick Weed built the first tannery in Elk County and named the town. The building in the foreground in this photograph is the old public school that has since burned down. (Christopher Dill.)

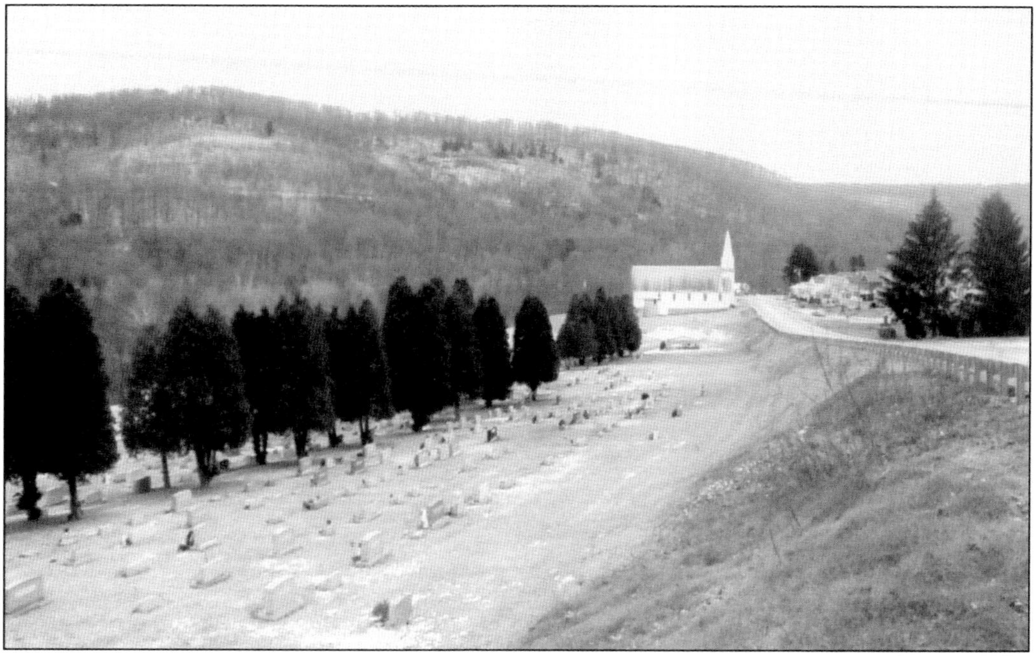

Force and Scattertown are two villages on Route 255 on the southern boundary of Elk County. The area was developed around the Shawmut Mining Company's coal mines. Scattertown was named because the houses were scattered around the area. St. Joseph Catholic Church dominates this photograph of the town of Force. (Dennis McGeehan.)

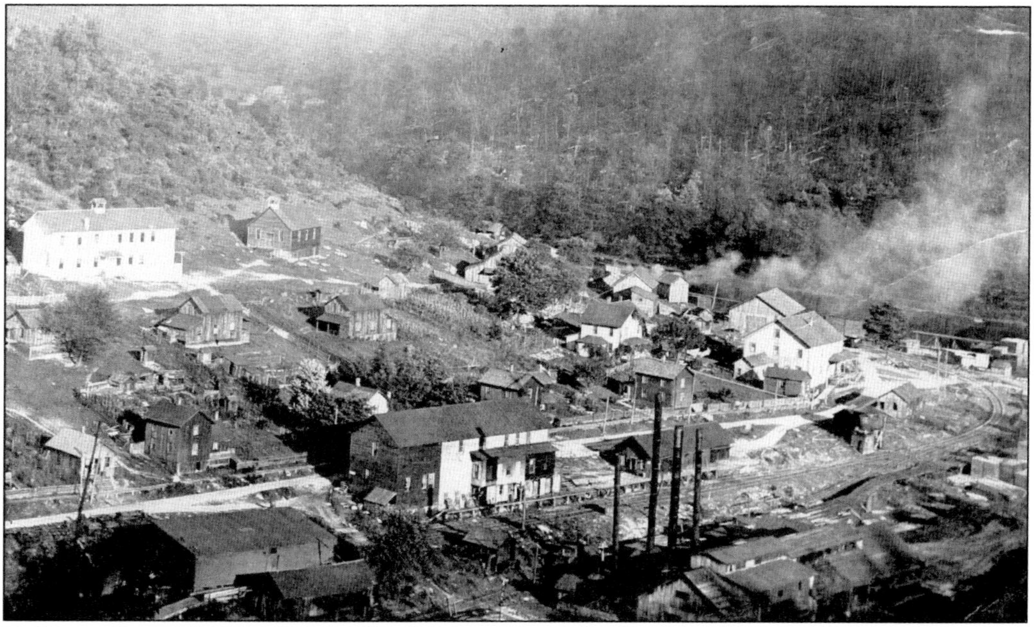

Hallton is located where Spring Creek empties into the Clarion River. It was a lumbering and rafting center for many years. This view from about 1900 shows the Hallton sawmill (smokestacks) on the lower right and the school on the upper left. The village also had chemical factories and a tannery. Several railroads served the businesses in the area. The village was originally called Spring Creek but was renamed after the J. K. P. Hall lumbering interests. (Dave Woods.)

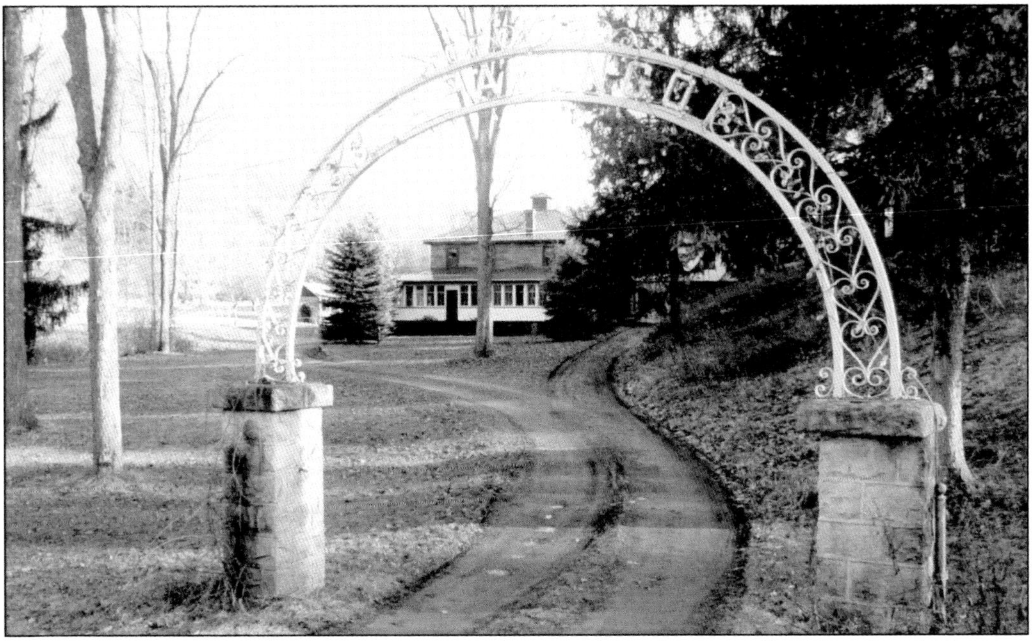

Portland Mills was the place where timber rafts started for the sawmills of Pittsburgh. Later it had its own sawmill and tannery, part of the Joseph Smith Hyde, J. K. P. Hall, and Andrew Kaul empire. It was an early gathering place for elk. Today elk are raised commercially at nearby Lake City. This photograph is of Tapawingo, a hunting lodge frequented for many years by wealthy Pittsburgh sportsmen. (Dennis McGeehan.)

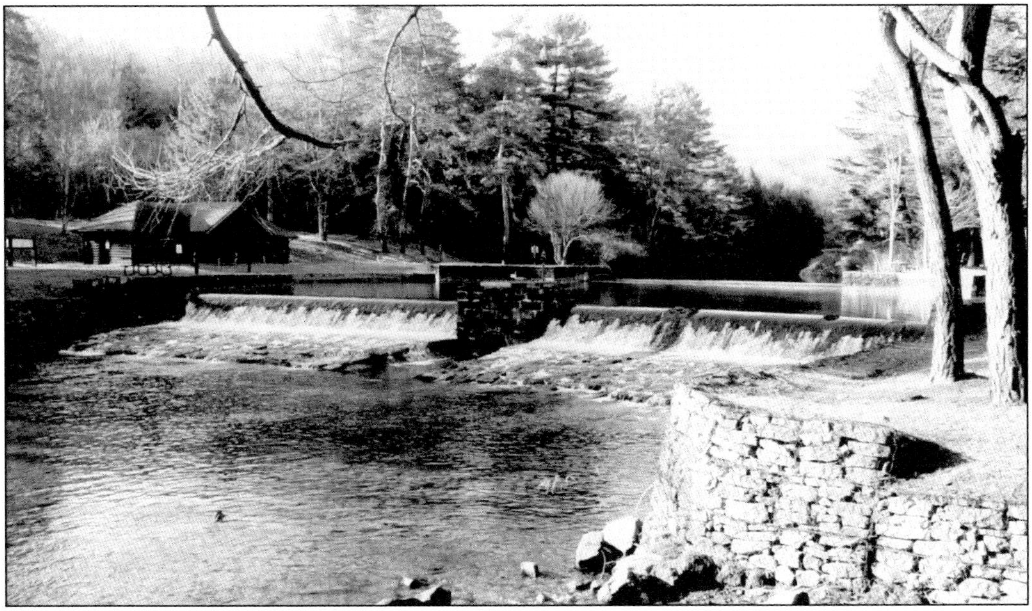

Civilian Conservation Corps (CCC) workers built this small dam at Loleta in the 1930s. It is now a recreational area in the Allegheny National Forest. Buzzard Swamp is another area that offers recreational opportunities. It has extensive waterfowl propagation ponds and hiking trails and is jointly managed by the Pennsylvania Game Commission and the National Forest Service. Both areas are in the Millstone Creek area. (Dennis McGeehan.)

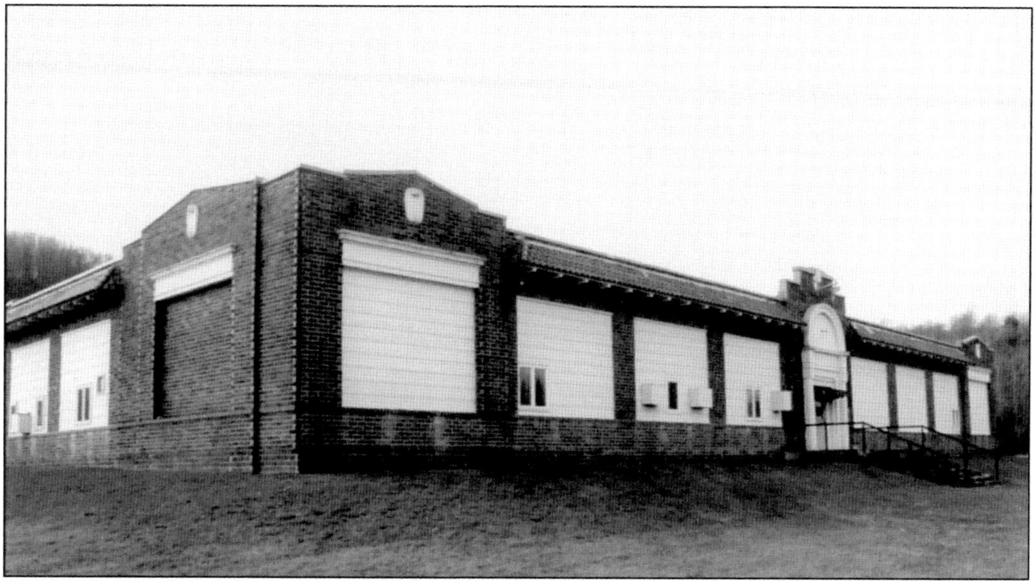

Brockport is on the southwestern border of Elk County and just north of Brockway in Jefferson County. The area's main industry was mining, both coal and clay. This photograph depicts the Horton Township School, which, like many rural schools, fell victim to consolidation. The BP Inn is located in Brockport. It was located on the Buffalo, Rochester and Pittsburgh Railroad and was located halfway between Buffalo and Pittsburgh. (Dennis McGeehan.)

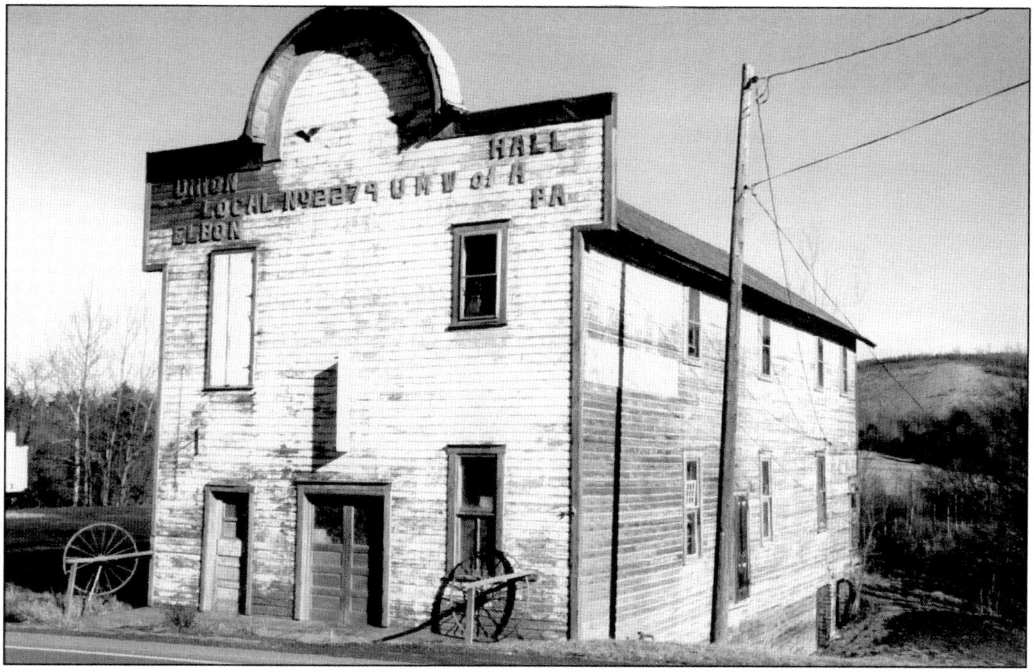

The union hall between Brandy Camp and Elbon was built after labor law reform in the 1930s. Before that, mounted private coal and iron police enforced owners' demands in the area. The local mining communities also used the hall for dancing, plays, music, and school activities. It later became an antiques store. Elbon was the company town of the Noble Coal Company. Elbon is Noble spelled backward. (Dennis McGeehan.)

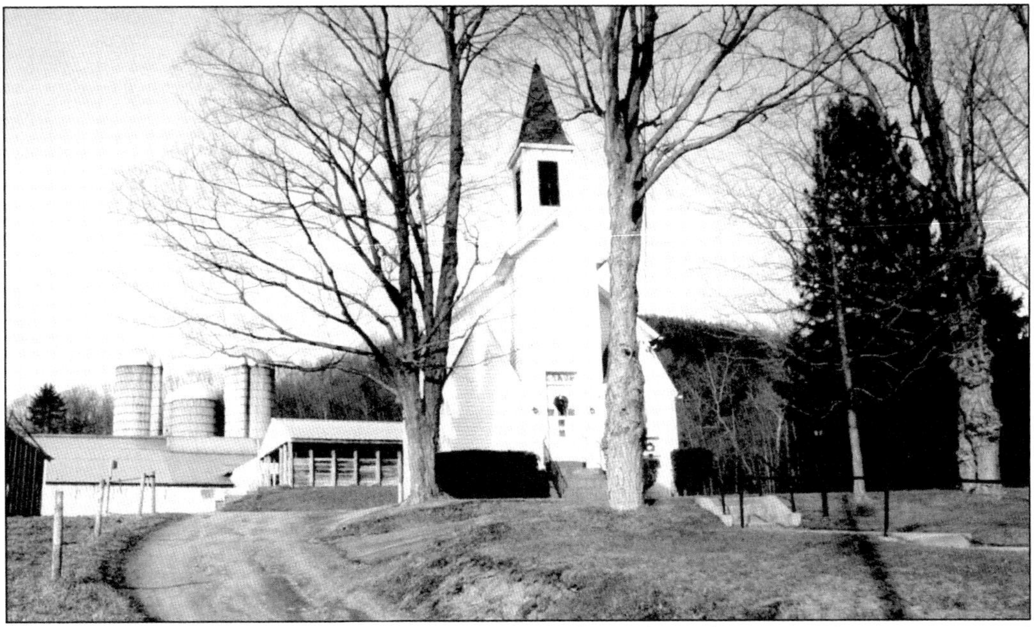

Toby was named after a legendary pioneer named Tobias whom the Native Americans trusted for his knowledge of herbs and home remedies. Timber, coal, and farming were the area's subsistence. A branch of the Erie Railroad served the area. The Toby Valley Methodist Church, seen here, was organized in 1876. Before that, the area was served by circuit riders, in the colorful era of ministry from horseback. (Dennis McGeehan.)

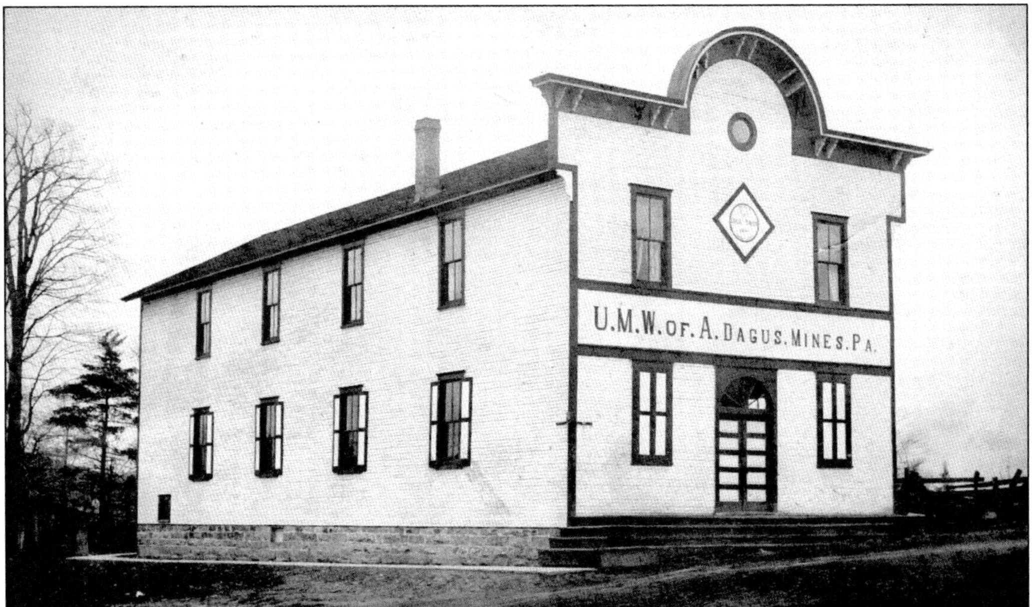

Dagus Mines was a company town built by the Northwestern Mining and Exchange Company. It was named for the spur of the Daguscahonda Railroad serving the mines. It was an early stagecoach stop on the Milesburg-Smethport Turnpike. The union hall, shown here, was not only the site of union activity but also hosted occasional medicine shows where singing and stage play accompanied sales of untested elixirs from traveling hucksters. (Mark Wendel.)

Coal Hollow is a small coal patch town located in Fox Township. It was built by the Northwestern Mining and Exchange Company to house the miners in the adjacent coal mines. The village included a company store, a public school, and the Guardian Angels Catholic Church. A spur of the Shawmut Railroad on Erie Railroad trackage served the location.

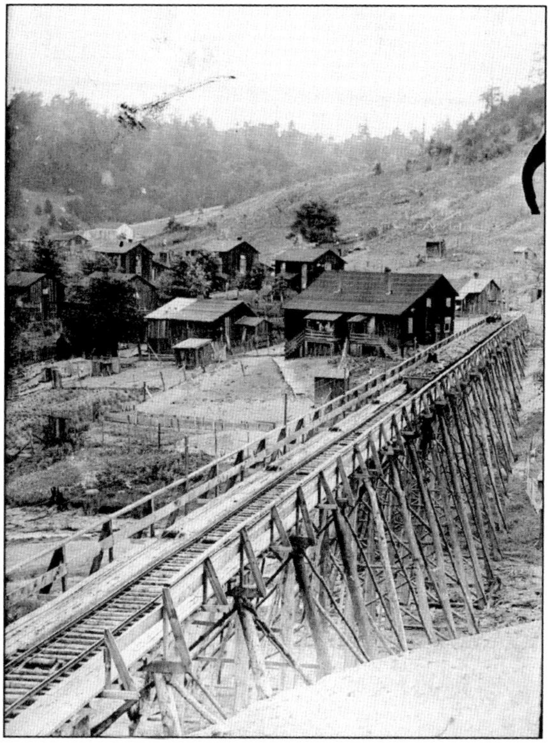

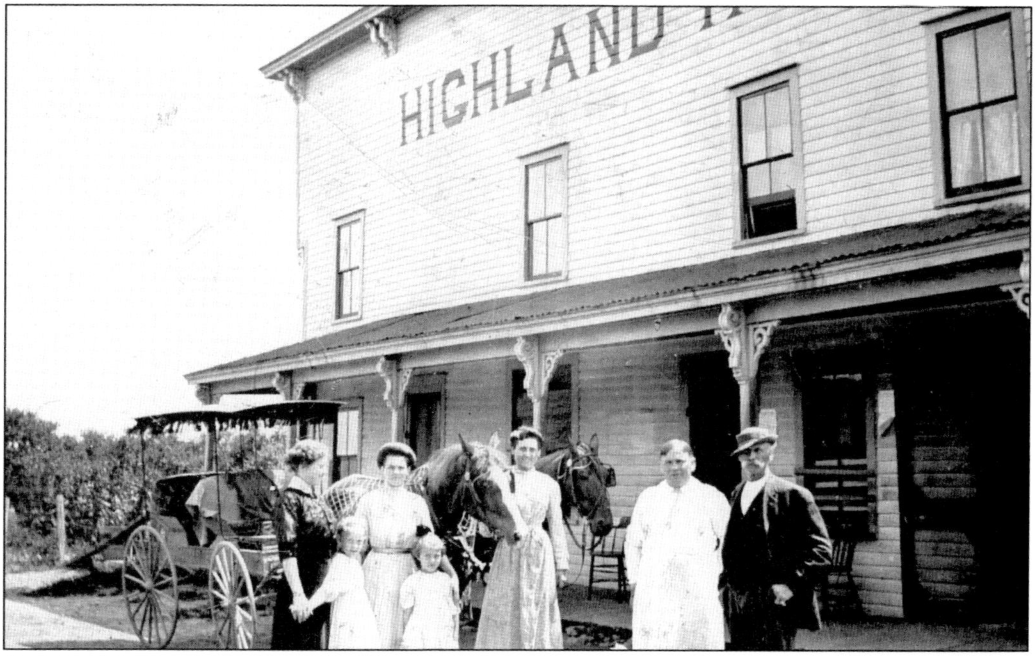

Highland Township's many small crossroads villages are mostly camps today. They include Highland, Russell City, James City, Lamont, Nansen, Sackett, and Pig's Ear. The Highland Hotel, depicted in this photograph, is the crossroads of the township's activity. A major Native American trail, the Iroquois Main Road used to pass close to the hotel. Archaeologists have excavated ancient Native American forts in the area.

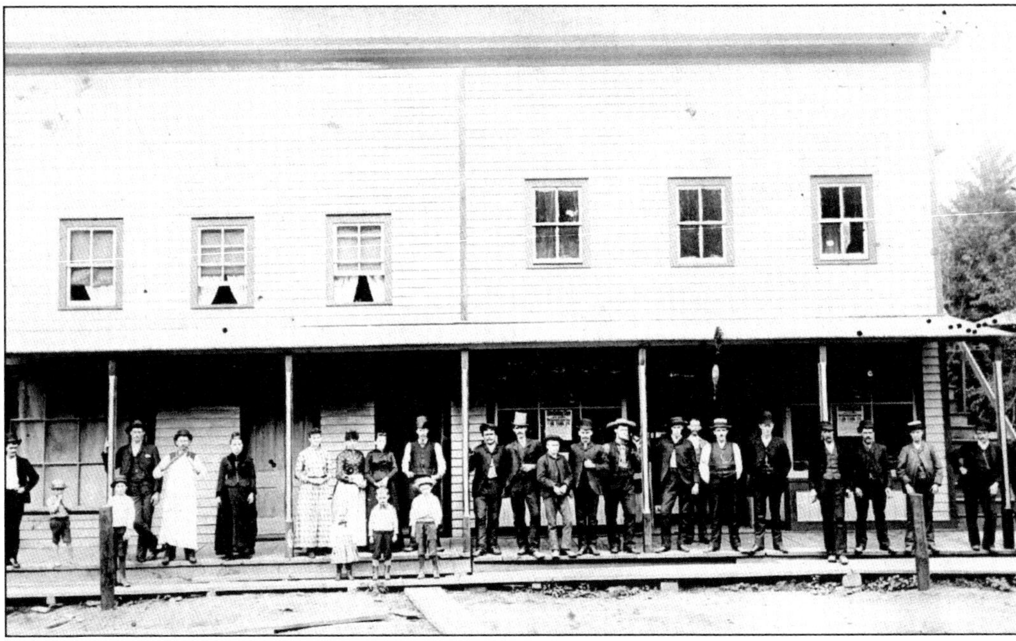

The settlement of Glen Hazel was started by a group of glassblowers sent by the Belgian government. The original name was New Flanders. However, lack of funds caused the colony to fail, and the Belgians drifted away to other communities. The site was renamed Glen Hazel when a sawmill was erected.

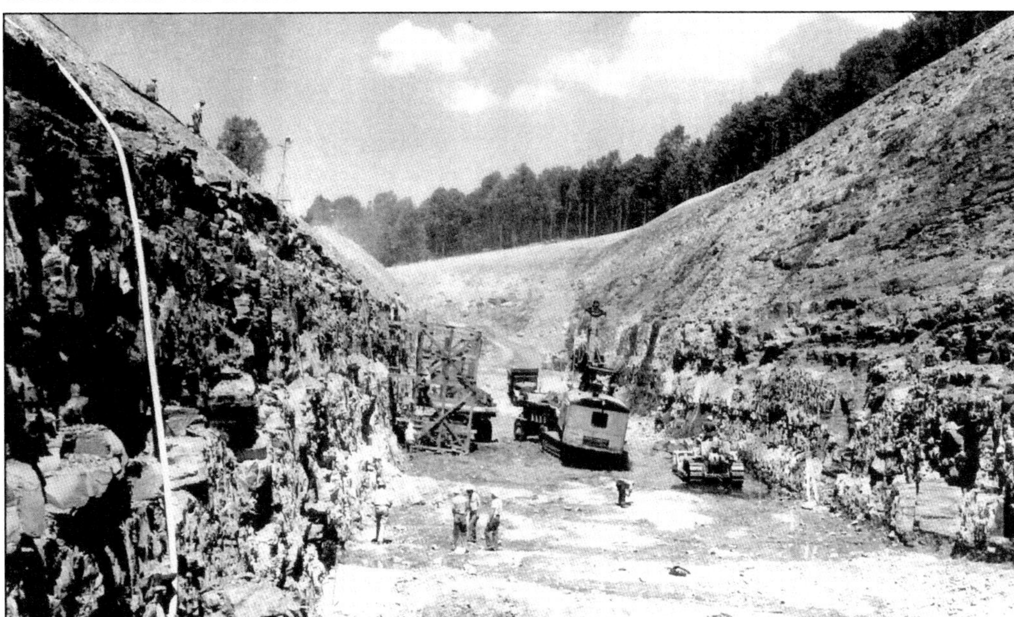

Construction workers dig the core trench for the East Branch Dam in the late 1940s. In 1936 and 1942, floods devastated western Pennsylvania and the United States Army Corps of Engineers began construction of a series of dams designed to protect the watersheds of western Pennsylvania and Pittsburgh. The dam has also provided tourism and recreation opportunities for the county.

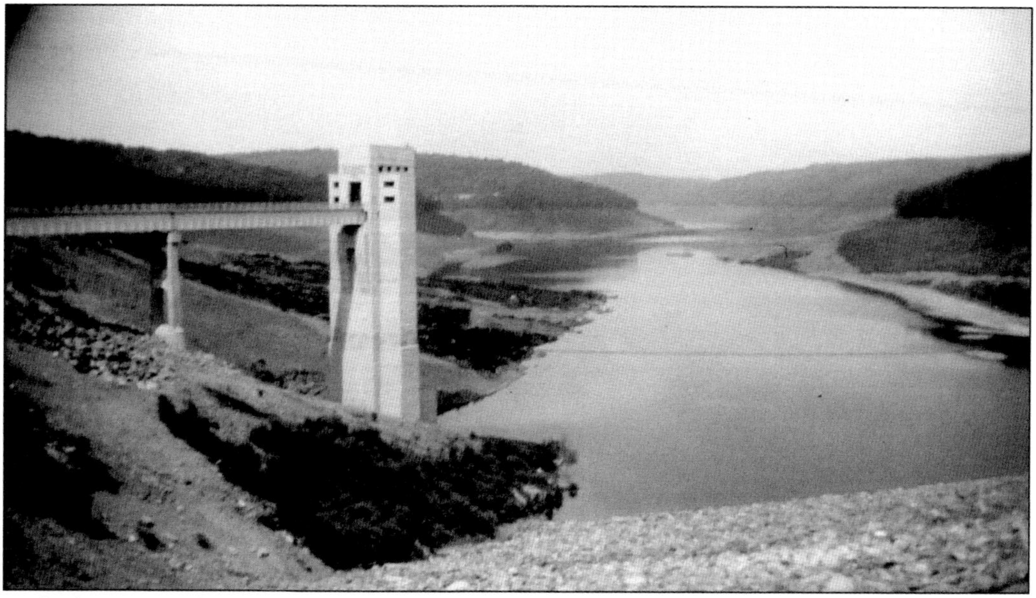

In the late 1950s, the East Branch Dam was ready to be filled. It became operational in December 1952. Surrounded by state forest, state game lands, and state park land, the dam has become the recreational magnet for Elk County. The first state game land purchased in Pennsylvania was just downstream of the dam. Three-fourths underwater, the control tower is the tallest structure in Elk County.

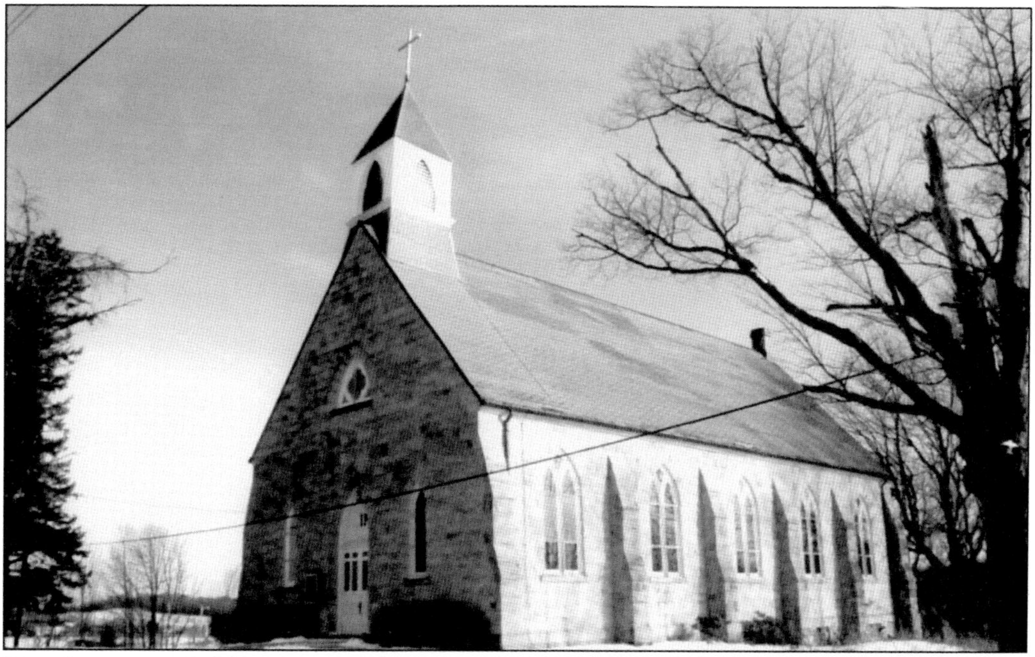

Rasselas was settled by pioneers when the area was still part of McKean County. One of the settlers was Rasselas W. Brown, after whom the village was named. The Holy Cross Catholic Church was completed in 1888 and replaced an earlier log church. Before this church was erected, the Benedictine priests from St. Marys traveled the 15 miles to serve the community. (Dennis McGeehan.)

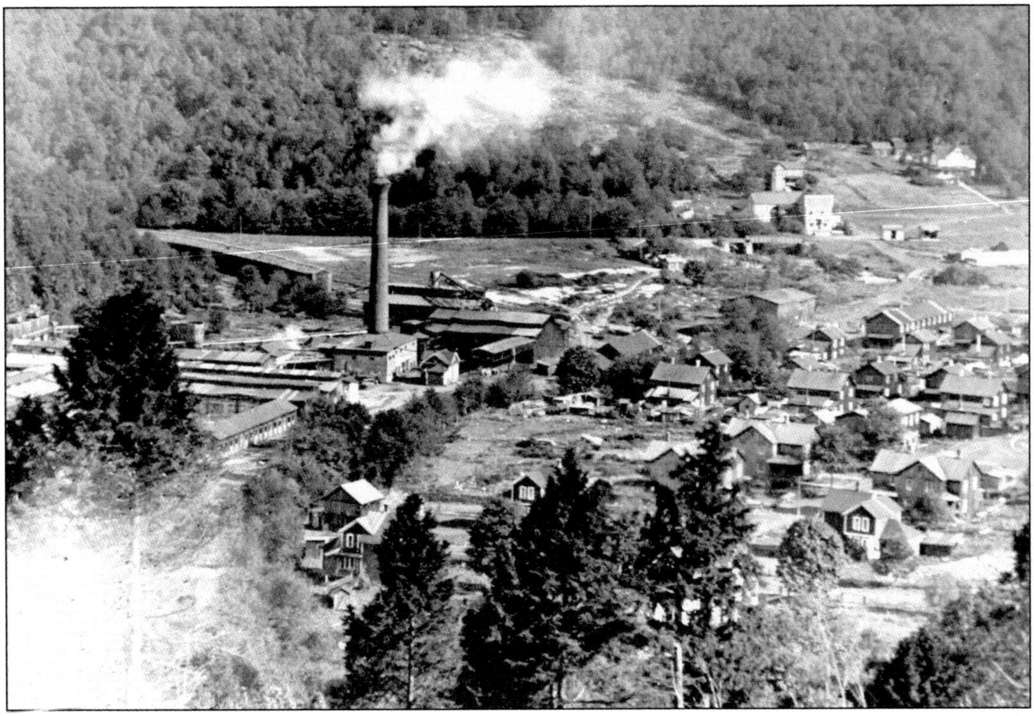

Instanter was a logging community on the upper East Branch of the Clarion River. In the early 1950s when the East Branch Dam was filled, Instanter disappeared under the waters of the new lake but not forever. It was located at the very end of the new impoundment, and whenever there are drought conditions, Instanter once again rises above the water and former residents stage a reunion.

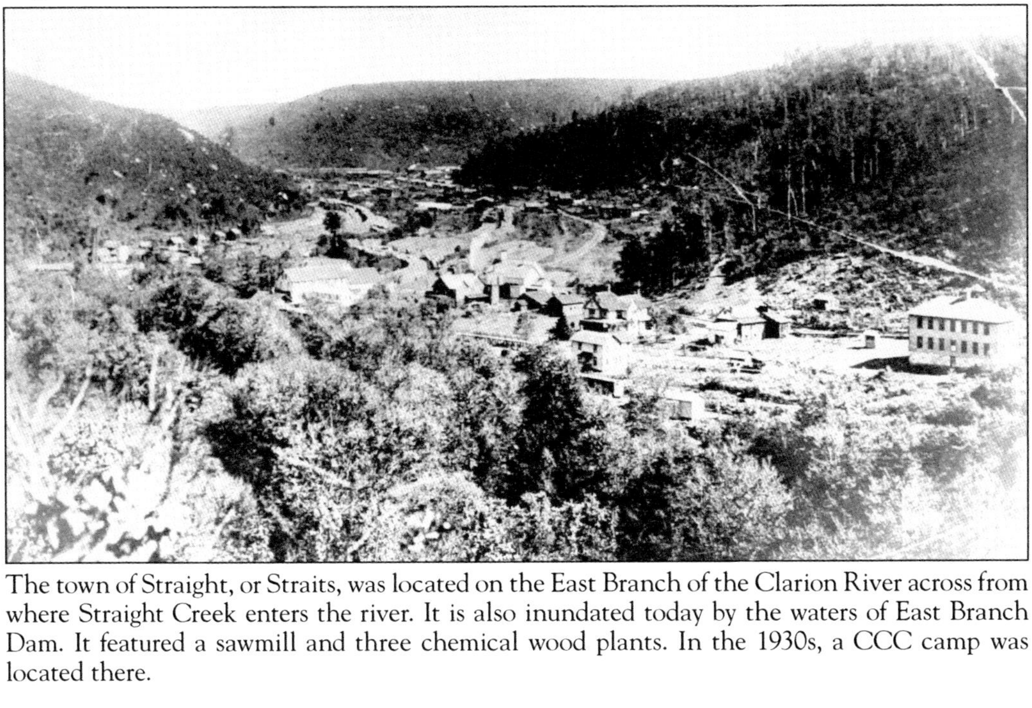

The town of Straight, or Straits, was located on the East Branch of the Clarion River across from where Straight Creek enters the river. It is also inundated today by the waters of East Branch Dam. It featured a sawmill and three chemical wood plants. In the 1930s, a CCC camp was located there.

Two

Business and Industry

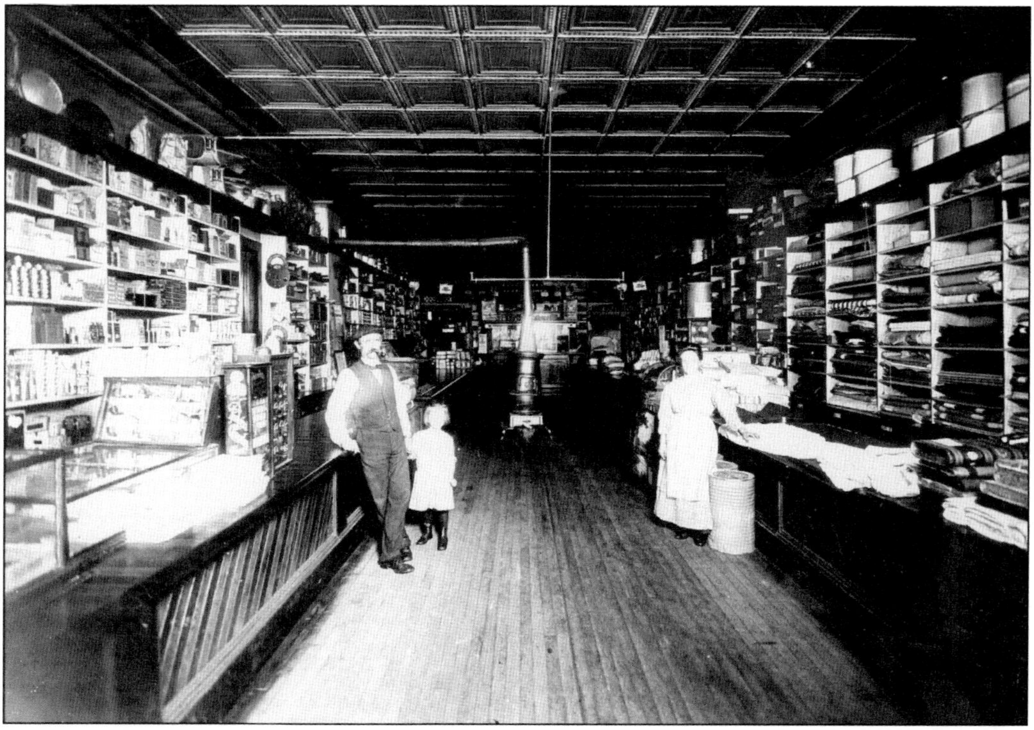

The M. J. Fuenfinger store in Kersey is pictured. This dry goods store was typical of the time with its decorative ceiling and hardwood floors. It sold numerous items, including bolts of cloth, visible on the right, and hats. Note the hatboxes stacked above. Also note the potbellied stove in the center of the store.

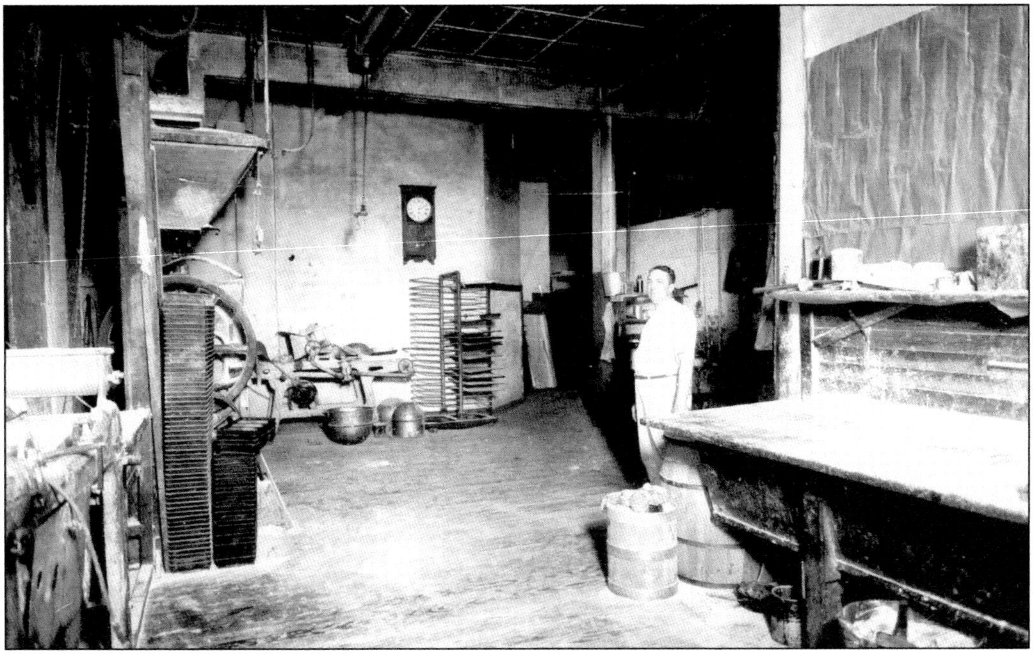

Ed Luhr, the manager of the New Baltimore Bakery on Erie Avenue in St. Marys, is shown amid the apparatus of his profession. Before bread was trucked in from outside the county, many local bakeries supplied the needs of the residents. Bakeries were always covered with a coating of white flour.

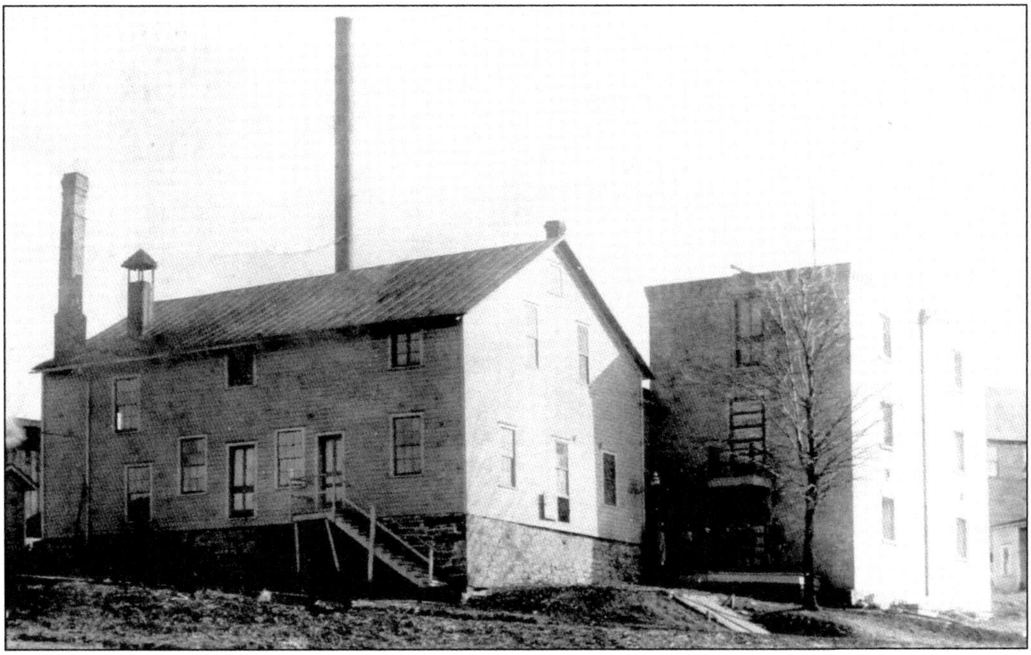

Straub Brewery is one of the premier tourist attractions of Elk County. Founded in 1872, the brewery has been satisfying local customers for over 100 years. Well known to local residents, it was eventually discovered by beer critics, and today beer connoisseurs from around the country and even the world make the pilgrimage to its "Eternal Tap" to sample the product.

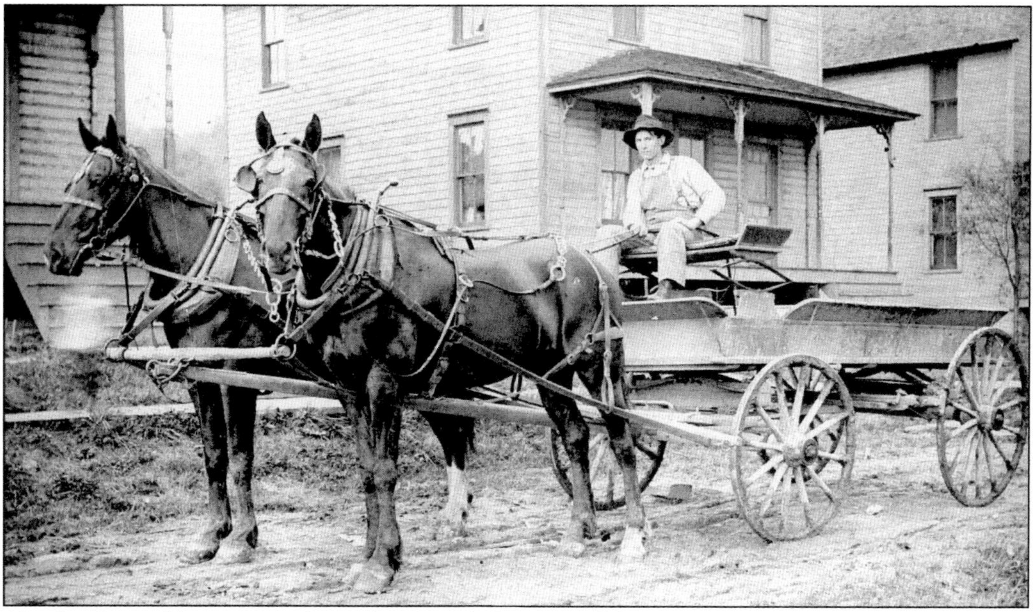

Charles Dippold is pictured on the Straub Brewery delivery wagon in 1906 delivering beer to local residents. The Straub Brewery is an old family-owned business that still operates in St. Marys. Many area residents still keep Straub Beer on tap in their homes to serve to guests.

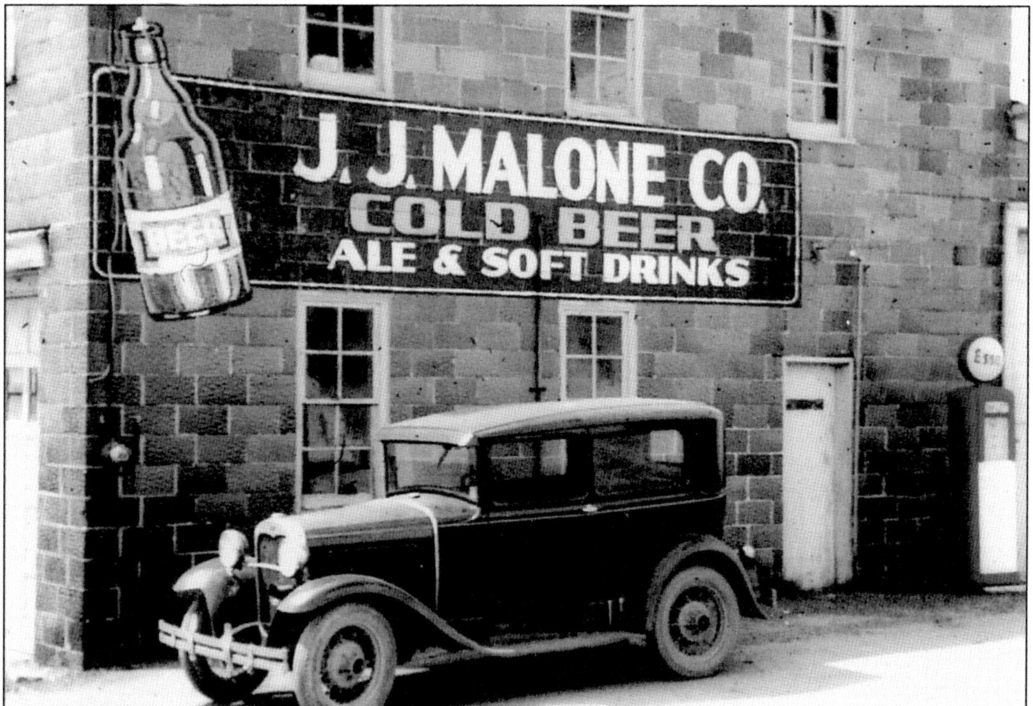

At one time there were seven breweries located in St. Marys. The residents were of German Bavarian ancestry and were knowledgeable in the brewing arts. Only the Straub Brewery survived the colorful era that was Prohibition in Elk County. The J. J. Malone beer distributor was located on Main Street in Kersey. The sign is faded but the building still stands. (Bill Krellner.)

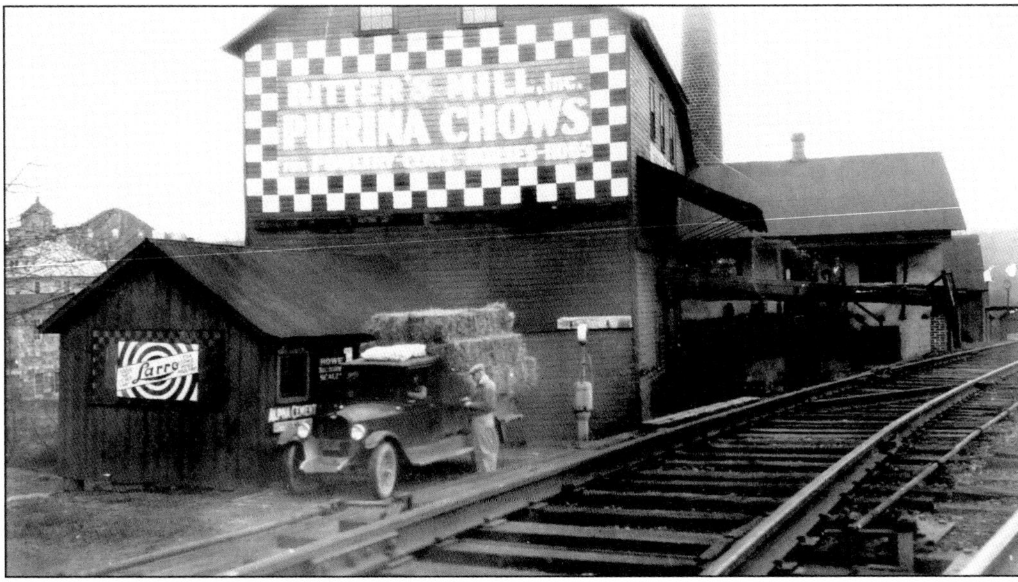

R. C. McGill ran a gristmill on Elk Creek at McGill and State Roads. However, most people remember the mill as Ritter's Mill after its next operator, Leohnard Ritter. The mill not only ground grain, but it eventually came to include a complex of allied services. During Prohibition, it was raided for making illegal whiskey.

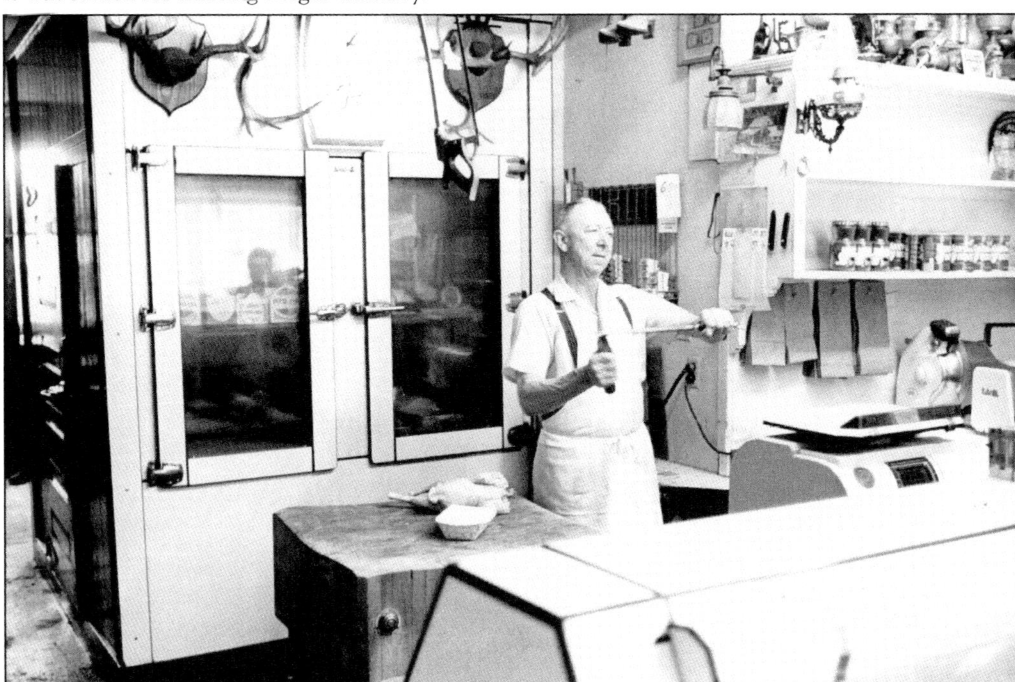

Small grocery stores used to abound before today's age of super-sized markets. These small operations provided all the services a local neighborhood needed. Many also butchered their own meat. One such was Philip "Fish" Herzing's market on Maurus Street in St. Marys. Fish is shown sharpening a knife by his butcher's block, with meat saw hanging handy. (Photograph by Ray Beimel.)

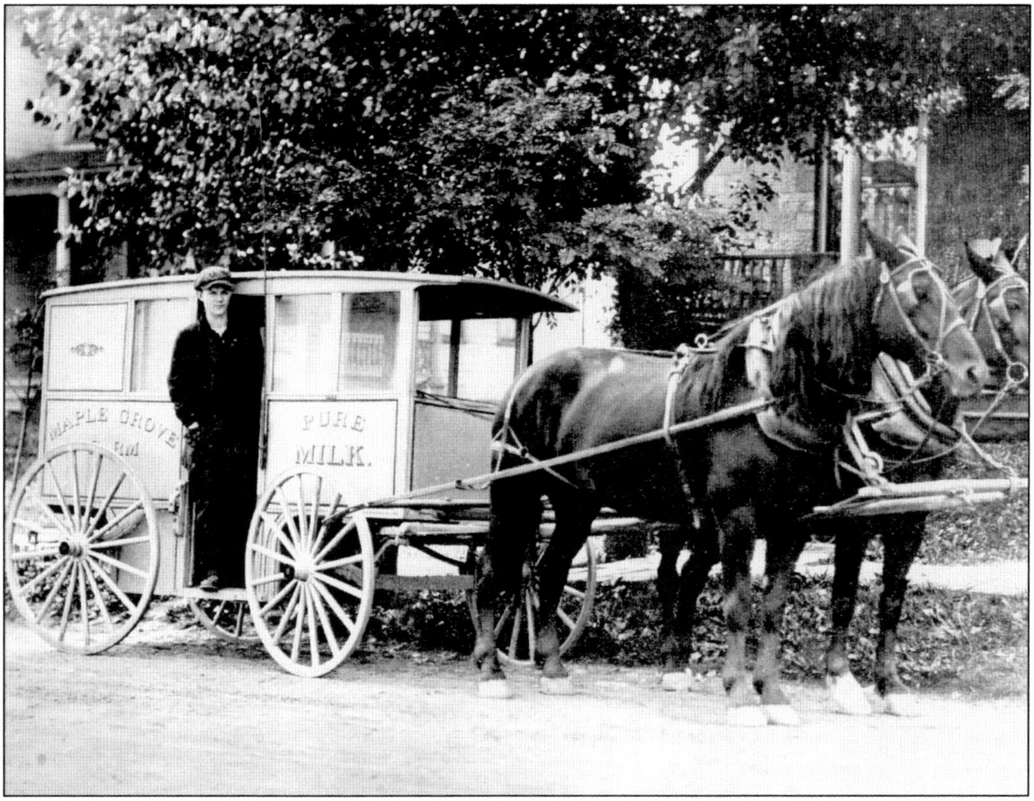

There were many dairies located throughout Elk County, and some had fleets of horse-drawn wagons that delivered milk to households throughout the area, usually early in the morning at first light. The Maple Grove Dairy was operated by the Coryell and Russ Store on North St. Marys Street in St. Marys.

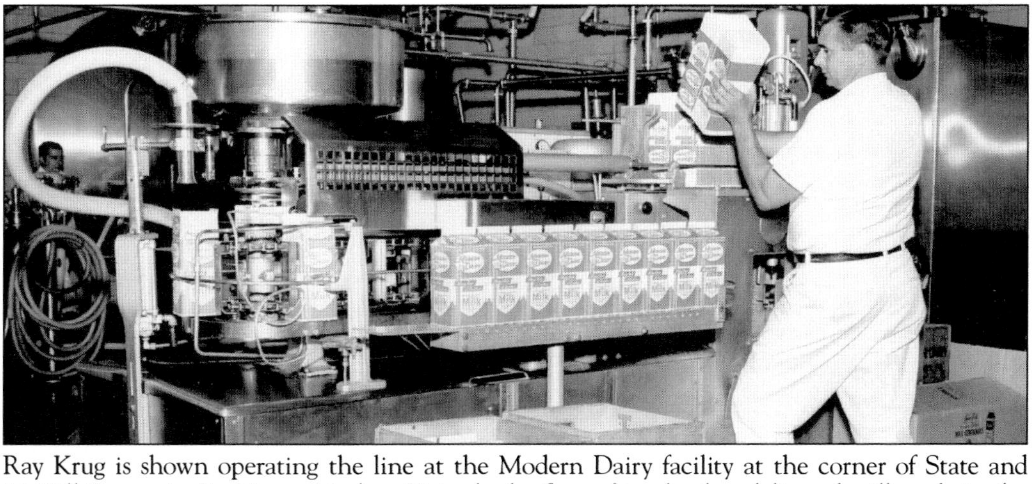

Ray Krug is shown operating the line at the Modern Dairy facility at the corner of State and McGill Streets in St. Marys. Modern Dairy had a fleet of trucks that delivered milk early in the morning throughout Elk County. The Gregory farm on Sugar Hill in St. Marys supplied milk to the processing plant.(Grotzinger Collection, St. Marys and Benzinger Township Historical Society.)

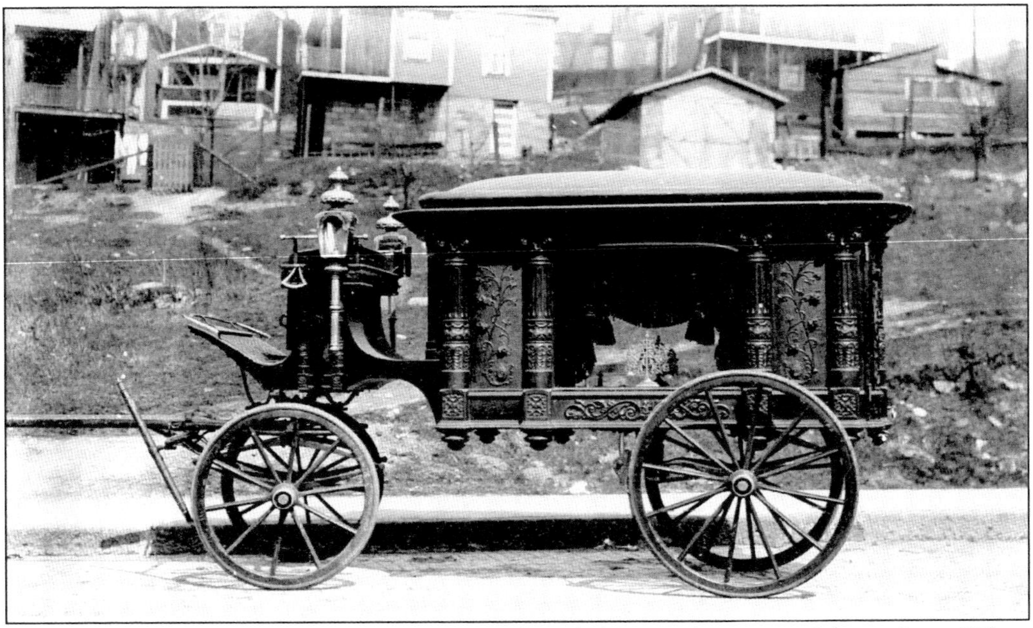

Here is a picture of a horse-drawn hearse from the Ubel Funeral Home in Johnsonburg. When a person travels to his or her final resting place, elegance is a fitting memorial. This vehicle is grandly decorated. Note the lamps and the viewing windows on the sides. Mourners would walk along beside the hearse to the cemetery.

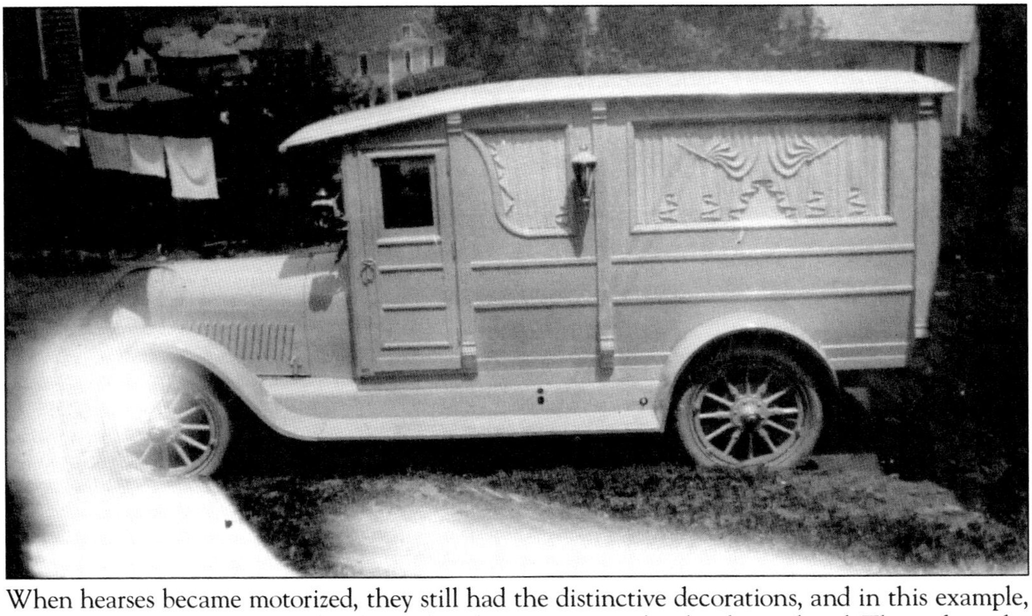

When hearses became motorized, they still had the distinctive decorations, and in this example, built right in. The hearse also has lamps but the viewing window has been closed. This is from the Weis Funeral Home in St. Marys. Most hearses were black. A white hearse was used for children.

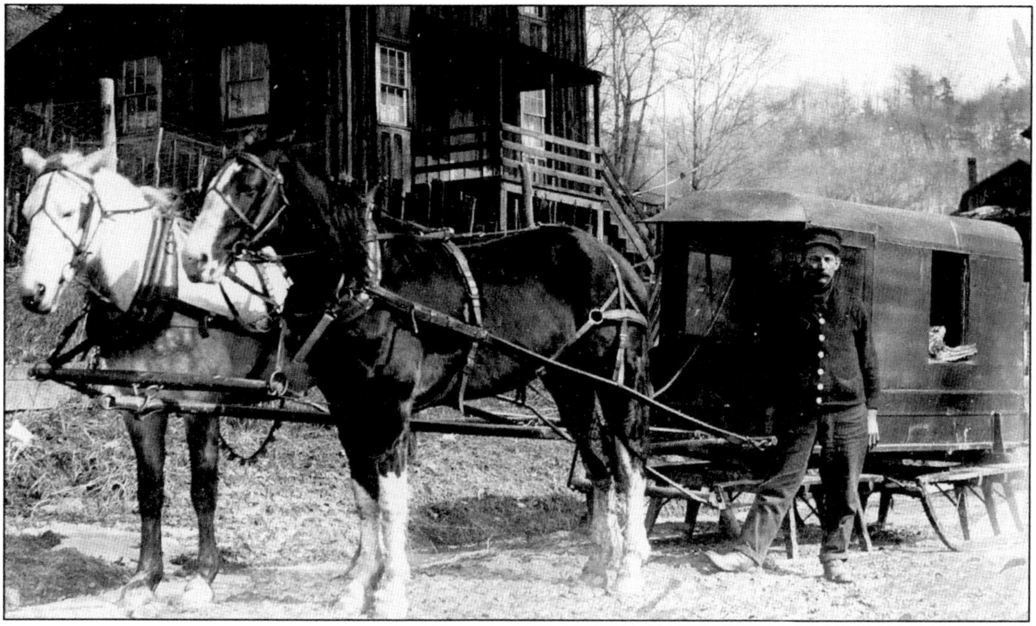

This is a photograph of a horse-drawn butcher's sled. Note the butchered meat hanging out of the uncovered window. The sled runners made it easier to haul by horse team in winter. It would have been converted to wheels during warm weather. The butcher was John B. Straessley of Fox Township.

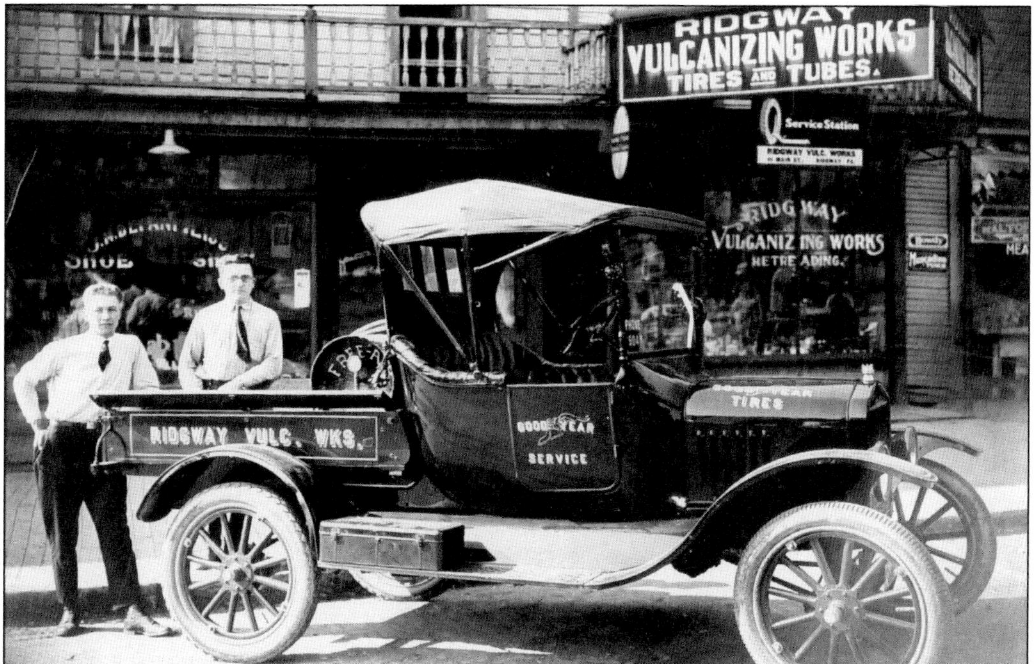

Employees of the Ridgway Vulcanizing Works pose outside the establishment beside their company vehicle. Vulcanizing refers to the process of heat-treating rubber to make it stronger and more durable. Back when tires were made of rubber, vulcanizing usually meant fixing flat tires and selling tires and tubes as well.

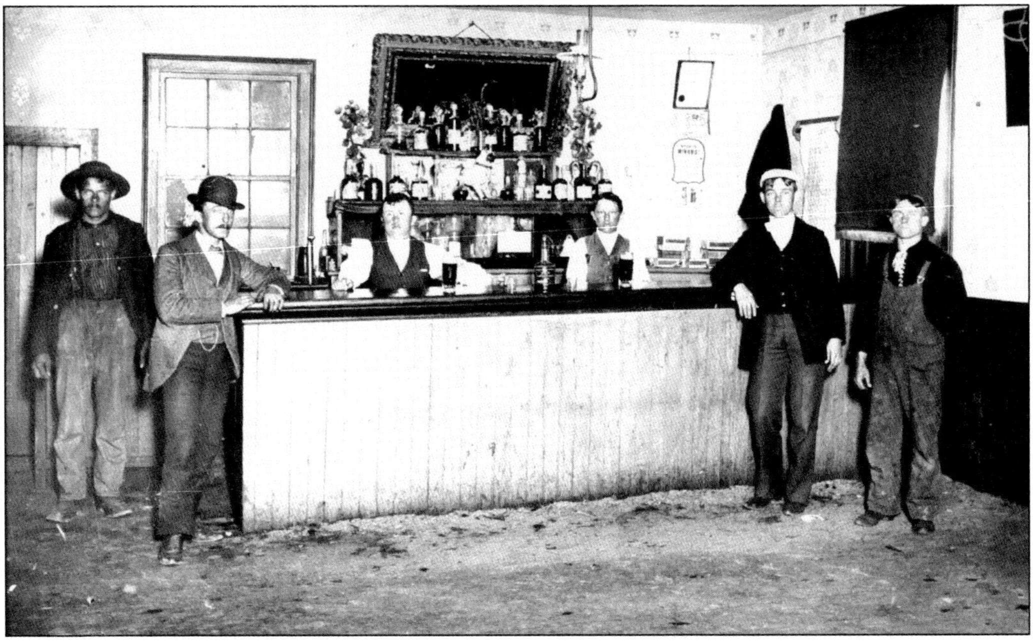

Bars were not fancy in the old days. This is the Zelt Hotel at the corner of South Michael and Chestnut Streets in St. Marys. It was later known as the Farmers Hotel and for many years the Corner Grill. Jake (left) and George Zelt are behind the bar. There are no stools or foot rail. Only a mirror has been hung to display the sparse selection.

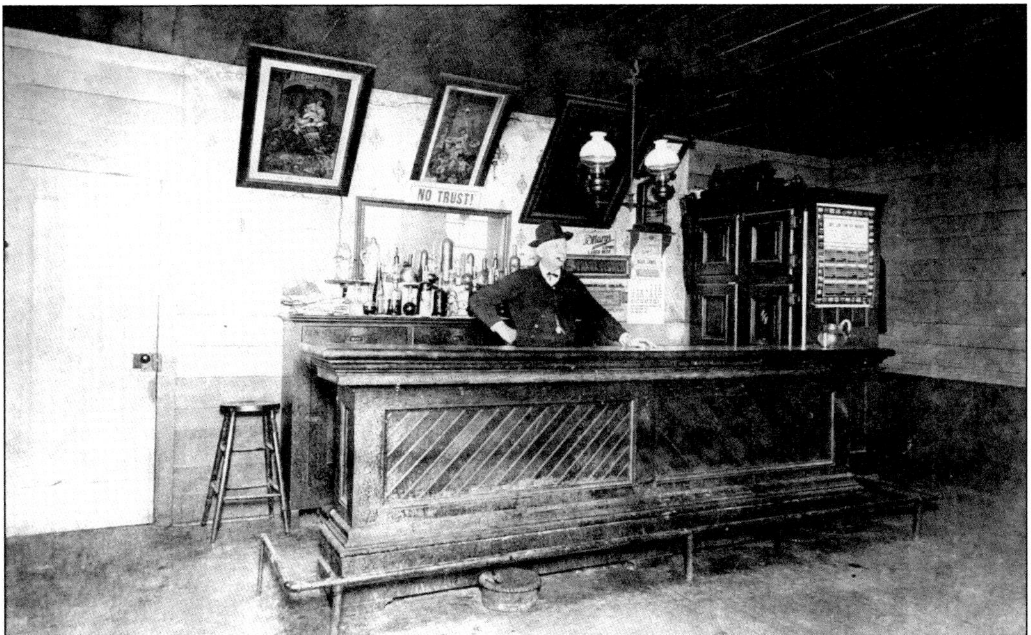

Frank Fisher is shown behind his bar on South Michael Street in St. Marys. This bar has one stool, a foot rail, and a spittoon. Some artwork has been hung behind the bar, and it features a fancy wood cooler. The establishment offers St. Marys Export Lager Beer but "No Trust!" No cash register is visible in this photograph or the previous one.

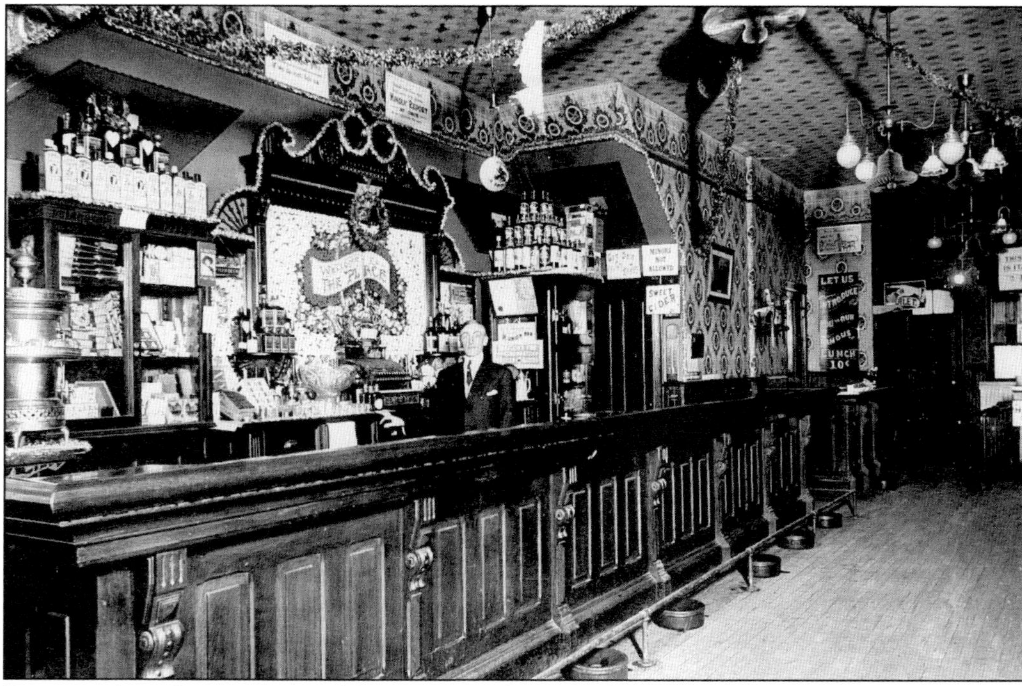

Barrooms have become more elaborate since the early days. This unidentified bar in St. Marys has a built-in mirror, fancy wallpaper, and lighting fixtures. The custom-made bar is much more ornate than the ones in the previous two photographs. The bartender is wearing a three-piece suit, he has a cash register, and the selection of beverages and cigars is greater. It has a fancy metal samovar, and the famous lunch is 10¢.

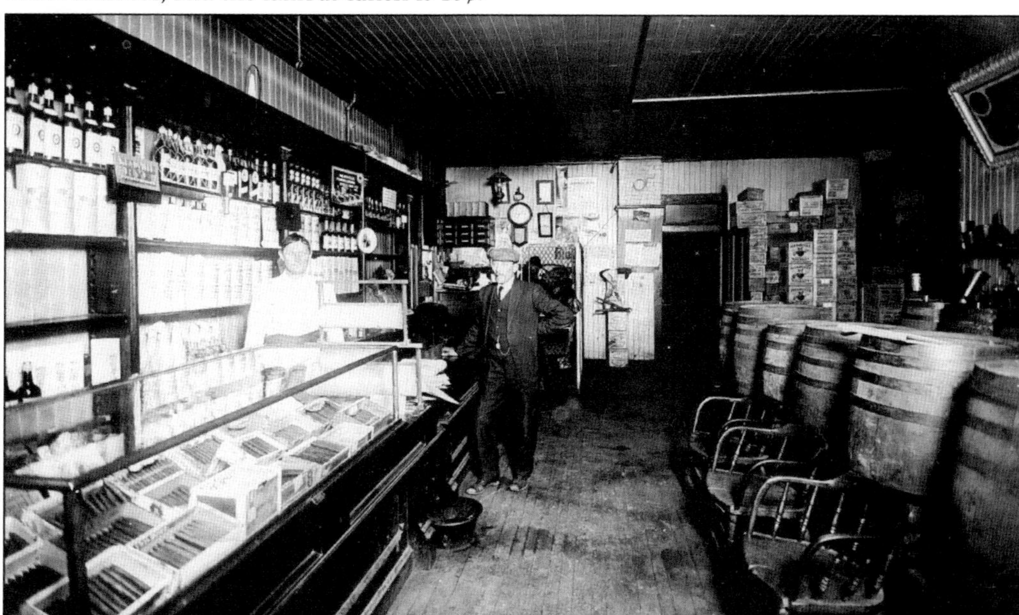

The M. J. Hacherl Liquor Store in Kersey appears to have a large selection of liquor in both barrels and bottles. Note the chairs and spittoon in front of the massive barrels. It also appears to offer a fine selection of cigars. Some of the products visible are Grappa and Meadville Rye.

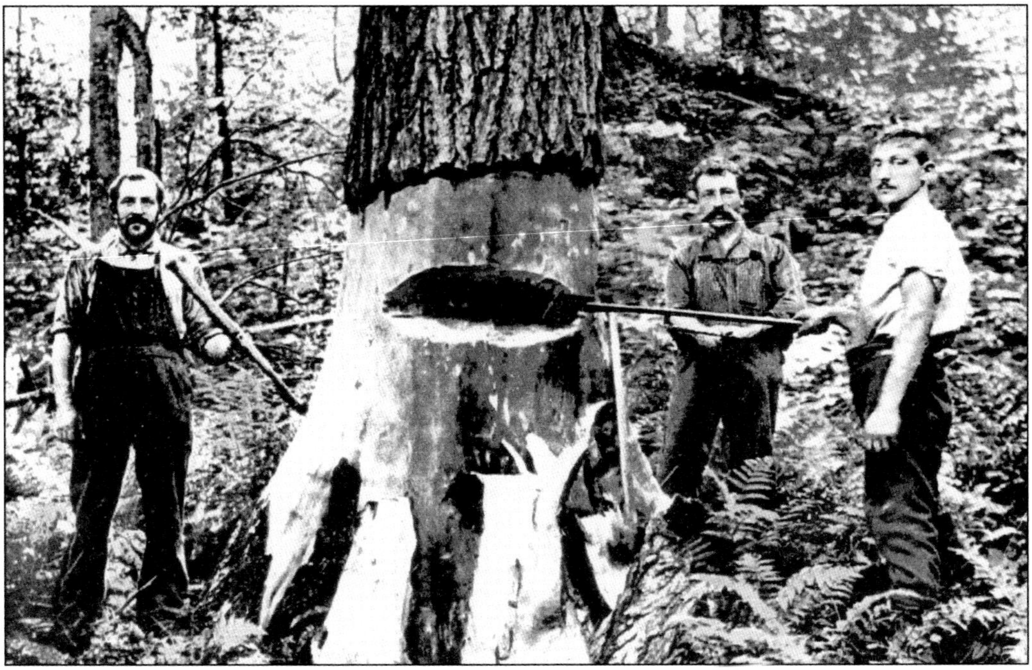

Woodhicks were the backbone of the logging business. It was tough, dangerous work, and there were often newspaper notices of lumberjacks killed or injured in the woods. Elk County was densely forested, and timber became the source of many fortunes. The double-bitted ax and crosscut saw slowly cleared the county to make way for farming and diversified industries.

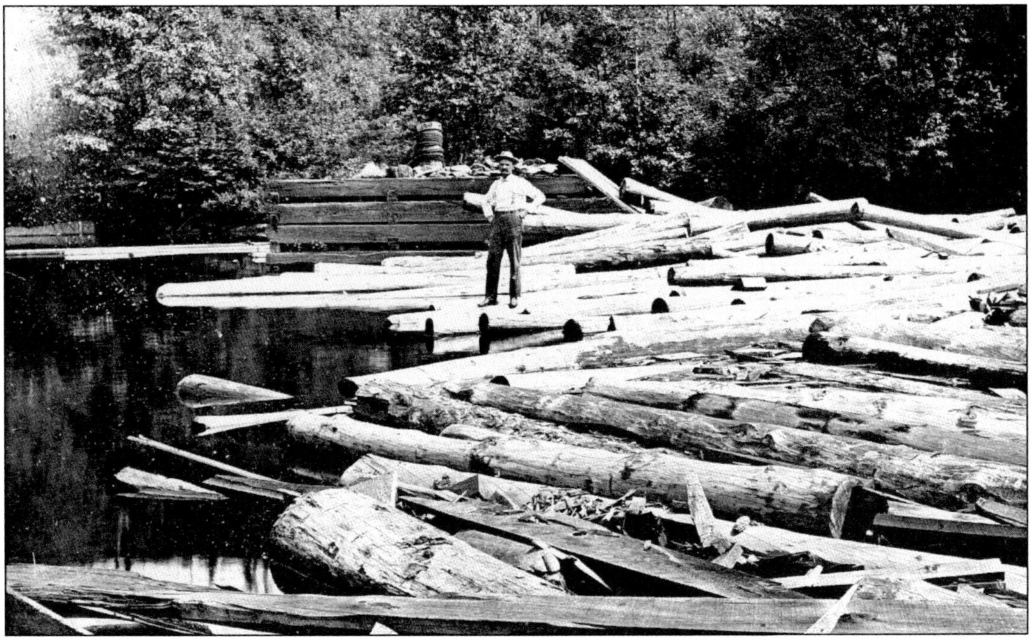

Logs were hauled out of the woods to a river landing where they were either constructed into rafts or floated individually downriver to sawmills. Both methods could not be used on the same river, and rivermen fought one another for the rights to watercourses. Keeping one's limbs from being crushed between the heavy logs was a constant preoccupation.

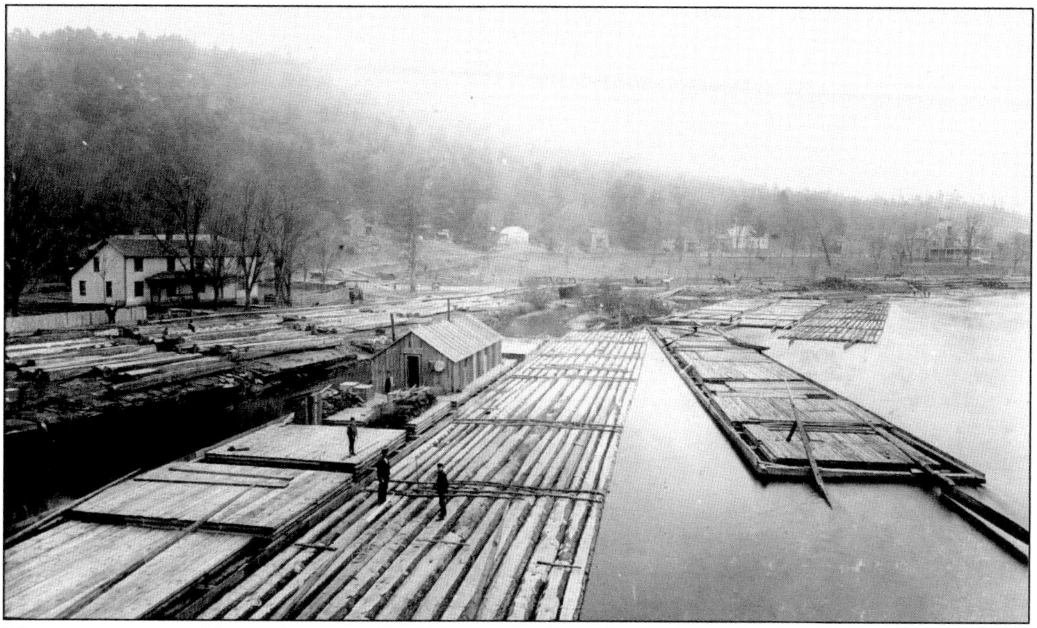

This is a scene of log rafting at Cooksburg on the Clarion River. Log rafts went down the Allegheny drainage west and the Susquehanna drainage east from Elk County. It was a colorful era and a tough, dangerous job. Log rafts formed immediately after the ice was off the rivers. Small dams were dynamited to increase the flow. Rafts were floated to sawmills downstream and the rafters walked back.

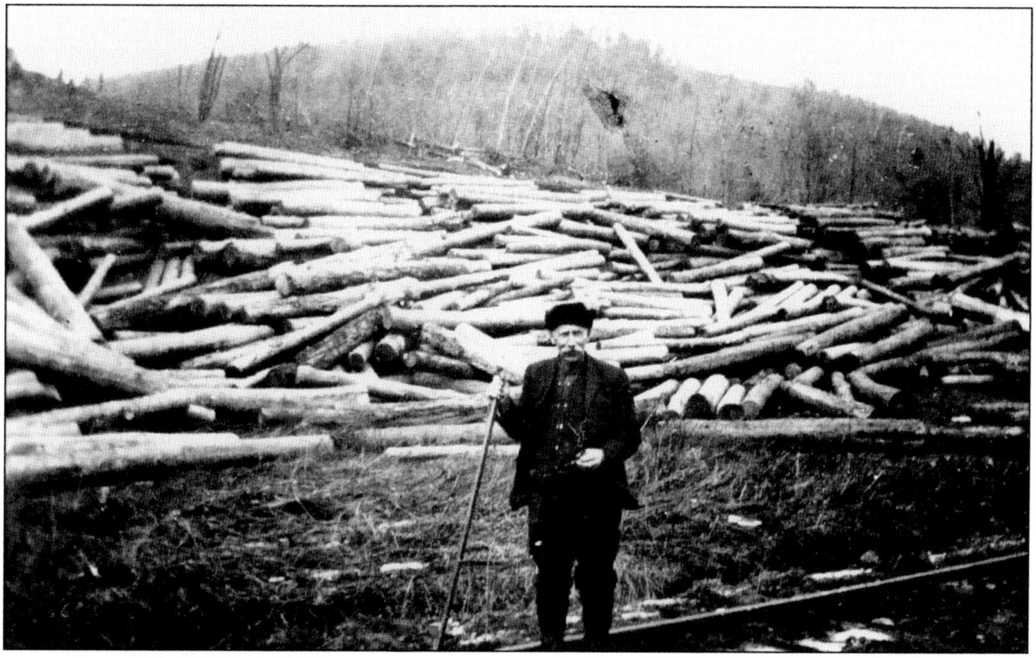

A timber cruiser carried a measuring stick and estimated the amount of board feet a tract of timber would yield. It was the first step in getting lumber to market after a speculator had bought or leased a piece of land. Shown here is Alois Kerner at the last landing of the Kaul and Hall Lumber Company in Rathbun on West Creek in 1922.

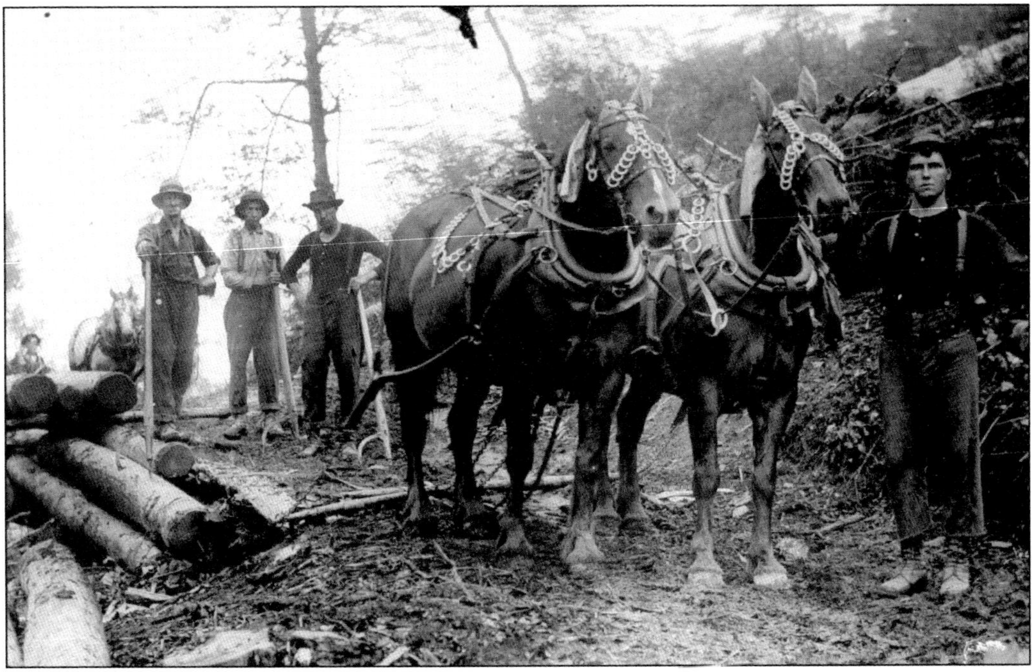

After a tree had been felled, it was stripped of its bark by a peeler. Horses then dragged logs to a water landing or rail siding. Dragging was easier in the winter when snow covered the ground. Note the ear covers on these horses and the cant hooks to roll logs held by the woodhicks.

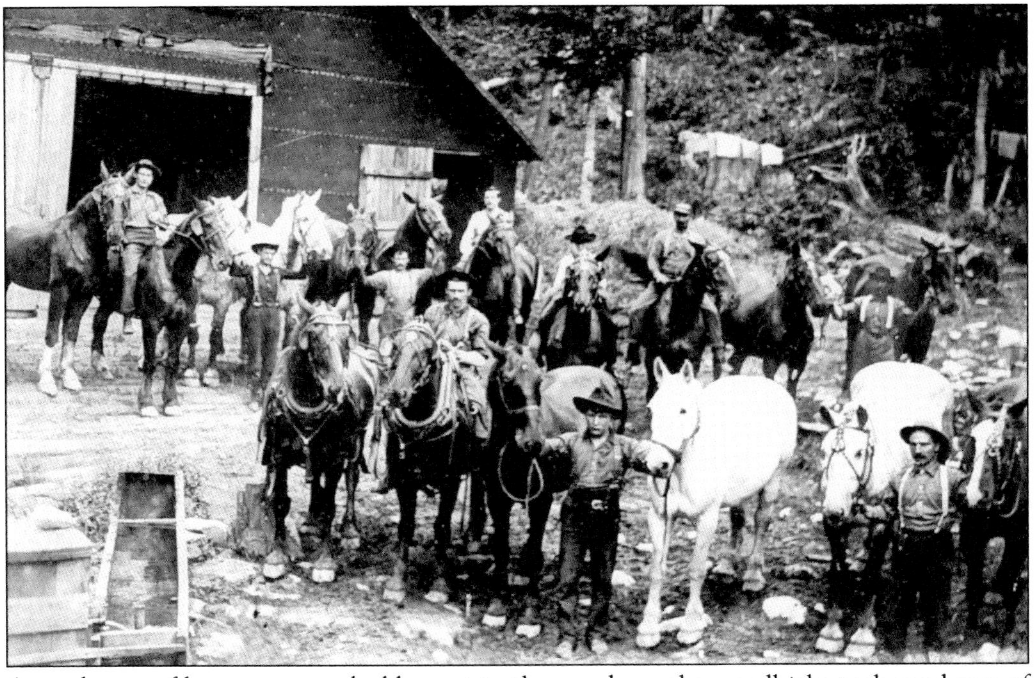

A good team of horses was a valuable asset in the woods, so the woodhicks took good care of their horses. The buildings may need some repair, but the horses are in fine shape. Here is a scene from a lumber camp that seems to have been a large operation given the number of horses assembled for this portrait.

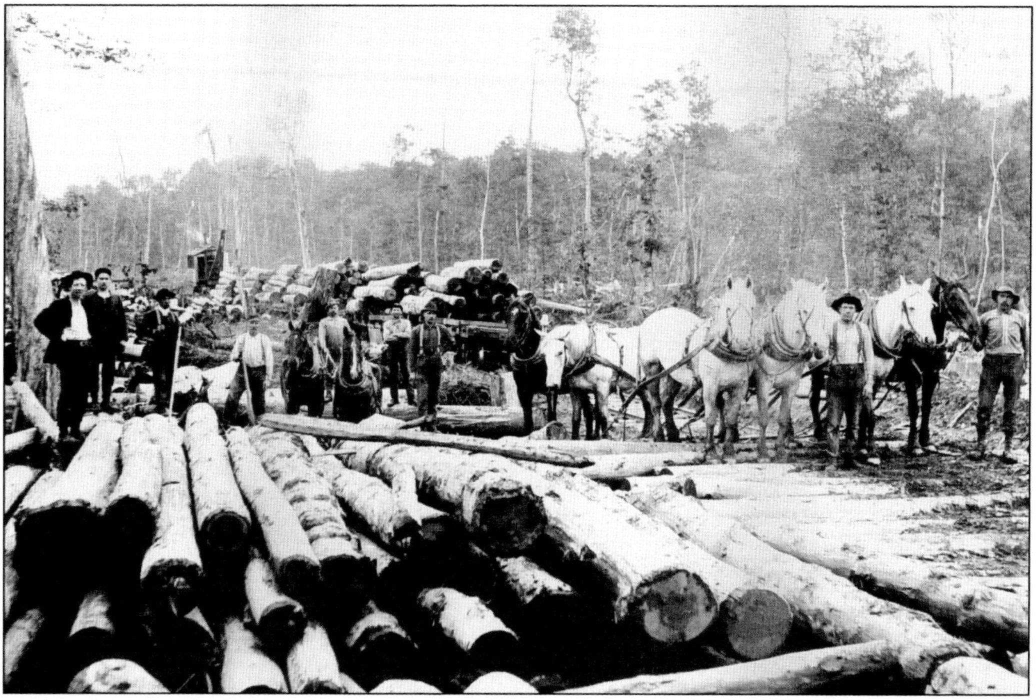

In this photograph, horse teams have dragged logs down to a railroad siding where they will be loaded onto flatcars. In the back left is a Barnhart loader, a unique invention used to load the logs. The teamwork between man, animal, and machine is evident in this photograph.

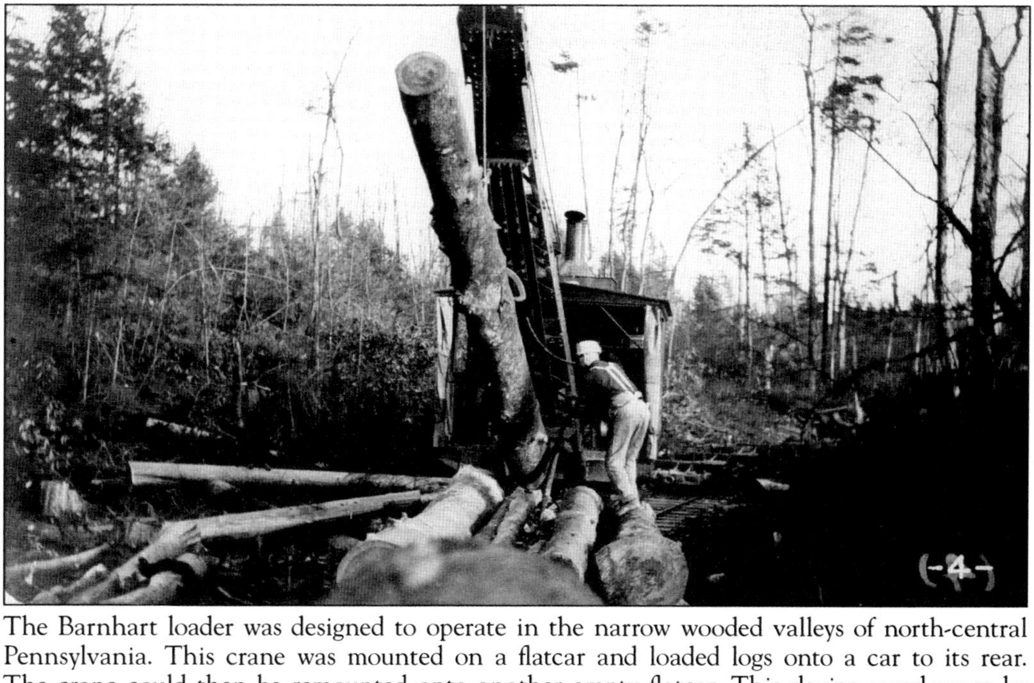

The Barnhart loader was designed to operate in the narrow wooded valleys of north-central Pennsylvania. This crane was mounted on a flatcar and loaded logs onto a car to its rear. The crane could then be remounted onto another empty flatcar. This device saved space by eliminating the need for a double track to get logs out of the woods. (Dave Woods.)

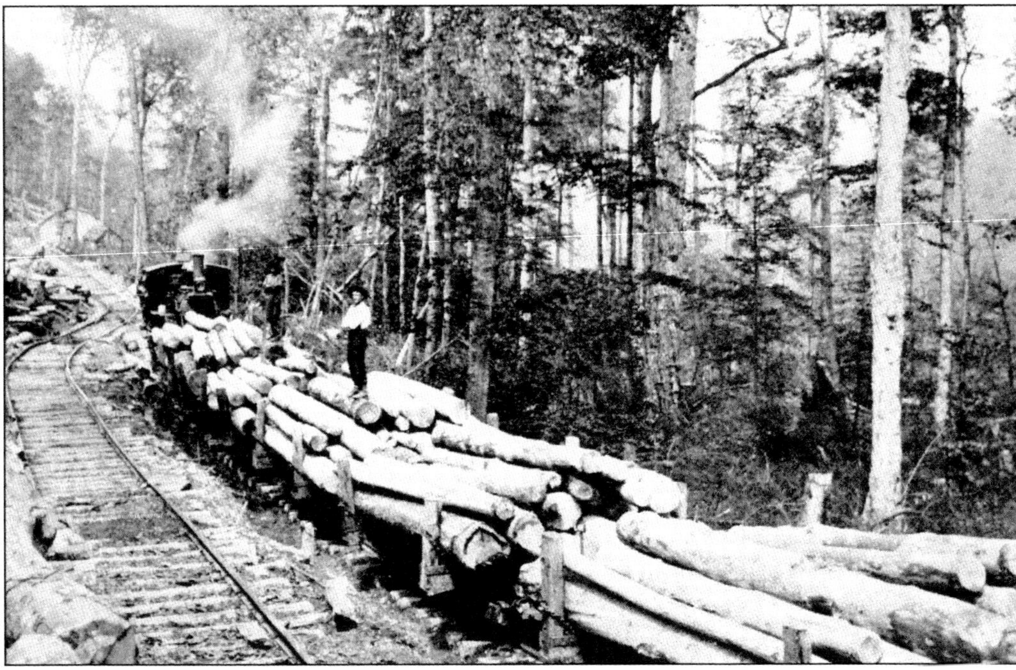

Here is a scene from a railroad siding after the flatcars have been loaded. They will then be transported to one of the many area sawmills for cutting into finished lumber. Originally the sawmills were located downriver before local sawmills sprang up all over Elk County. The traces of abandoned railroads are still noticeable in many area hollows. Some have been turned into hiking and biking trails.

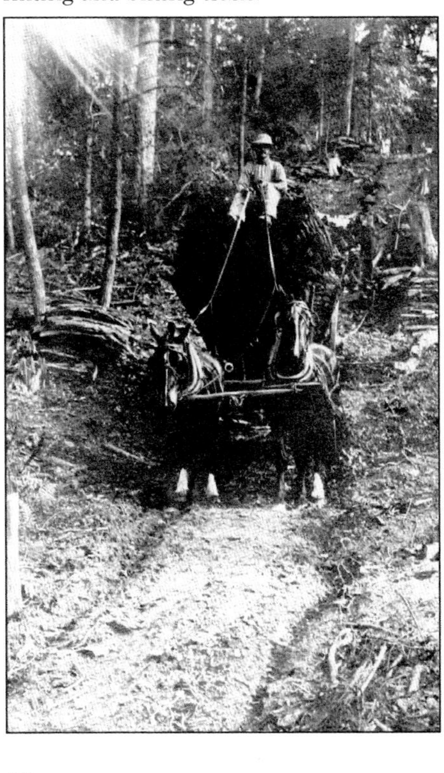

A large stack of hemlock bark is being hauled out of Sawdust Run by an overloaded team of horses. Hemlock bark was valuable for its high tannin content. The bark was used in the tanning industry to tan animal hides into leather. Bark peelers removed the bark from the trees as soon as the tree was felled.

In this photograph a Shawmut Railroad car is being loaded with hemlock bark to be sent to area tanneries for use in the tanning process. For a short time, hemlock bark became more valuable than the wood, and the wood was left behind in the forest as demand for bark increased. Note how high the workers are stacking this load of bark.

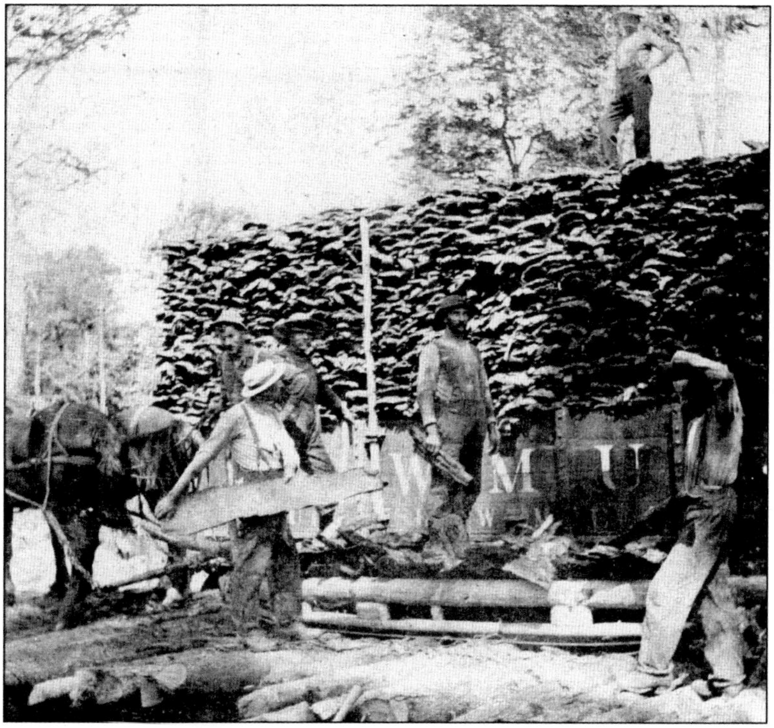

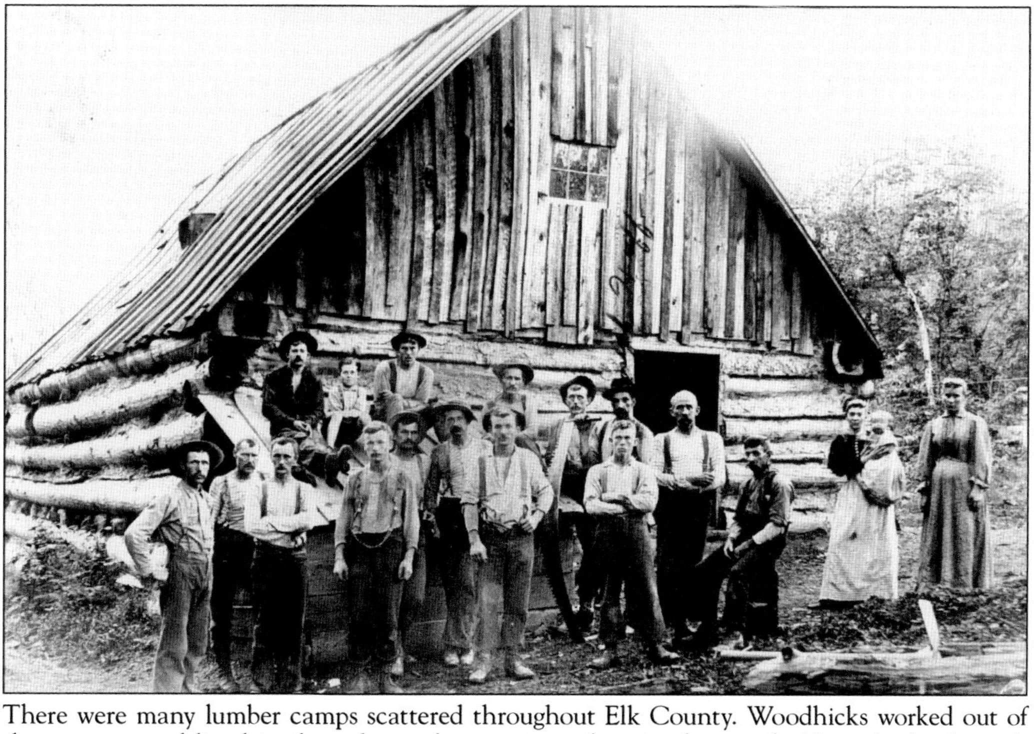

There were many lumber camps scattered throughout Elk County. Woodhicks worked out of these camps and lived in them for weeks at a time, deep in the woods. Note the lumberjack holding a crosscut saw, one of the principal tools of the trade. This camp is a crude structure, as the logs have not even been finished. A woman holding a baby is also visible.

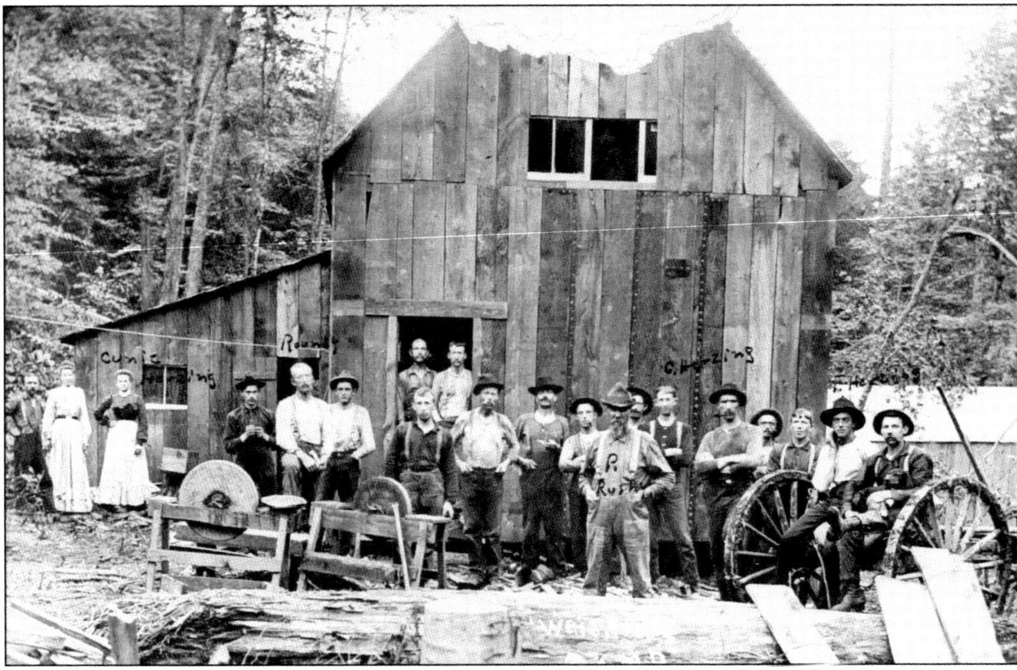

Here is a view of the Weisner Lumber Camp. Lumber camps usually had women cooks who lived at the camp, often with their children. The men always raved about the quantity and quality of the food served. Note the two grinding wheels used for sharpening the lumberjack's double-bitted axes, which were another essential tool of the job.

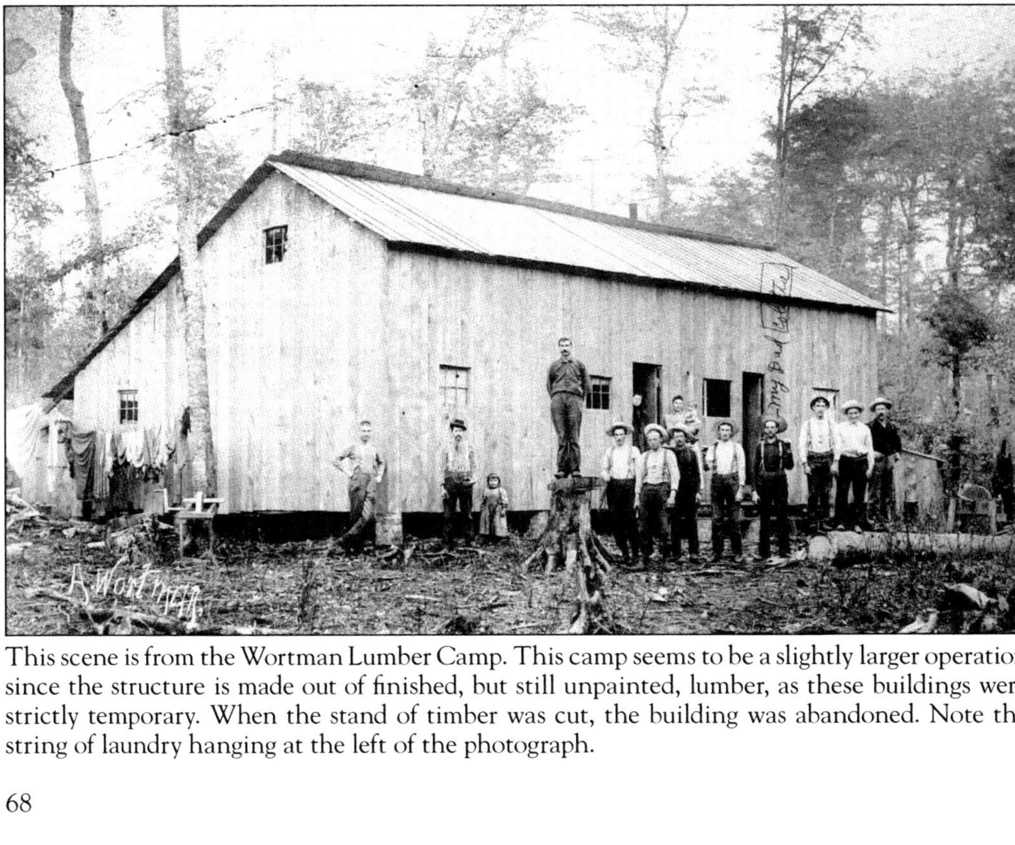

This scene is from the Wortman Lumber Camp. This camp seems to be a slightly larger operation since the structure is made out of finished, but still unpainted, lumber, as these buildings were strictly temporary. When the stand of timber was cut, the building was abandoned. Note the string of laundry hanging at the left of the photograph.

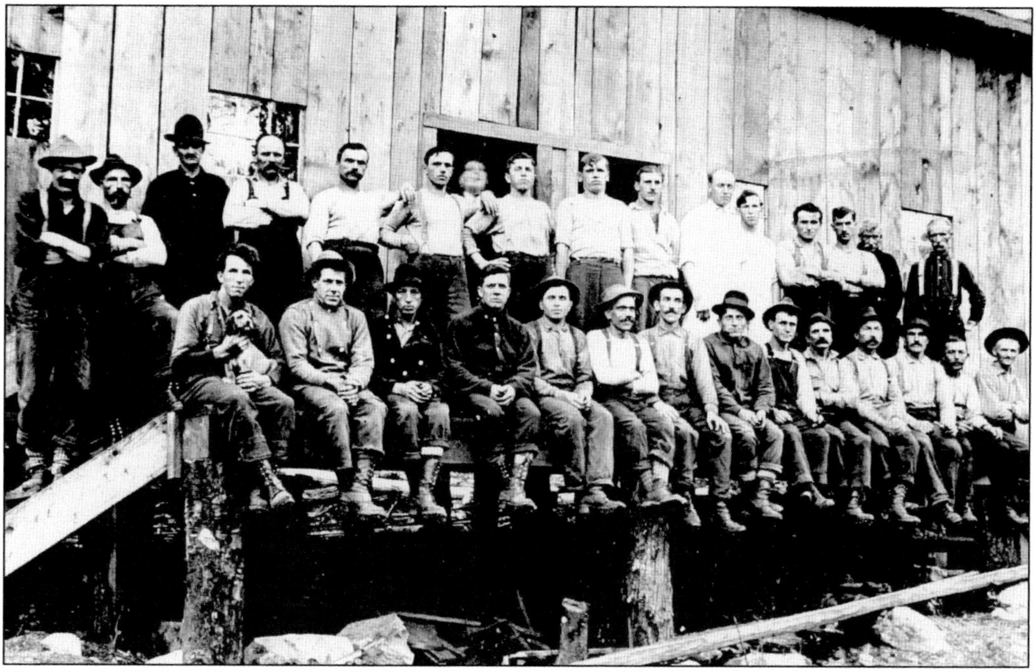

If a photographer showed up, all the woodhicks tumbled out for a group photograph. Many of the lumber camps were manned by immigrants. Much labor was needed in the big woods of north-central Pennsylvania, and the area attracted recent immigrants to the available jobs. Note the woodhick at lower left holding the camp mascot dog.

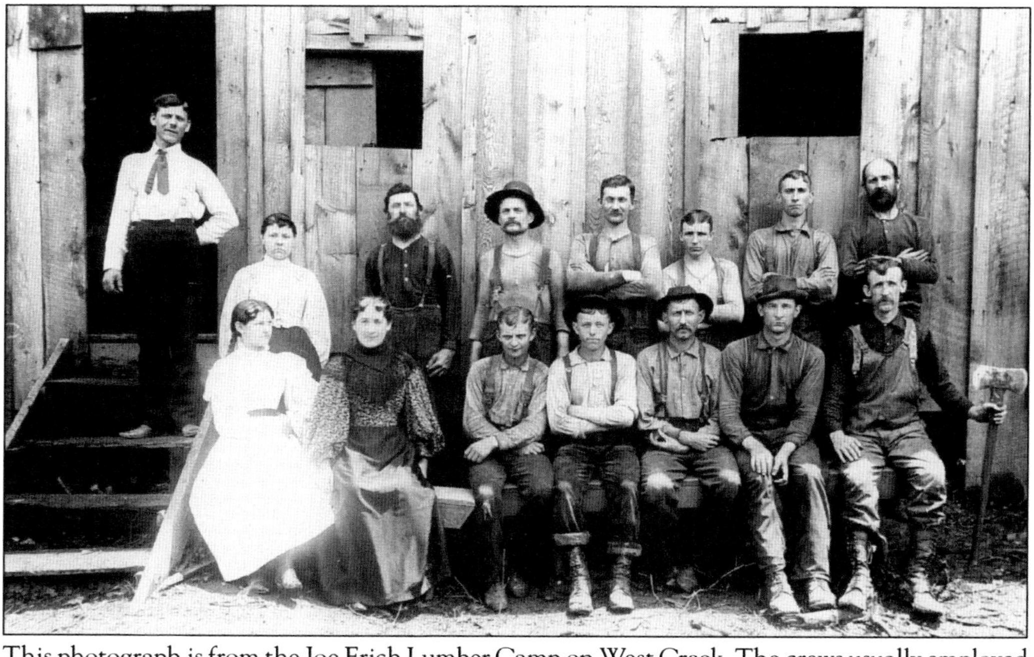

This photograph is from the Joe Erich Lumber Camp on West Creek. The crews usually employed a wide range of ages from young to old plus the usual female cooks. Note the woodhick on the far right holding a double-bitted ax, a lumberjack's primary tool. The job of the man in the tie is unknown.

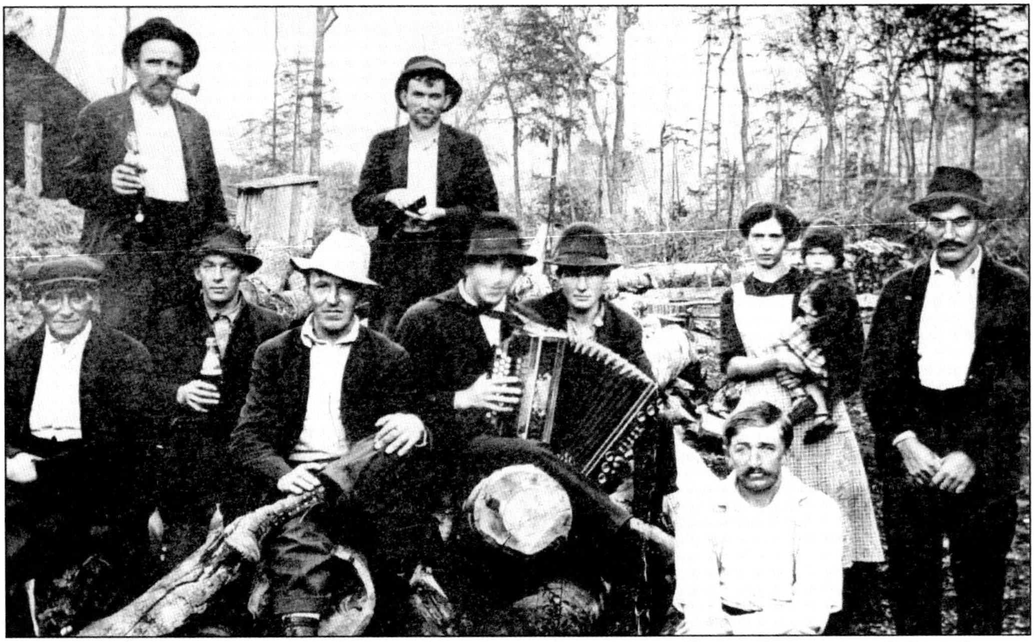

Lumber camp life was hard work, but when the work was over, the workers enjoyed their leisure time. In this photograph, a woodhick entertains the residents with his accordion. Notice there are men and women, old and young, at the camp. One is smoking a pipe while another is dipping into his tobacco pouch. Several are enjoying a beverage.

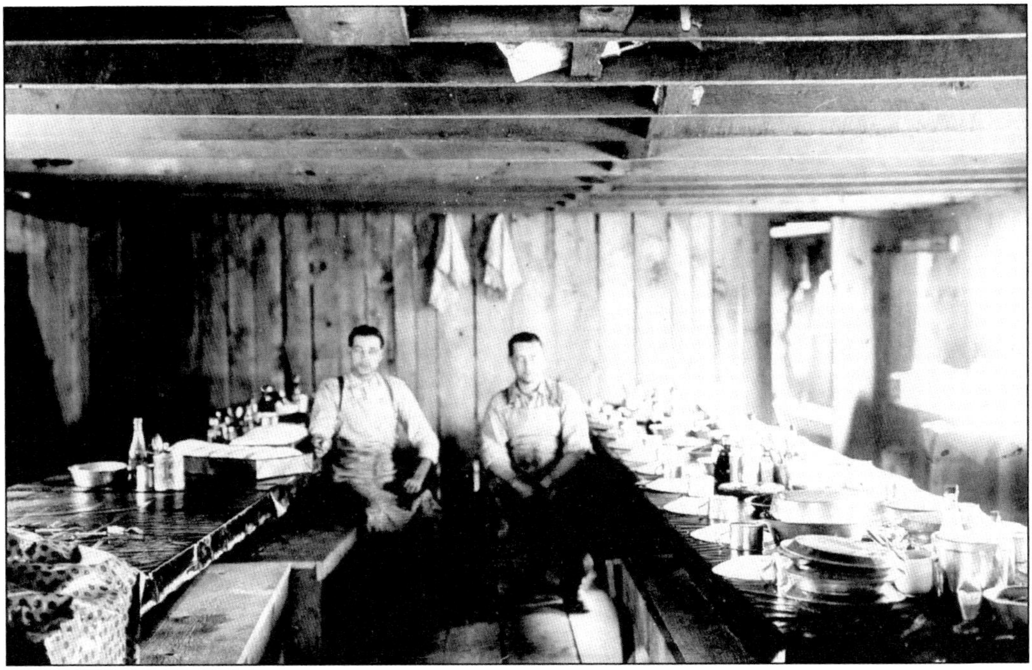

Here is an interior view of a lumber camp mess hall. Although most camps hired female cooks, this camp was an exception. Feeding a large group of men who have worked at a difficult job was a major undertaking. The food was simple, plentiful, and good. Men went to sleep soon after they were fed and had a smoke because they started a new day's work at first light.

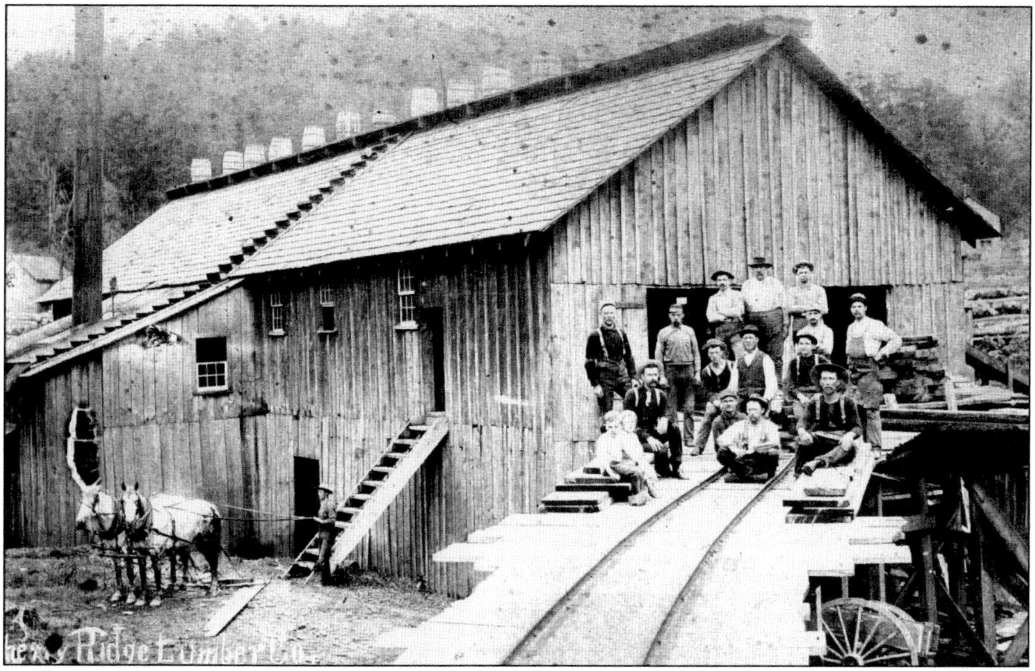

Here is a scene of the Cherry Ridge Lumber Company sawmill. Sawmills and lumber camps were scattered throughout Elk County. Note the line of barrels on the roof to catch rainwater and the built-in ladder to reach the barrels. The barrels were kept full of water in case of a fire; they would fall through the roof and help put out the fire.

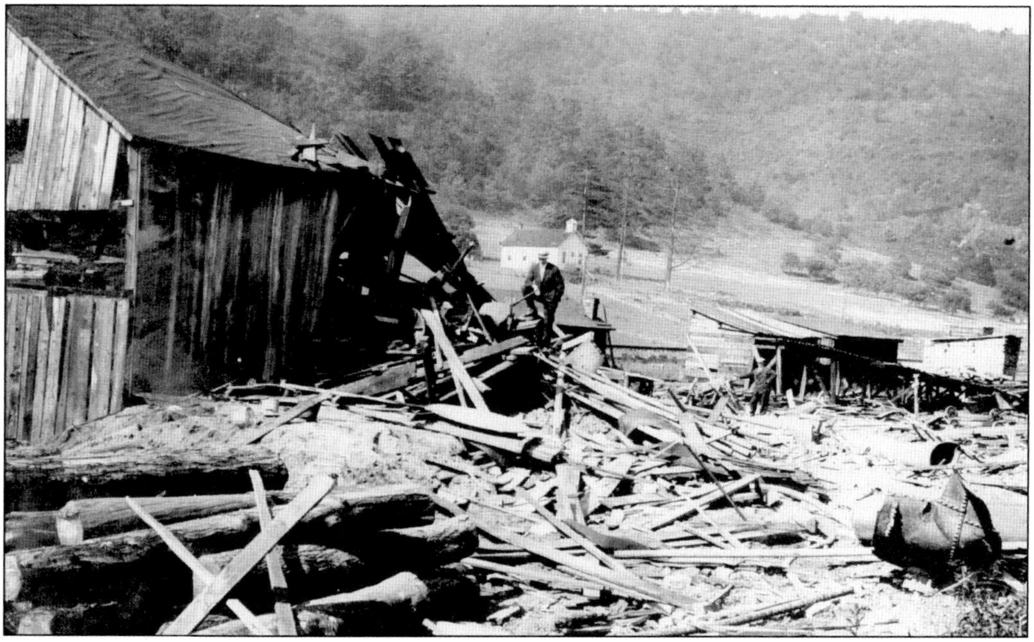

North-central Pennsylvania became the lumber capital of the world for a time and many fortunes were made. Much of the timber went downriver to Williamsport or Pittsburgh. Later many small area sawmills handled the work locally. This photograph shows a boiler explosion at Joe Erich's sawmill on West Creek.

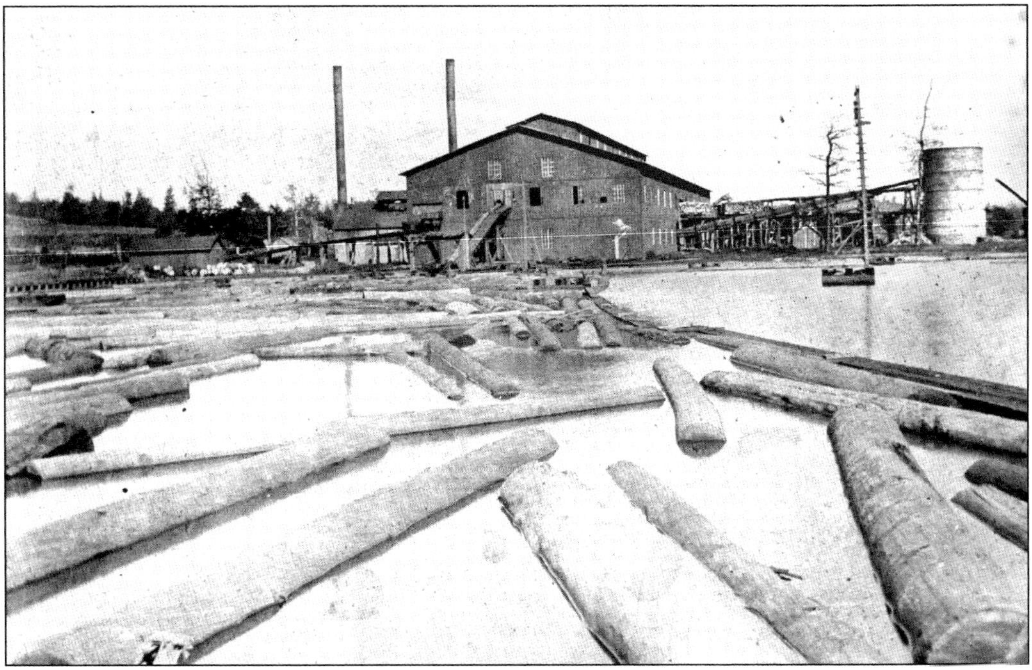

The Hall and Kaul Sawmill on Theresia Street in St. Marys was one of the largest in the state. It was built in 1896 and destroyed by fire in 1924. The company was formed by a partnership between state senator J. K. P. Hall and Andrew Kaul. This is a view of the log pond. The logs would be guided up the jack slip, visible on the mill, to be sawn.

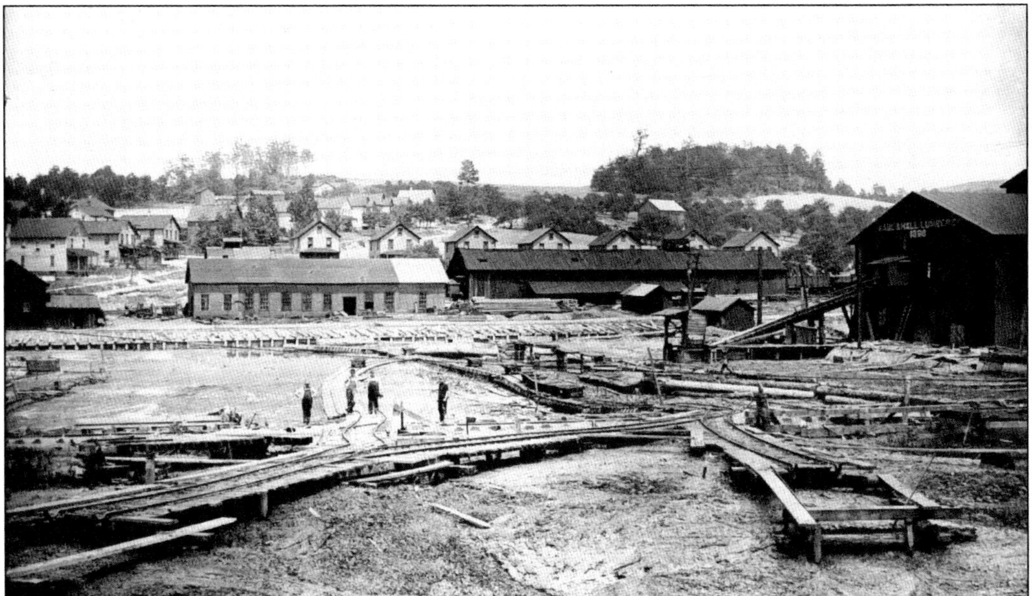

The Kaul and Hall Sawmill in St. Marys is pictured. The company changed its name from Hall and Kaul to Kaul and Hall in 1899 when J. K. P. Hall retired. The sawmill is on the right with a drying and sorting shed top center. Note the maze of structures to deliver logs and wood to various sections of the mill. The last logs were cut in 1922.

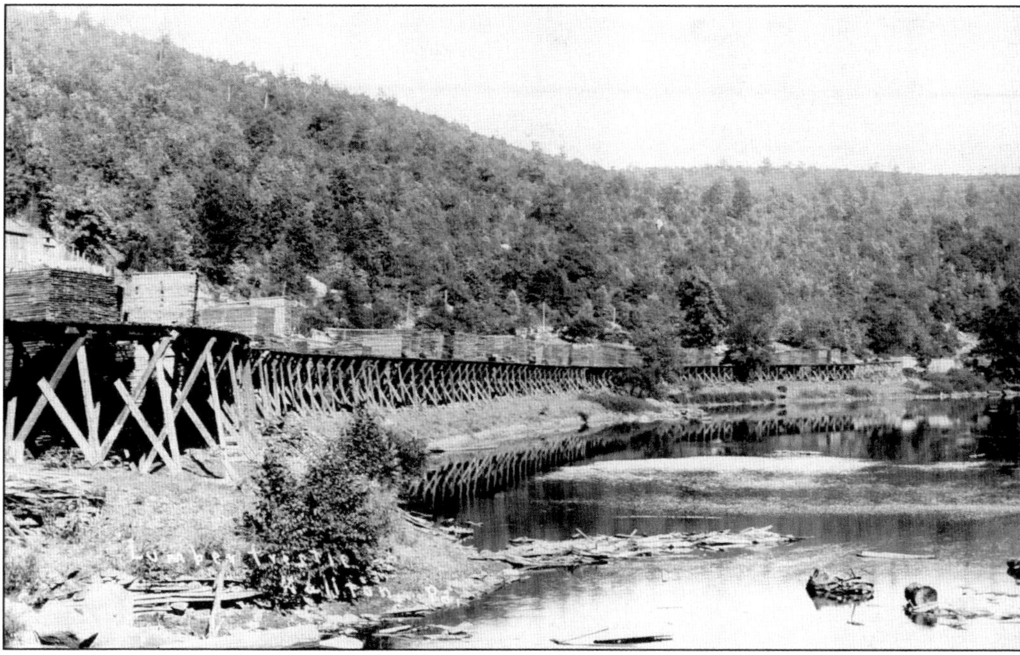

The Clarion River is a beautiful stream popular with canoeists today. Part of the river in Elk County bordering the Allegheny National Forest is designated wild and scenic. There are many developed river access points, including one at Hallton. A canoeist from the past would have met this scene of finished lumber, stacked on trestles, at Hallton. (Dave Woods.)

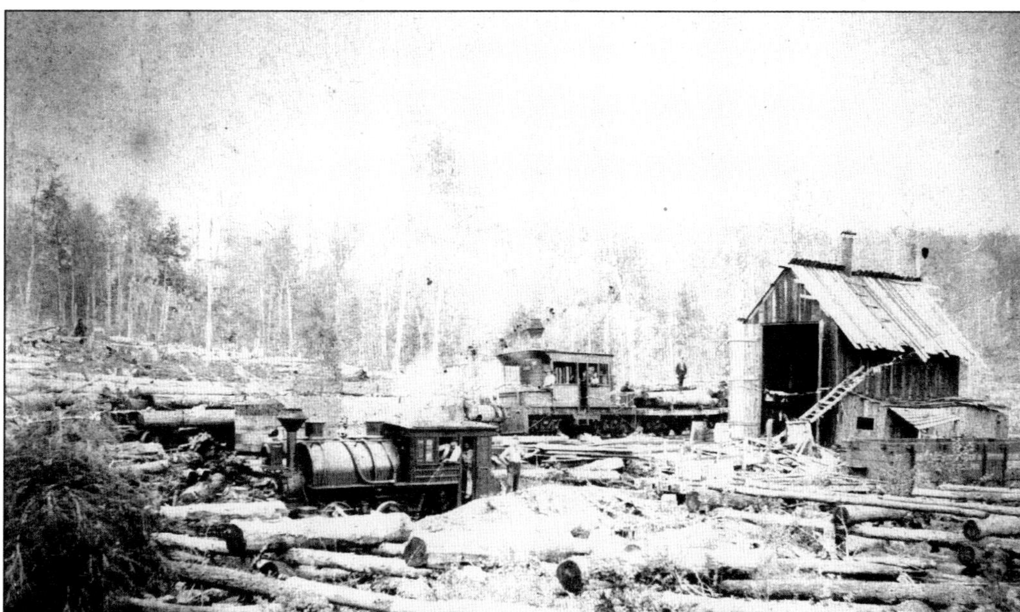

This photograph provides an impression of the logging era in Elk County. Horses, men, and machines are working together. Locomotives are shuttling logs around standard- and narrow-gauge railways with log piles everywhere and temporary shacks and shanties for tools and equipment. Entire forests were sent to mills to be processed into products for a growing country. This is a scene from the Johnsonburg area.

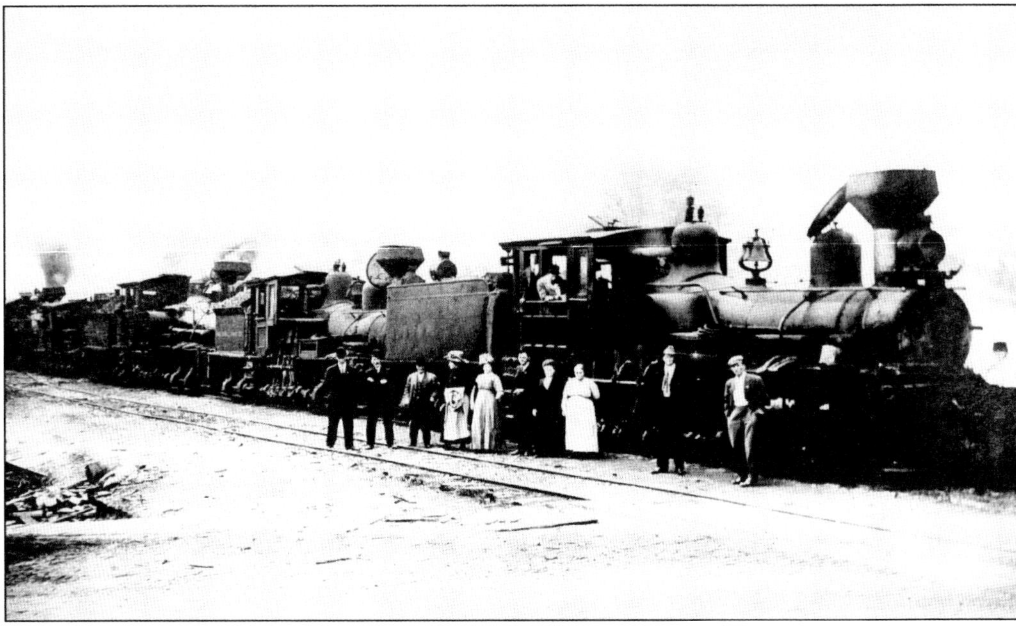

Here is a lineup of four shay-geared locomotives known as "stemwinders" from the Kaul and Hall Lumber Company. These rugged, powerful locomotives were specially designed for the steep, narrow valleys of north-central Pennsylvania and were used to haul logs from the forest to the mill. This occasion was in 1911.

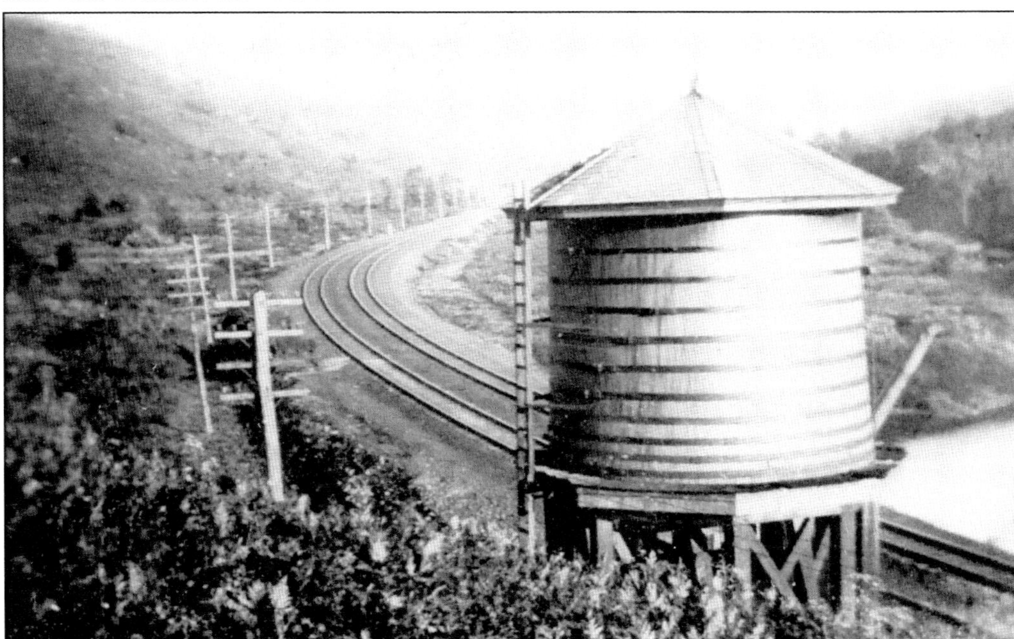

Prosperity arrived in Elk County in the form of the Philadelphia and Erie (later Pennsylvania) Railroad. The main line from Sunbury to Erie came through St. Marys, Ridgway, and Johnsonburg. The low-grade secondary track came later across southern Elk County and was a more logical route. Politics enabled the main line to serve the county's important towns. Shown is the Scahonda water tank with Elk Creek on the right.

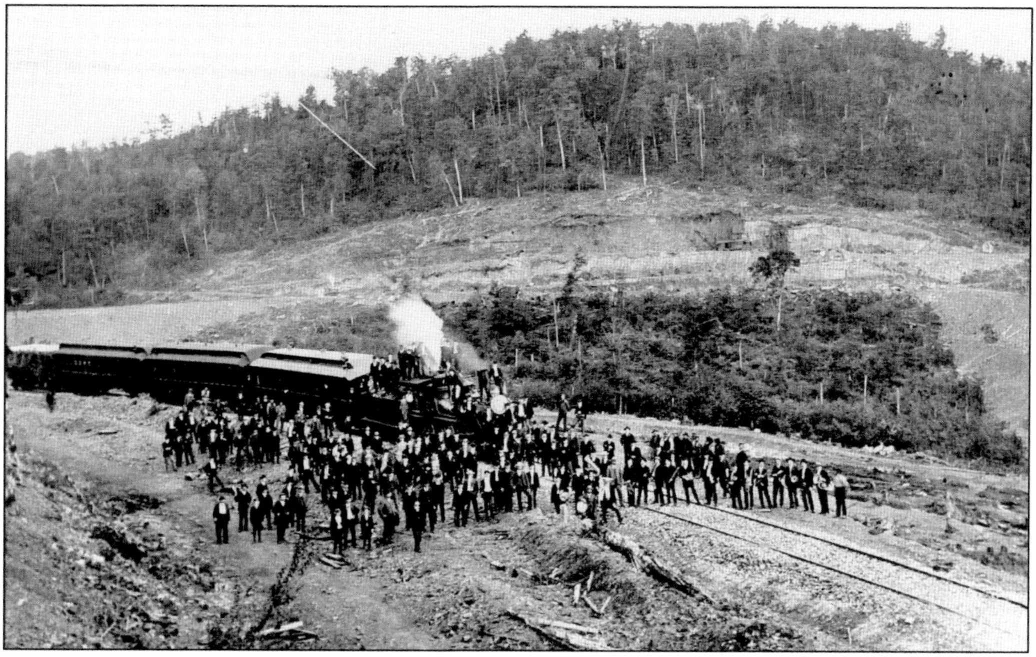

When the Pittsburg, Shawmut and Northern Railroad completed the loop at Kasson, it was deemed significant enough to celebrate with marching bands and many dignitaries and onlookers. The loop was an almost 360-degree circle of track to avoid building the line over rough terrain. The loop had a horseshoe curve and shortly after its completion was the scene of a fatal train wreck.

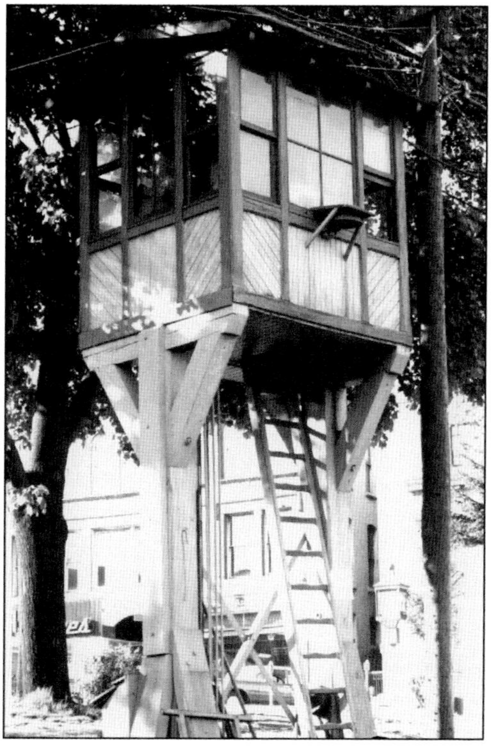

Between the years 1919 and 1958, this gateman's tower operated on the diamond in St. Marys. A crew manned the tower and raised and lowered gates when trains passed through town. The gates were installed after a fatal car-train accident when St. Marys started to have a lot of automobile traffic. After the last passenger train of the night, a kerosene-burning light was used.

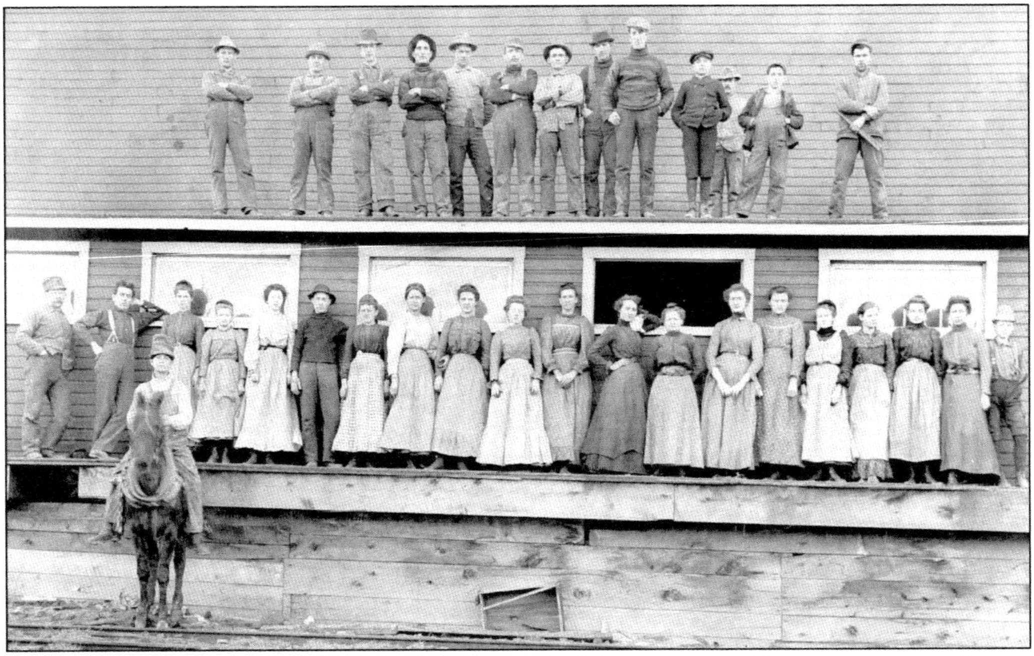

A group of workers poses outside the Kindling Wood factory in St. Marys on Theresia Street. This facility was one of the many operations that utilized by-products of the timber business. Wood that was too small for lumber was bundled into kindling for sale in cities to start fires. Note that most of the workers are women.

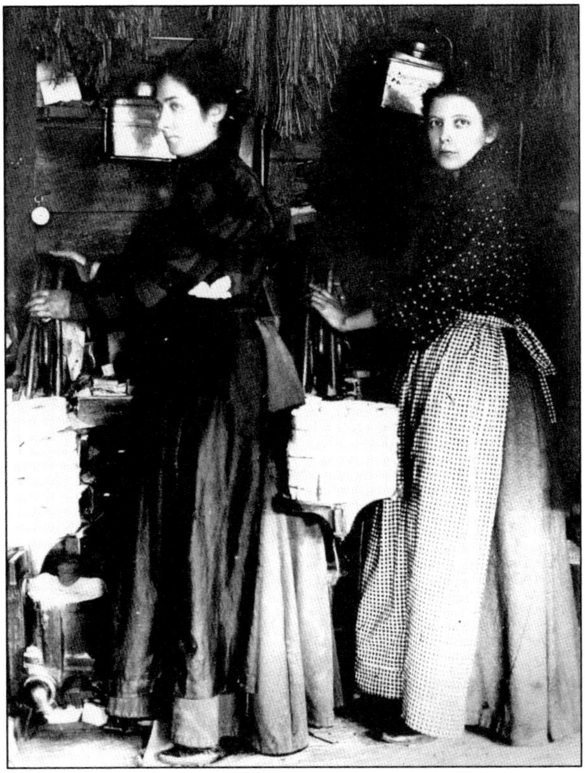

Here is a scene inside the Kindling Wood factory in St. Marys. This was one of the first businesses in the area to hire women. Visible in the photograph are two bundles of the type that the company produced. The bundles were sent to cities that had little local firewood to start home and cooking fires.

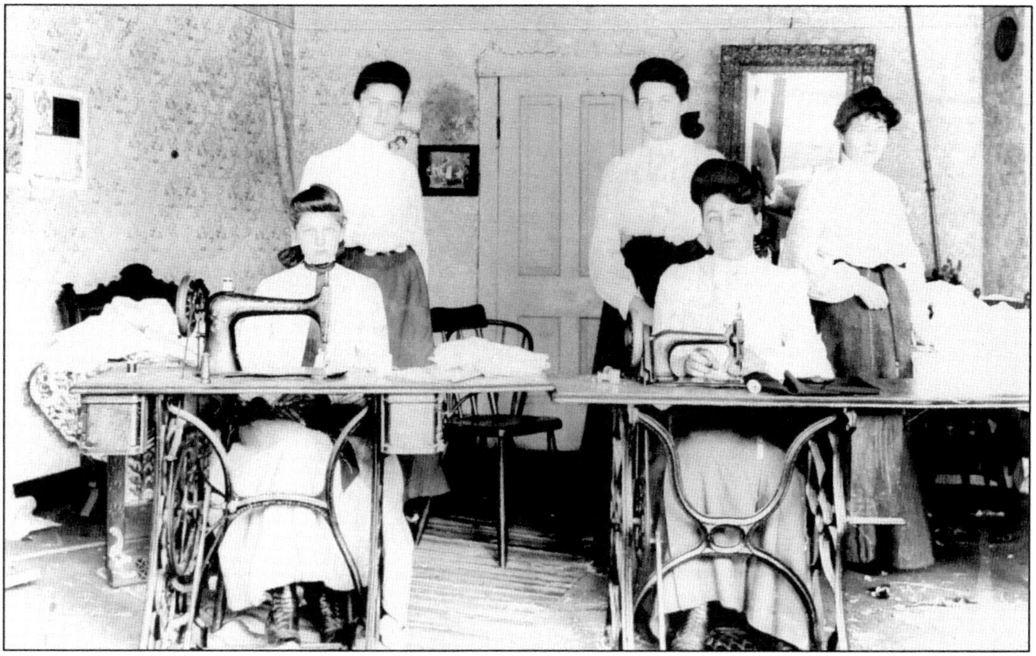

As women began to move into the workforce more and more jobs were open to them, many jobs were segregated by gender. The job of seamstress was one that was dominated by women. When the world wars of the 20th century sent many men overseas, women found increased job opportunities, including jobs that had been male dominated.

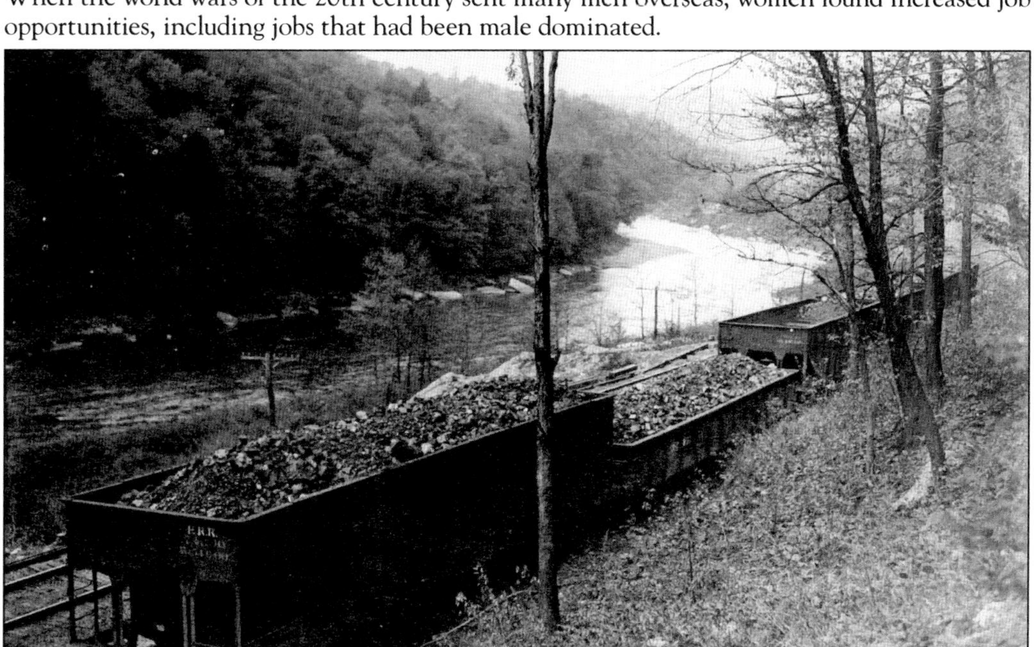

Coal was another natural resource within Elk County that was valuable and extensively mined. Various railroads served the county. The two main coal carriers were the Pittsburg, Shawmut and Northern Railroad and the Pennsylvania Railroad. Over the years, much coal came out of Elk County, and coal trains were a common sight.

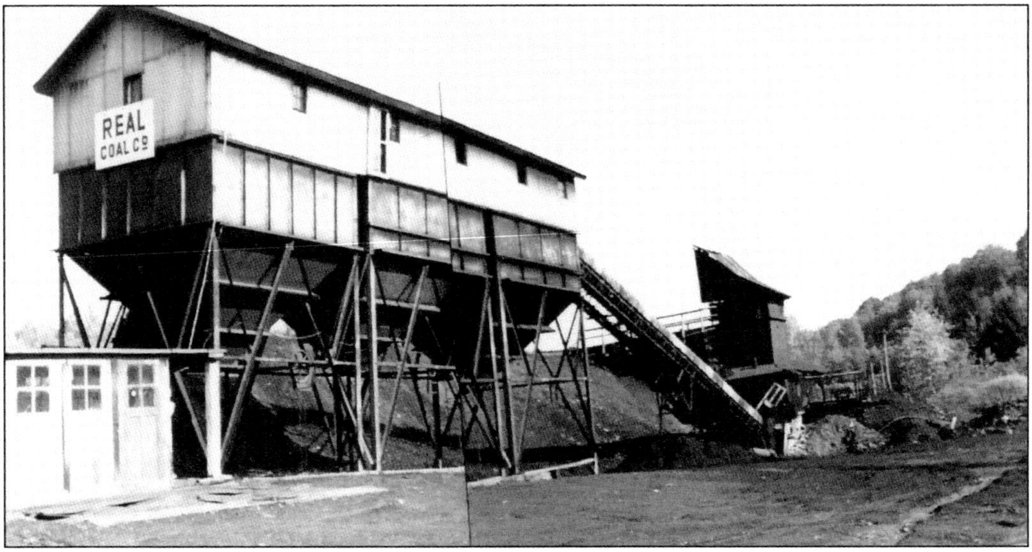

Both strip-mining and deep shaft mining were common in Elk County. Coal is still being mined in the county, but today it is usually strip-mined. The last deep coal mine in Elk County was the Real Coal Company shaft in the Drummond/Shawmut area. It closed in the early 1970s. (Bill Krellner.)

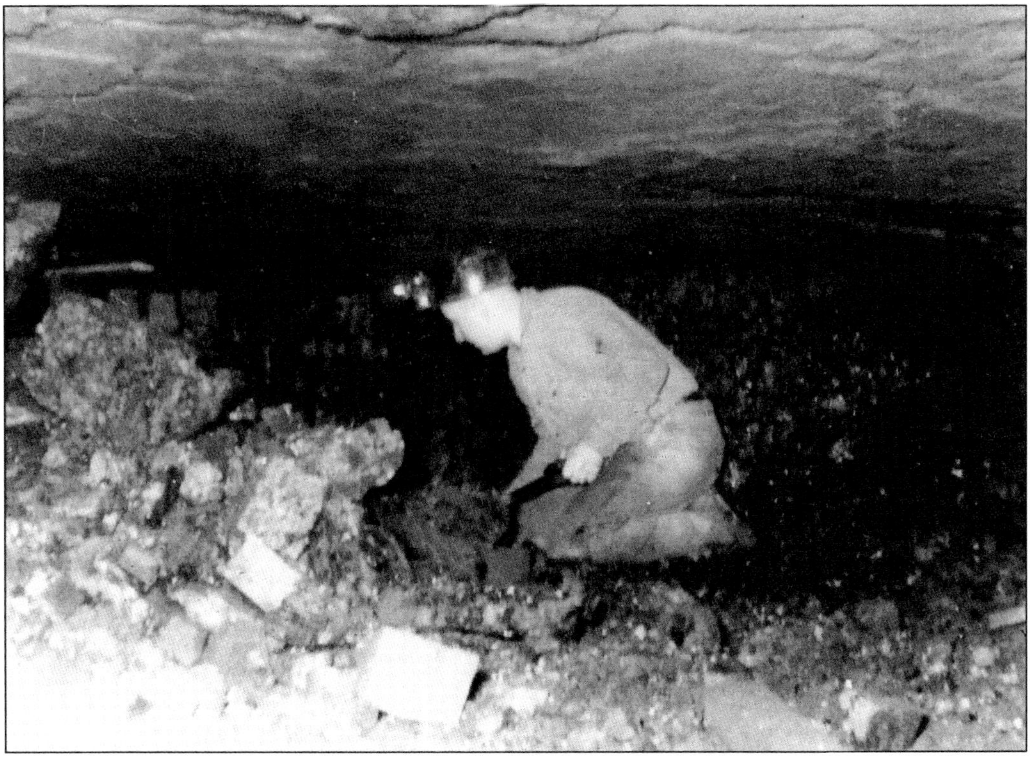

Elk County has a lot of underground history as there were valuable deposits of coal under much of the county. Deep mining was a difficult, hazardous job. Miners with their carbide headlamps worked in cramped quarters with the constant threat of cave-ins and poisonous gases. This scene is from a mine in the Byrnedale Hill area. The miner is Francis Schreiber. (Bill Krellner.)

Here is the first oil well shot in the St. Marys area. Elk County is close to the site of the first commercial oil well in the world, which was drilled in Titusville. There are still working oil wells in Elk County, mostly in the northern section of the county. There are also many natural gas wells in Elk County.

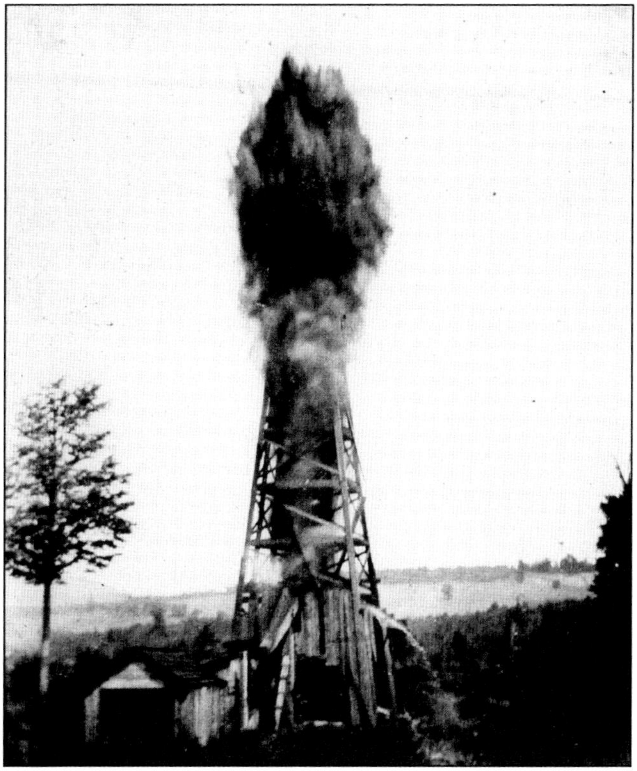

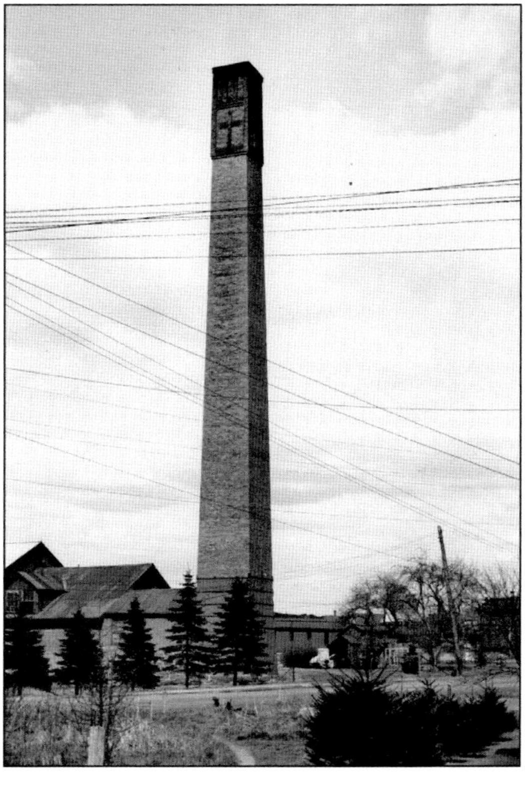

The St. Marys Tannery was built in 1884 and closed in 1955. Tanneries were a natural complement to a town that had a sawmill, as the hemlock bark from the logs was used to tan animal hides. The landmark tower had a cross design in brick near the top, to honor a construction worker who had died in a fall and could not afford a proper memorial. (Grotzinger Collection, St. Marys and Benzinger Township Historical Society.)

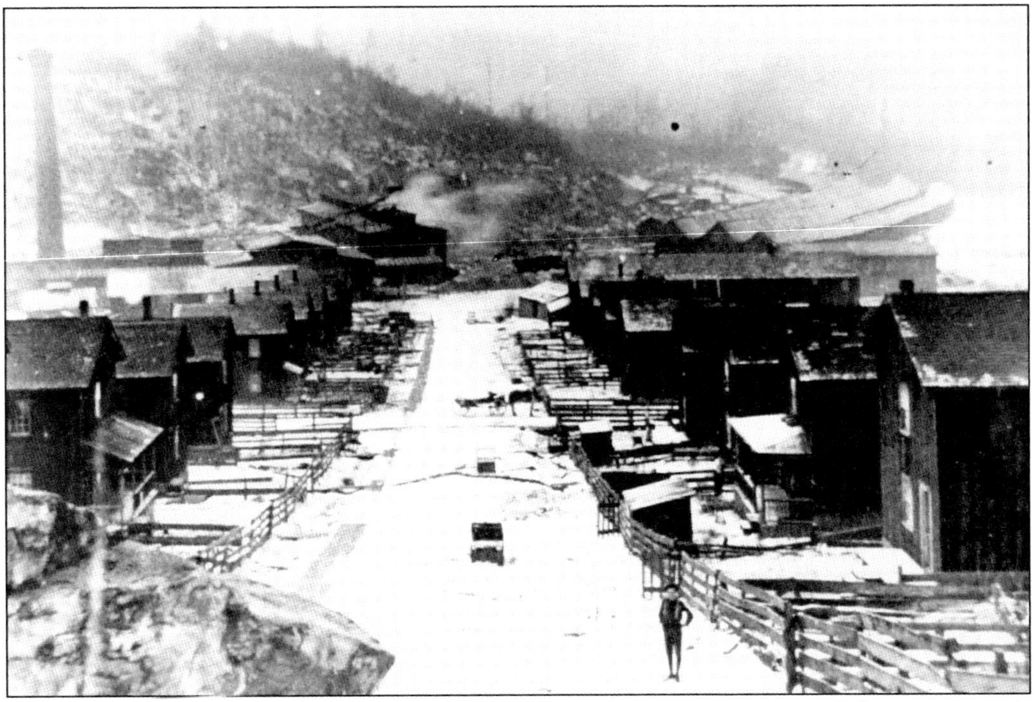

The town of Instanter was located at the juncture of Five Mile Creek and the East Branch of the Clarion River. Today it is under the waters of the East Branch Dam where Elk State Park is located. The town was served by the Quinn, the Johnsonburg and Clarion, and the Pennsylvania Railroads and featured a sawmill and tannery. Timber was taken out of Five Mile and Seven Mile Creeks.

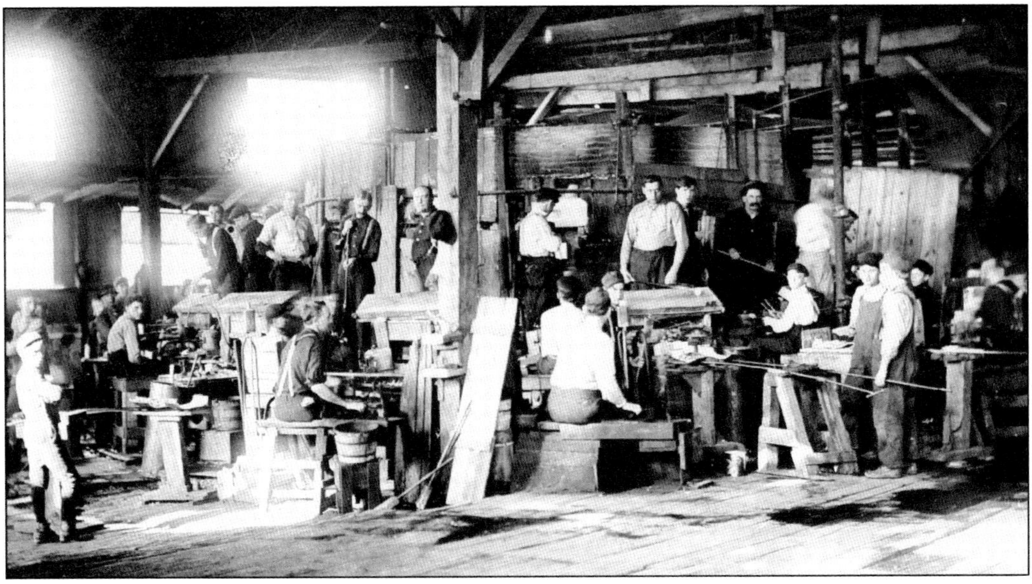

This is a scene from inside the Pierce Glass Works on Fourth Street in St. Marys. Early immigrants to Elk County included a group of Flemish glassworkers that settled in Glen Hazel in the northern part of the county. Another remnant of the Belgian migration is the name Brussells Street in St. Marys.

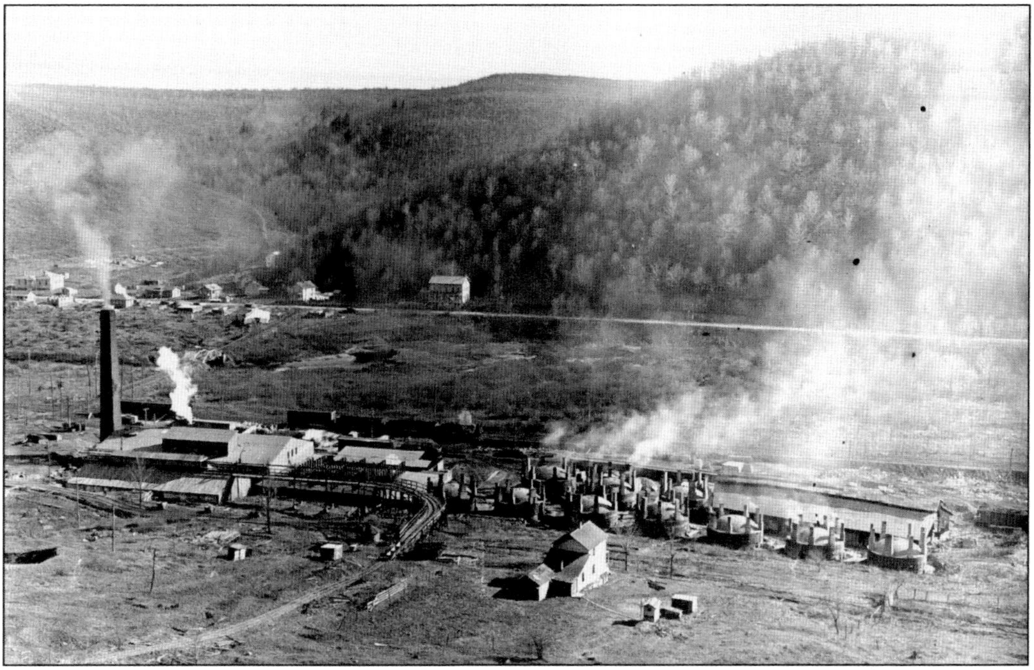

The small village of Daguscahonda is located on the Ridgway–St. Marys road. A small cluster of residential houses existed to work the Elk Fire Brick Company's Daguscahonda plant. In this aerial photograph from 1920, the entire operation is visible. A narrow-gauge railway enters the plant from the bottom of the photograph, clay products are baked in beehive kilns, and finished products are shipped out on the Pennsylvania Railroad.

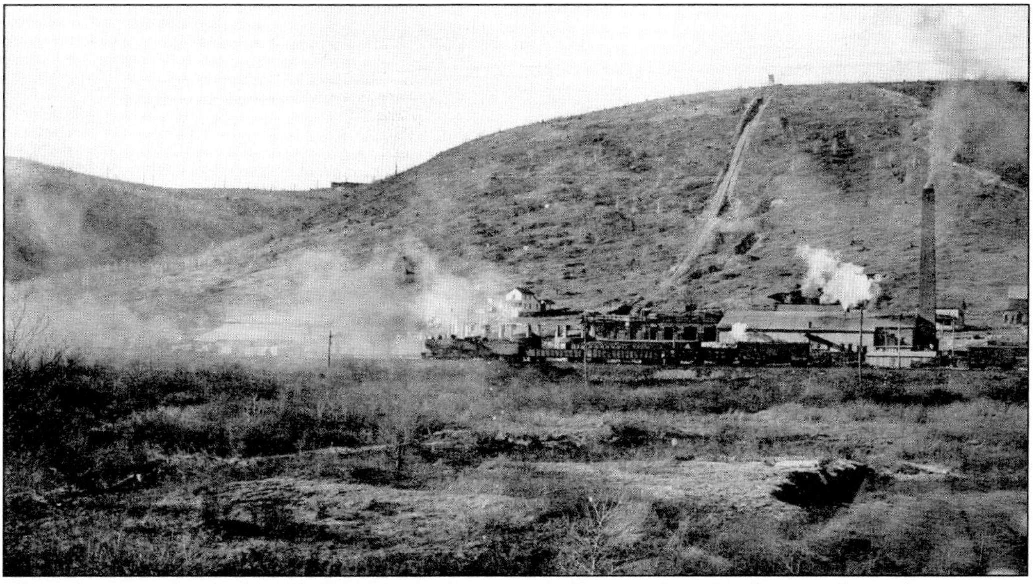

This photograph of the Elk Fire Brick Company's Daguscahonda plant is from the opposite perspective than the previous view. Visible in this scene is the narrow-gauge railway that climbed the hill behind the plant, giving access to the facility's clay diggings. The factory was located along Elk Creek. Note the absence of trees on the hillsides as frequent fires, sparked from trains, burned them off.

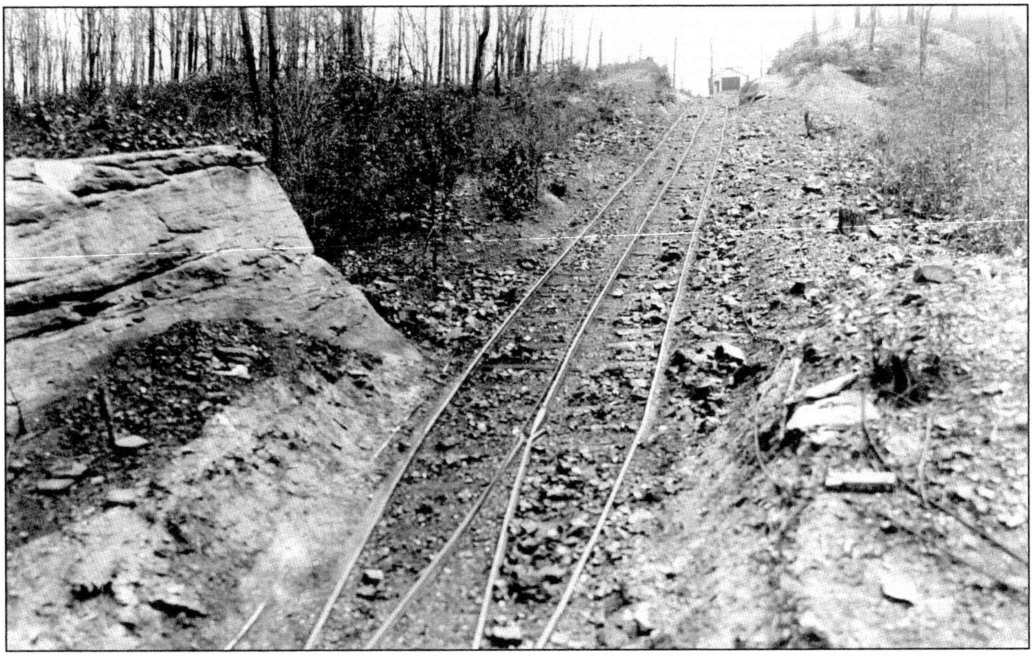

Here is a view of the narrow-gauge incline gravity railway that served the Elk Fire Brick Company's Daguscahonda works. Cars loaded with clay-bearing rock were lowered to the factory as empty cars were raised up the opposite track. Clay mines on top of the hill furnished the facility with its raw material.

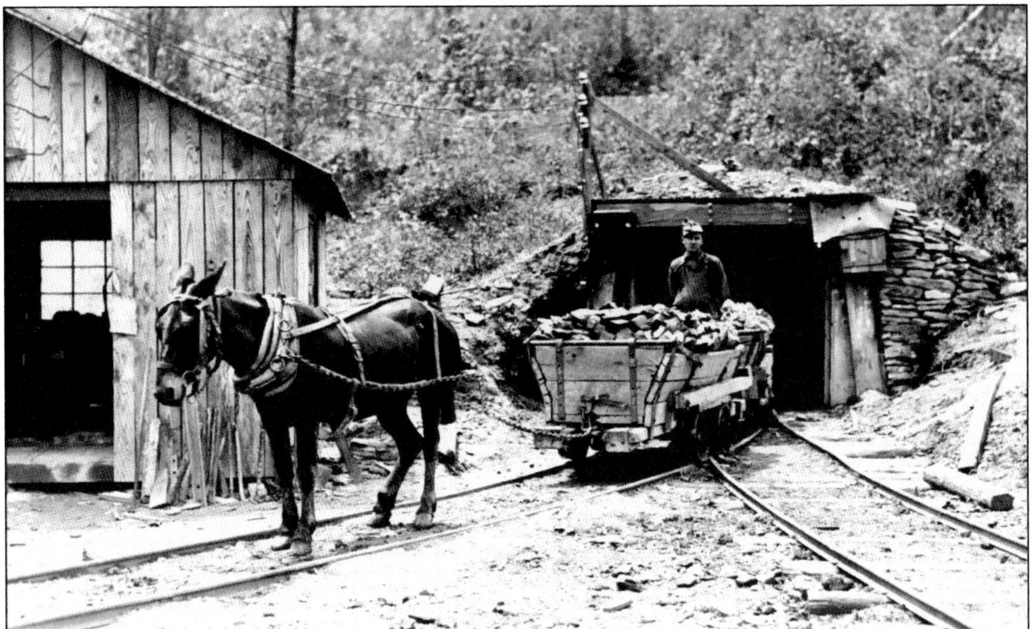

Clay can be found under most of Elk County. Clay products companies were located in many areas of the county, making such items as fire-resistant brick, tiles, and sewer pipes. In this photograph, a miner, wearing a headlamp, is just emerging from the mine with his mule hauling a car filled with clay-bearing rock.

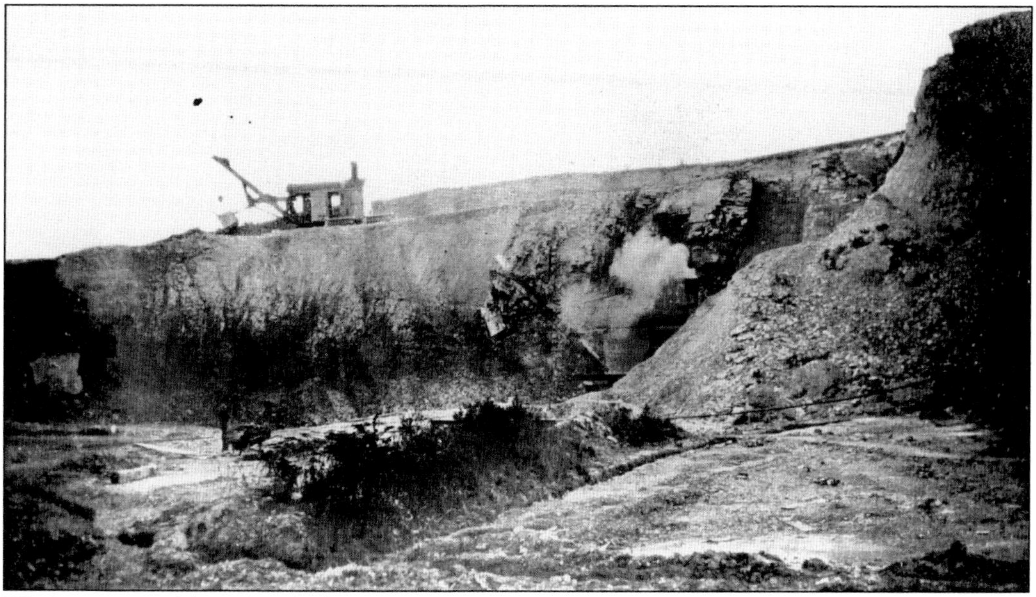

Elk County was blessed with clay, which was used for baking many different types of fire-resistant products. There were four different clay products plants located in St. Marys and others scattered throughout the county. This quarry scene is from the clay digging behind the Pennsylvania Fireproofing Company on Brussells Street in St. Marys.

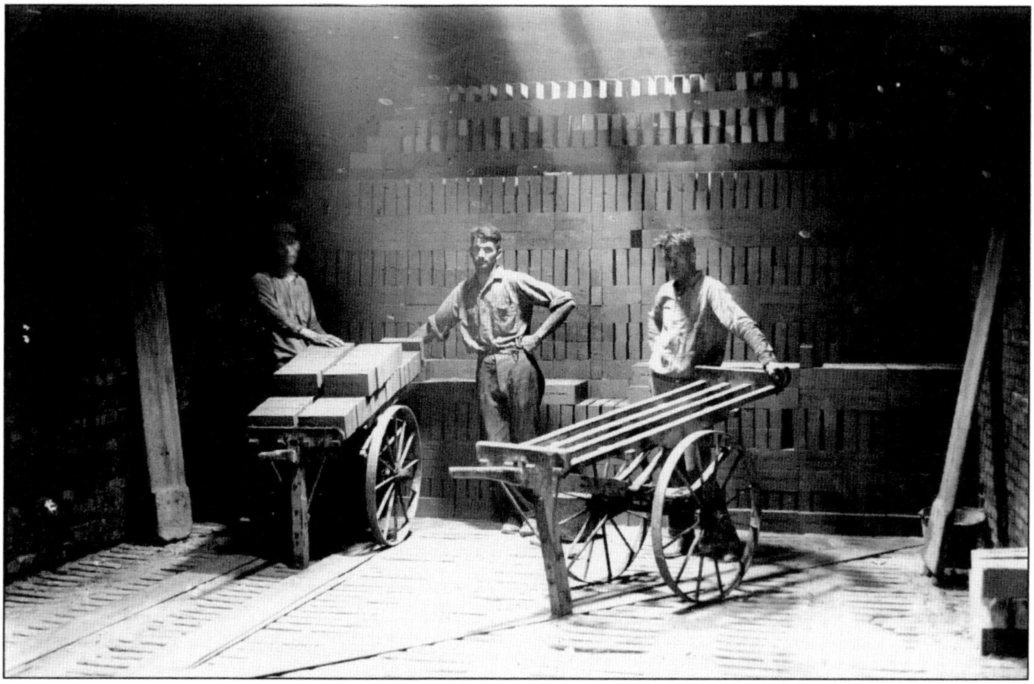

This scene is from inside the Elk Fire Brick Company's St. Marys plant located on State Road. This facility baked the clay in beehive kilns after it was shaped into bricks. The bricks were eventually used to line ovens where bricks resistant to high temperatures were needed. Specially designed handcarts were used to move the bricks. The workers are (from left to right) Conrad Greendorner, Hans Auman, and Fred Prechtl.

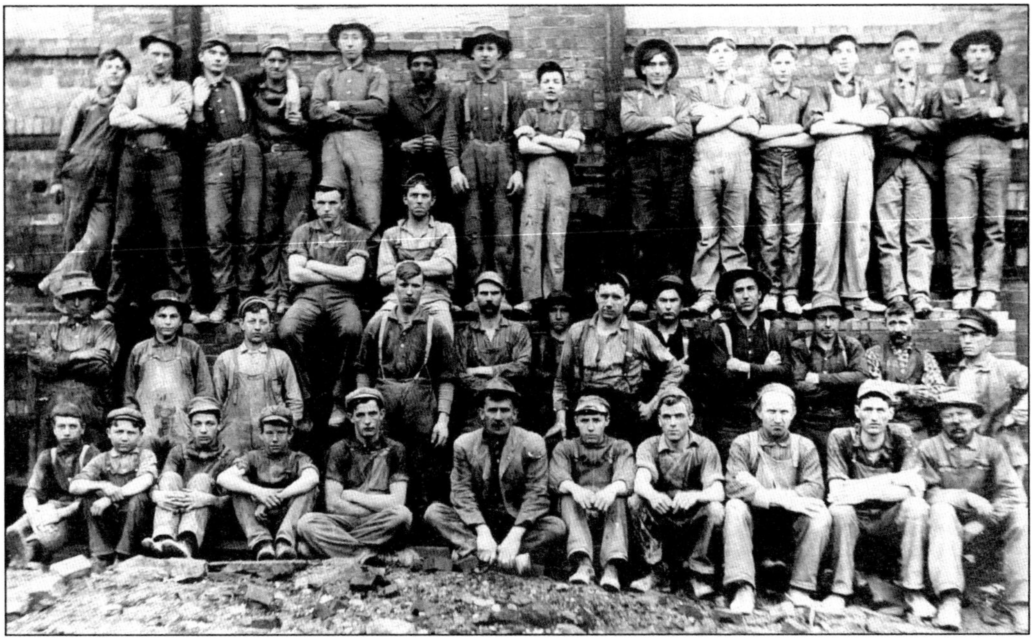

If every picture tells a story, then every face is its own chapter. These kiln workers from the Elk Fire Brick Company's Daguscahonda plant exhibit every shade of human emotion: happiness, sadness, excitement, resignation, age, youth, hope, and fear. Their ethnic faces are typical of the men and boys who worked the clay kilns around Elk County.

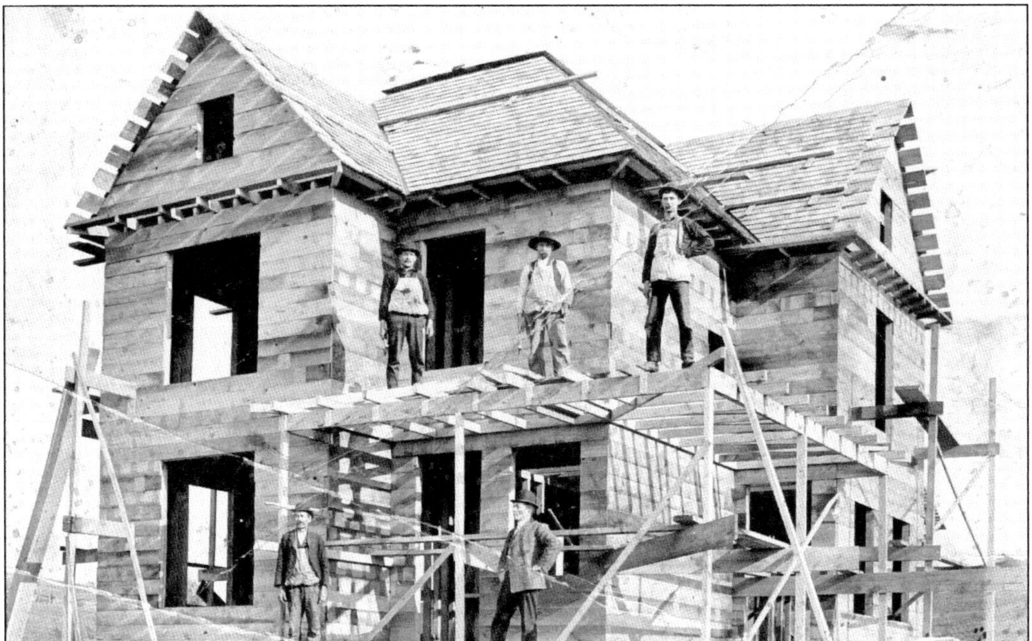

As Elk County prospered, many more people were attracted to the county's growing economic success. House construction became a booming business as the population increased. Valentine Neubert II built many houses in the St. Marys area. He is pictured here at top left on a house he was building. The man in the suit, bottom right, is possibly the homeowner.

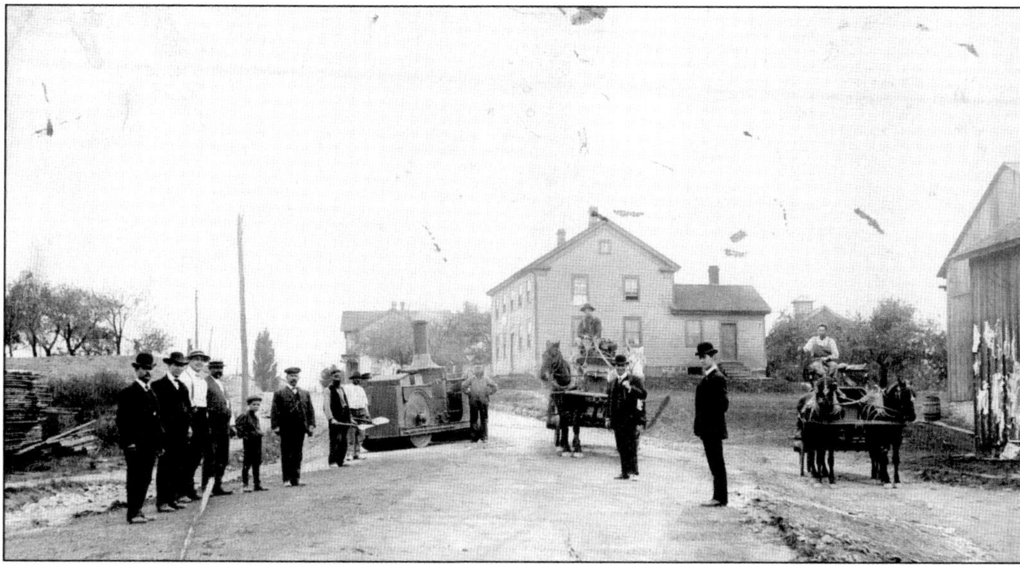

When Main Street in Kersey was being paved, the horse-drawn era and the mechanized era met head-on. Note the horse eyeing the newfangled iron horse in the form of a steamroller. The event seems to have drawn a crowd of onlookers in their Sunday best although it could not have been a Sunday since the construction crew is working.

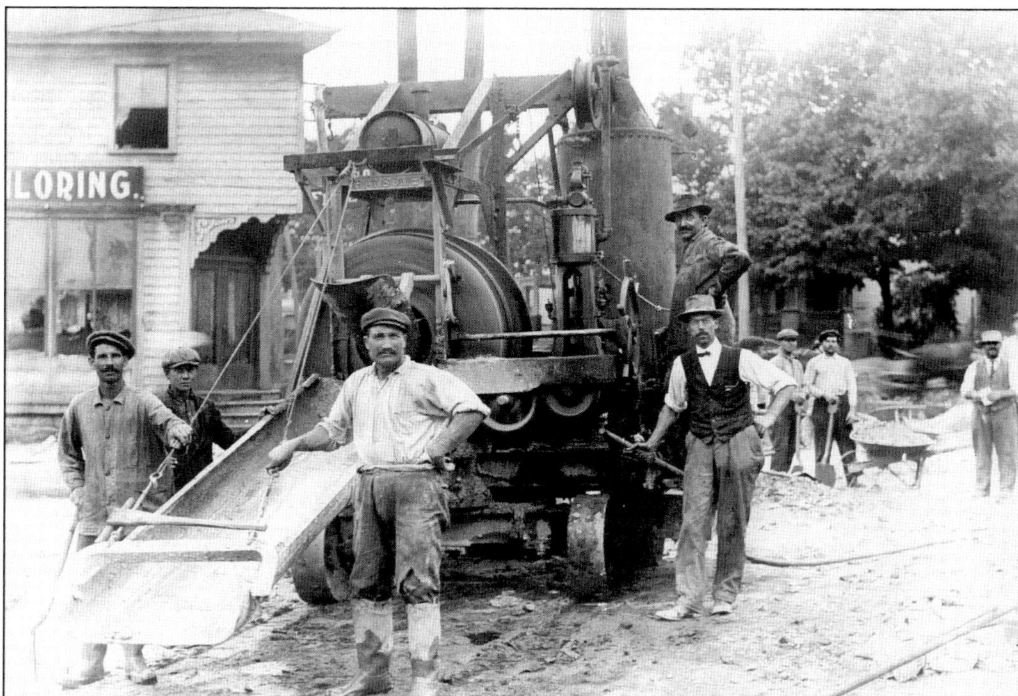

The diamond in St. Marys was paved in 1913. A steam-driven mixer is shown in operation. When the railroad came through, it created a diamond shape of intersecting streets in downtown St. Marys. The paving of the diamond eventually led to more traffic and automobile congestion. However, in this photograph, a blurred image of a horse moves through the right background of the still unhurried center of town.

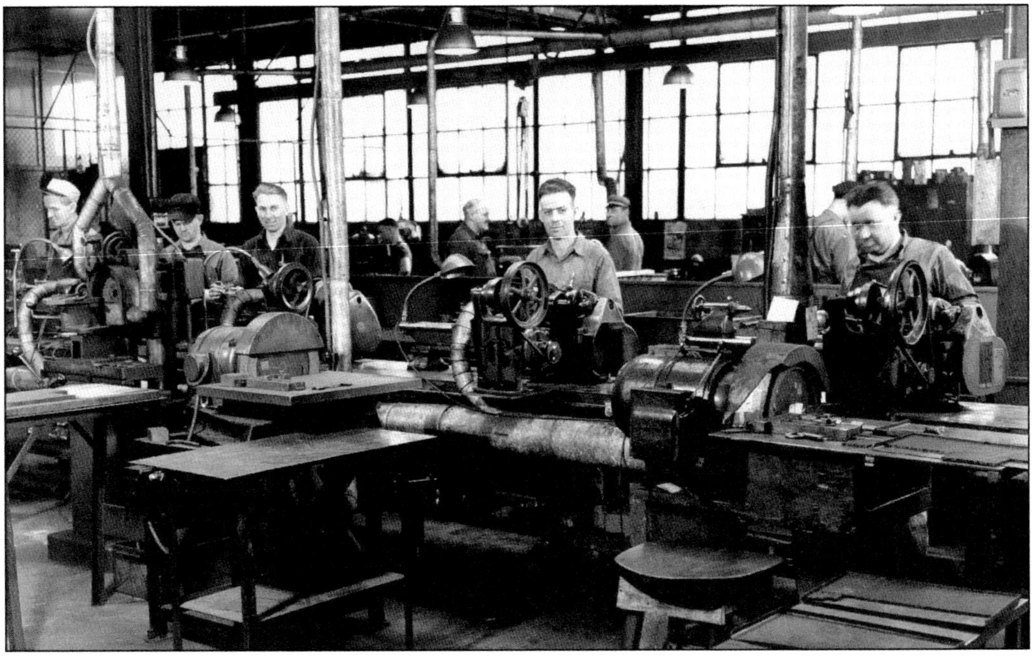

St. Marys has been called the "carbon capital of the world." In 1899, Andrew Kaul and John Speer founded the Speer Carbon Company. Soon many other carbon factories flourished in St. Marys. Eventually numerous powdered metal and tool and die businesses complemented the industrial landscape of the county. This scene is from the Speer Carbon Company in 1945.

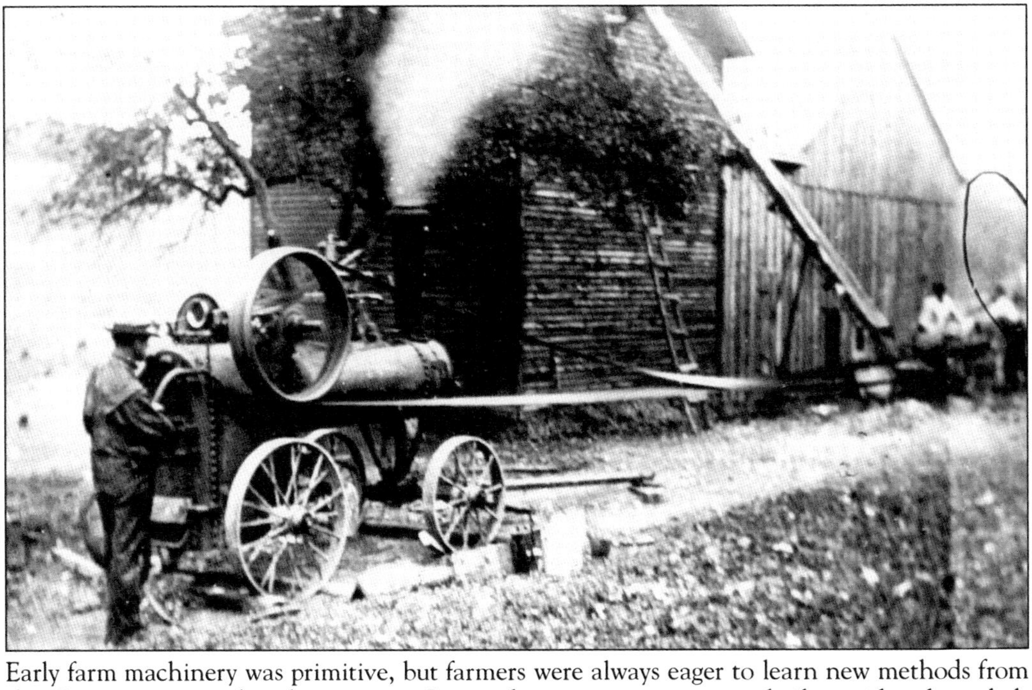

Early farm machinery was primitive, but farmers were always eager to learn new methods from the Grange or agricultural extension. Pictured is a stationary steam boiler, with a large belt attached, to drive silage into a barn in the Sugar Hill area. Note the iron wheels on the engine for transportability.

Three

Social and Sporting Life

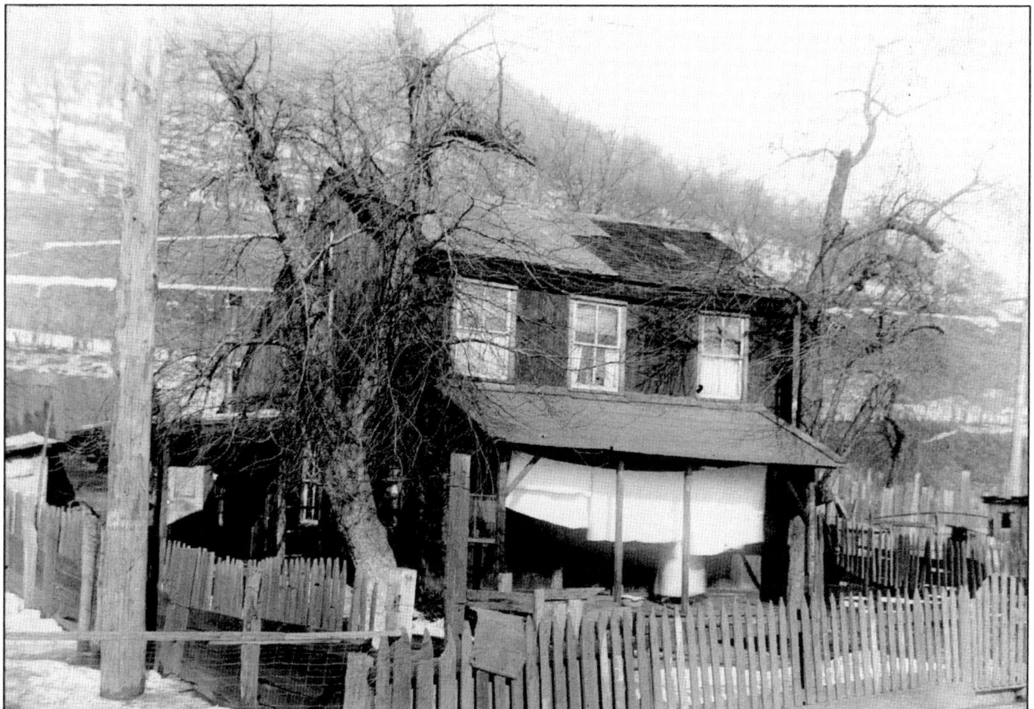

Here is a scene of a house from Daguscahonda. The frame structure is unpainted and only half shingled, but the windows are curtained and an industrious woman is hanging wash on a sunny early-spring day. The house is surrounded by fencing to keep the chickens in the yard and the pigs out of the garden. Note the outhouse on the right of the photograph.

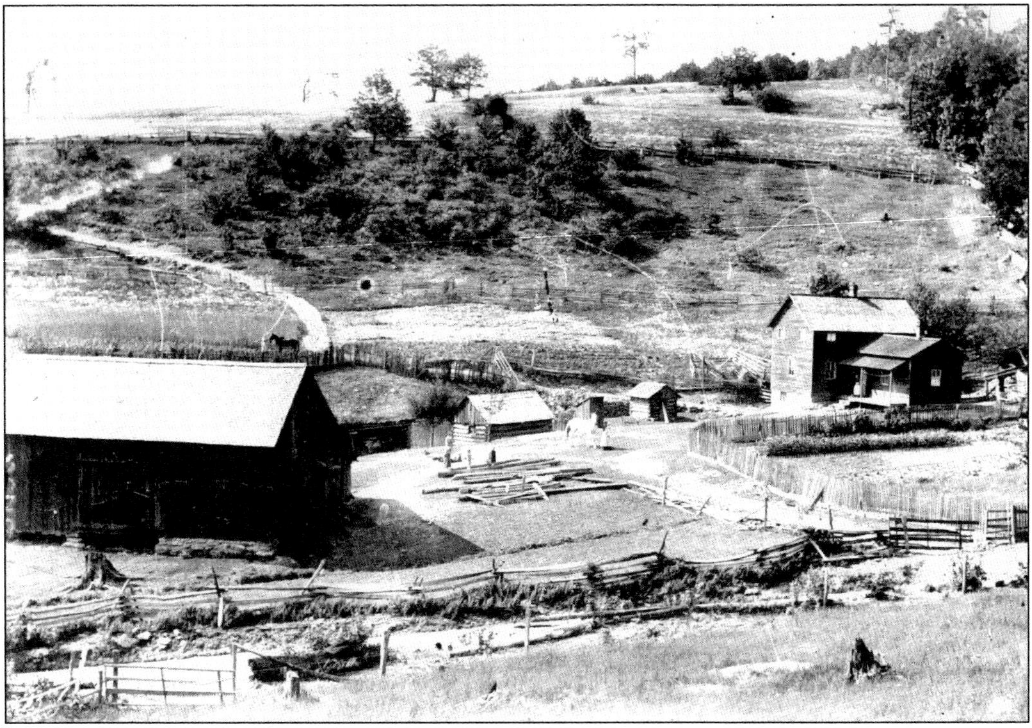

The first occupation in the Elk County area was farming. The land and topography of Elk County was not conducive to agriculture, and the settlers soon took to extracting natural resources and other pursuits. However, farmers never gave up and continue to till the soil. Most farms are second incomes or hobbies. This photograph depicts the Breindel farm in Flower Valley.

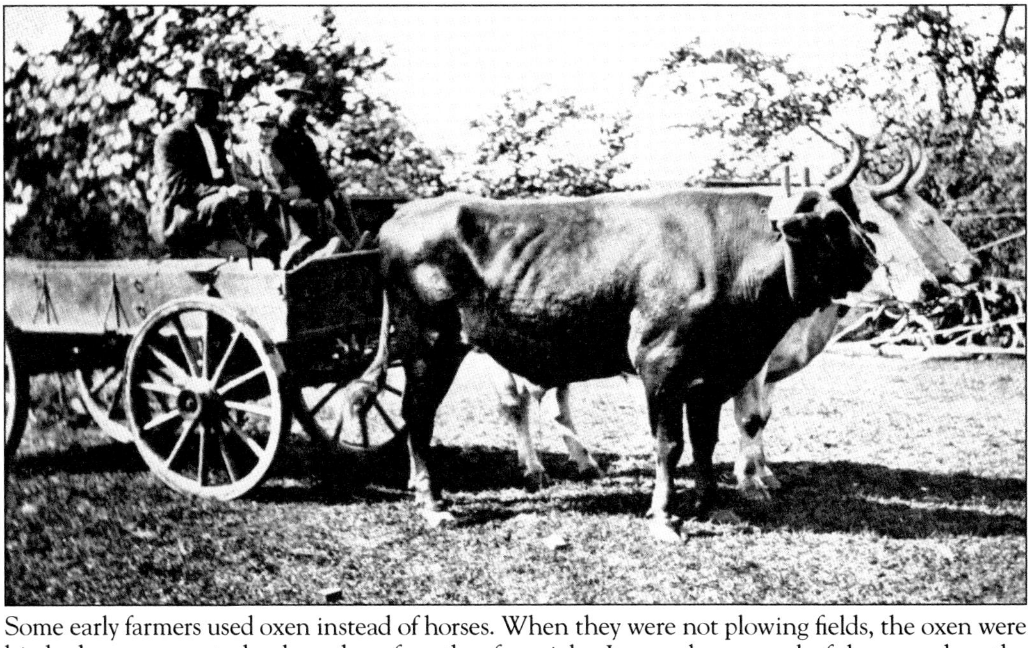

Some early farmers used oxen instead of horses. When they were not plowing fields, the oxen were hitched to a wagon to haul goods or for other farm jobs. It was always a colorful scene when the oxen team was driven to town for supplies. Mike Willert owned the last span of oxen in the area.

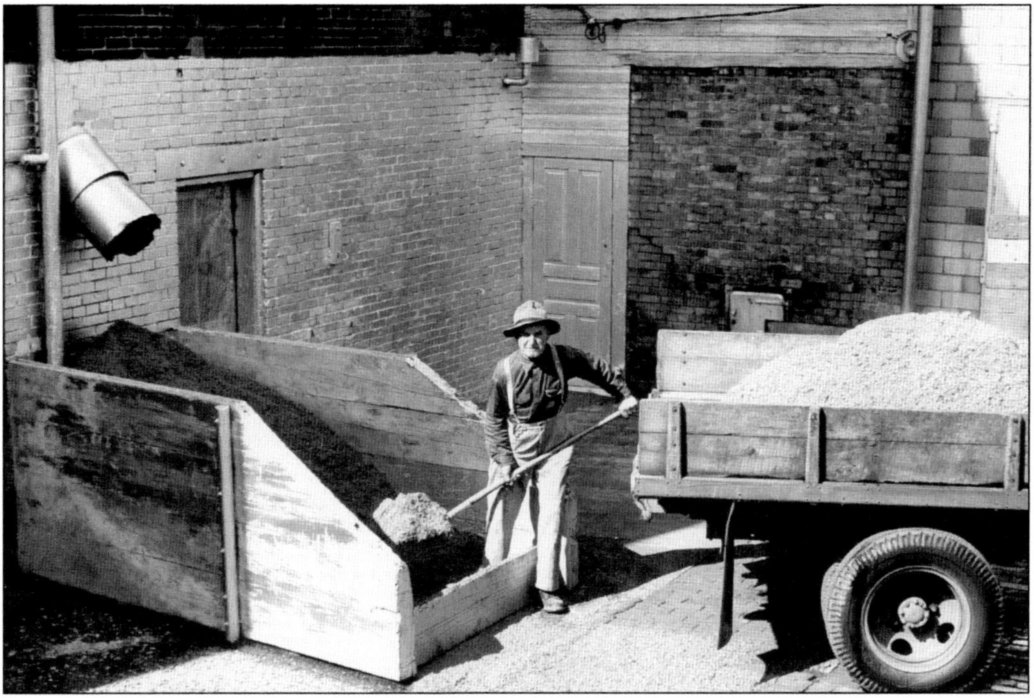

Ed Sarginer is shown shoveling corn mash from the Straub Brewery for use as cattle feed. There were many farms in the Elk County area and a few are still thriving. Corn was a staple crop of the county. Dairy products such as milk and cheese were common local products. Area livestock farmers supplied butcher shops. Chickens and eggs were also sold. (Grotzinger Collection, St. Marys and Benzinger Township Historical Society.)

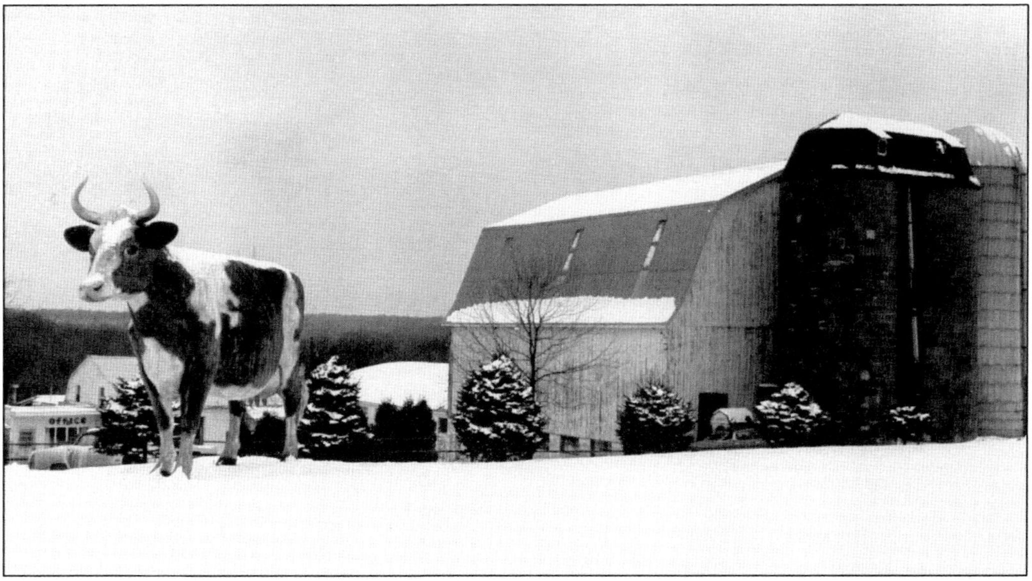

The "big cow" was an area landmark in Kersey. It was so large that pilots used it to navigate, although it needed some explanation to anyone who had not yet seen it. The cow stood for many years next to the Ayrshire Dairy Farm's retail store. Sadly, the farm closed its retail store and the cow has moved away.

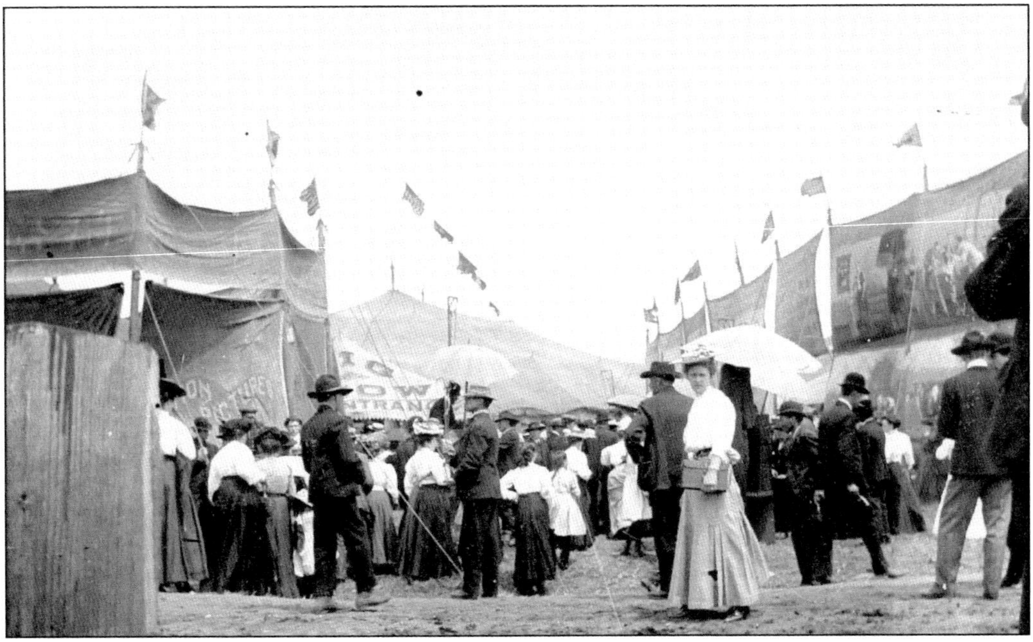

County fairs are a high point of the year for rural areas, and Elk County is no exception. Before the age of transportation and communication, rural areas were often isolated and country folk yearned for entertainment and excitement. Local products were featured along with touring companies of entertainers. Games, shows, exhibitions, trinkets, and oddities were available to one and all.

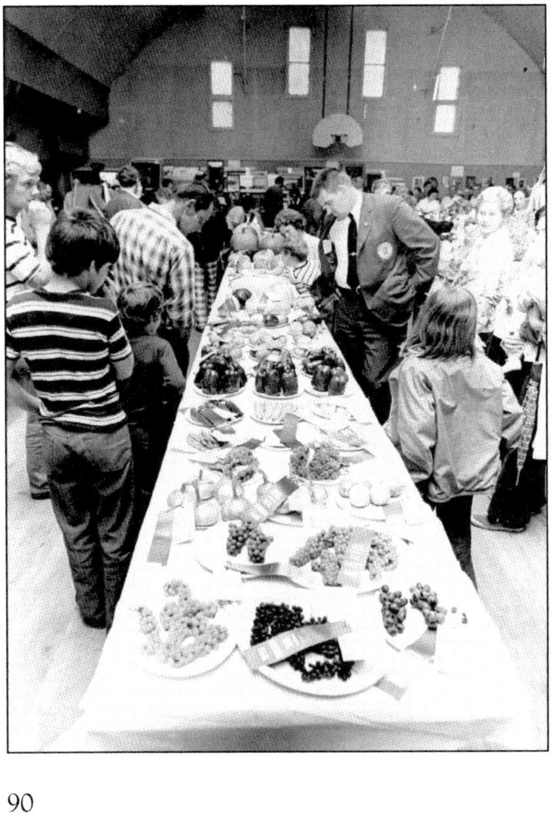

The Elk County Fair is held in Kersey. Much of the agricultural output of Elk County is from small farms and household vegetable gardens. The Grange and 4-H are active in Elk County, and these part-time farmers are very proud of their products. Pictured is the public inspection of products inside the Kersey Community Building. (Ray Beimel.)

After a lifetime of serving the community and passing their work on, this elderly couple is shown relaxing. Joseph F. and Kate Windfelder are shown in front of their residence on Center Street in St. Marys. Joseph started a brewery and operated the Arcade Saloon on South Erie Avenue. He also served as mayor of St. Marys.

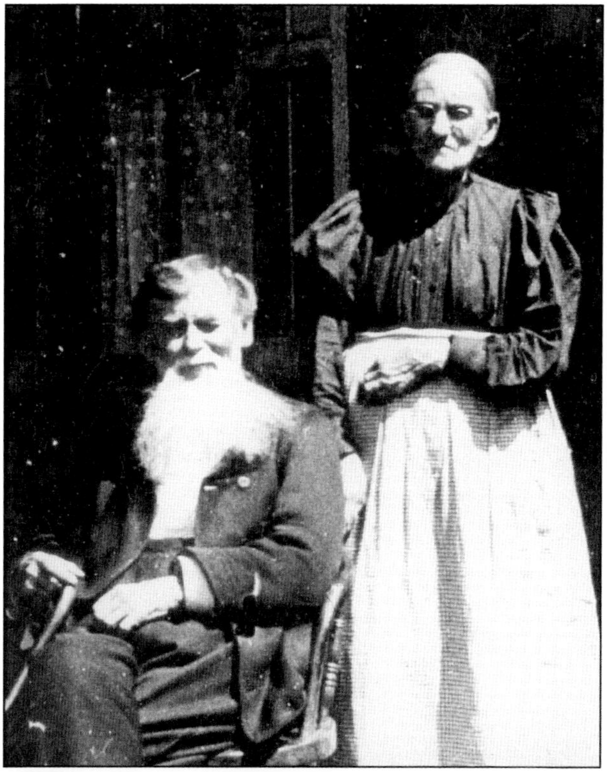

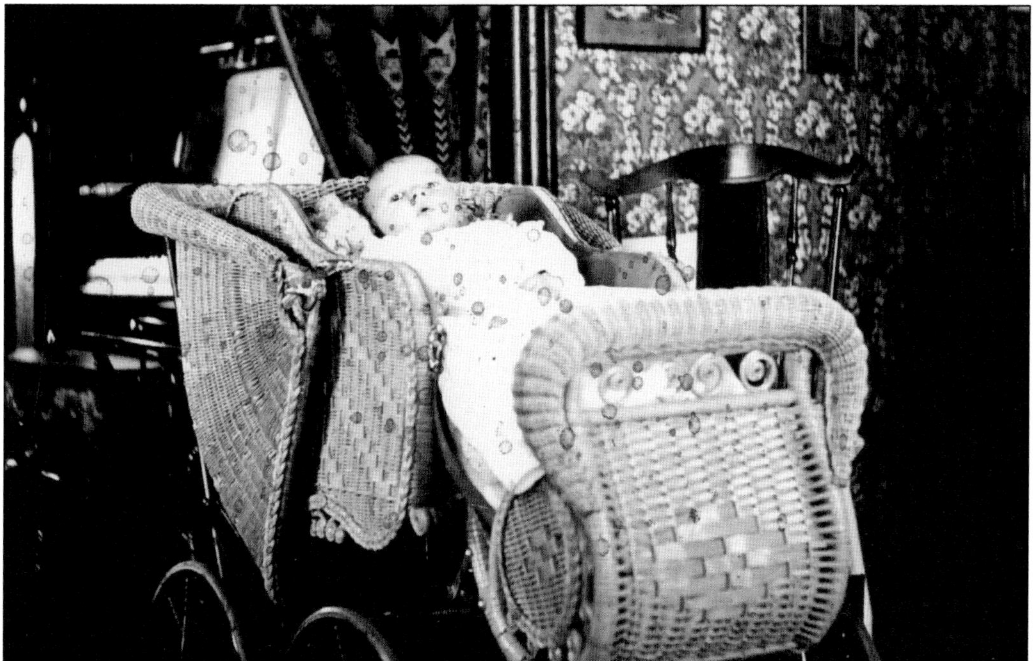

All people are excited about an addition to the family, and a photograph of the newest arrival was the same then as it is now. This child gazes in bewilderment at the world that has welcomed it. The furnishings of this house reflect the times in 1900, as does the ornate baby carriage.

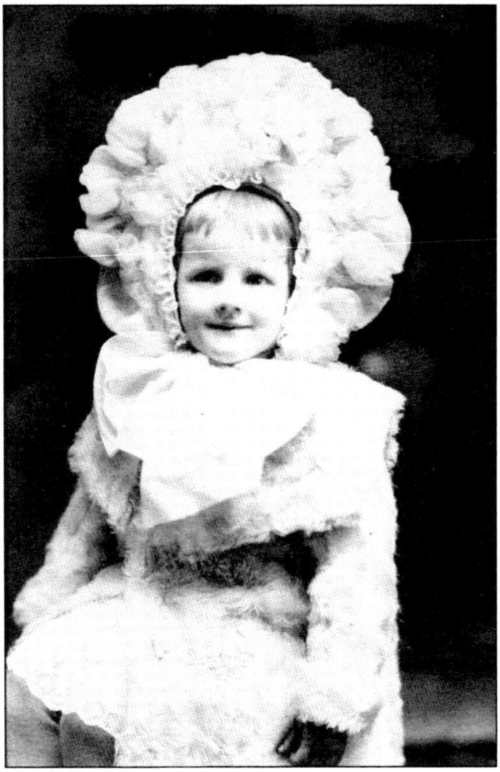

Any community's survival depends on building a business and social network and preserving it for the next generation. All generations like to pamper their children and raise them in their own particular culture and ways. This smiling little girl looks as proud of her fancy bonnet as her parents must have been of her.

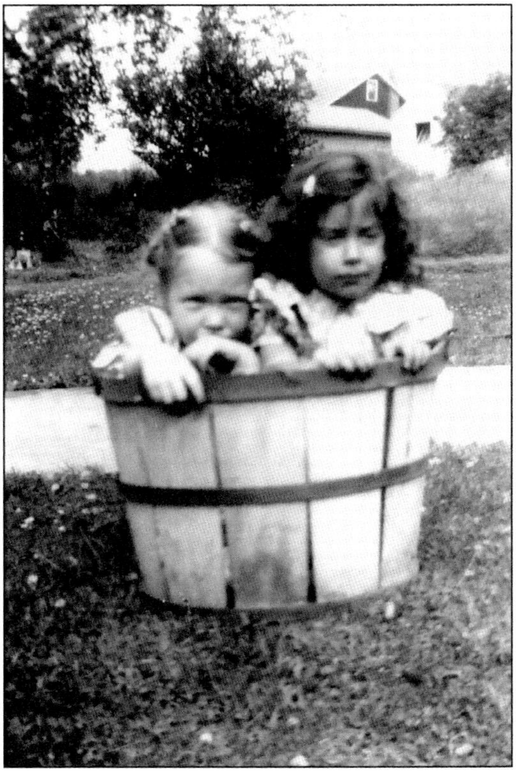

Countless photo albums are donated to historical societies with no descriptions of the precious memories of years gone by. Elk County residents, whose names are now unknown and who may have grown up and left the county or stayed and lived among later residents, are represented by an unidentified basketful of children.

Elk County was always a rural area, much more so in the past than now, and the pace of life was much different than today. If every child's wish came true and they really did get a pony, it did not matter that one's feet could not reach the stirrups yet or that one had to share the ride.

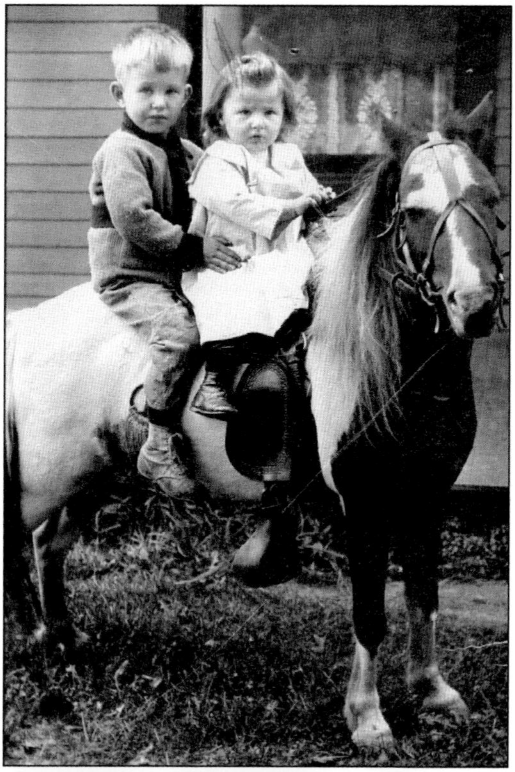

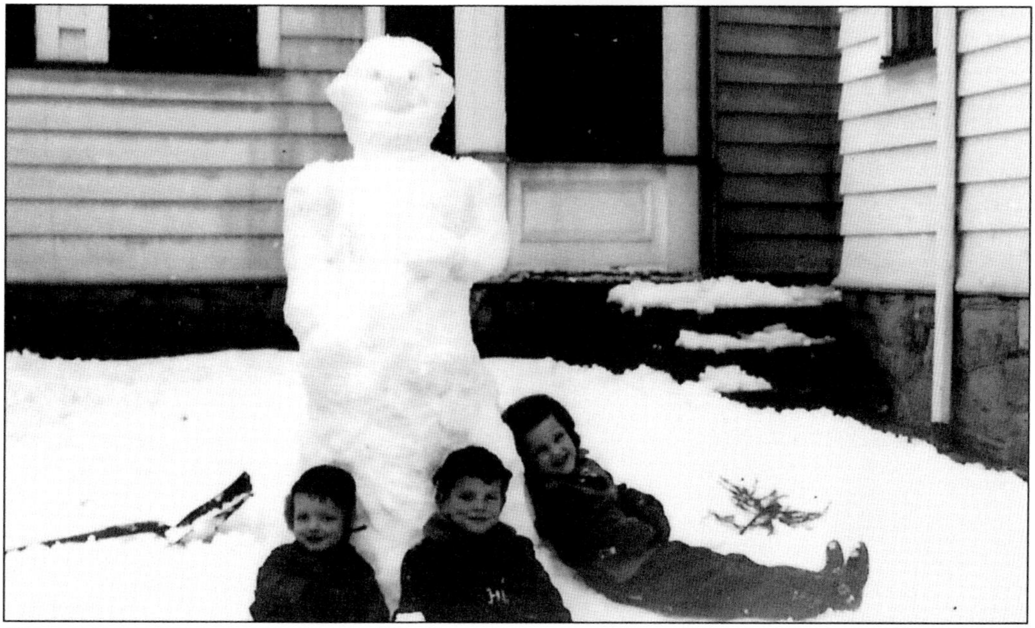

Winter carnivals are popular in Elk County, and most residents enjoy the colder months. Young scholars especially celebrate the cancellation of school, and after a deep snowfall, many snowmen and other temporary sculptures sprout in area yards. These children are relaxing after their artistic efforts and seem to await only the addition of a magic top hat to see their creation come to life.

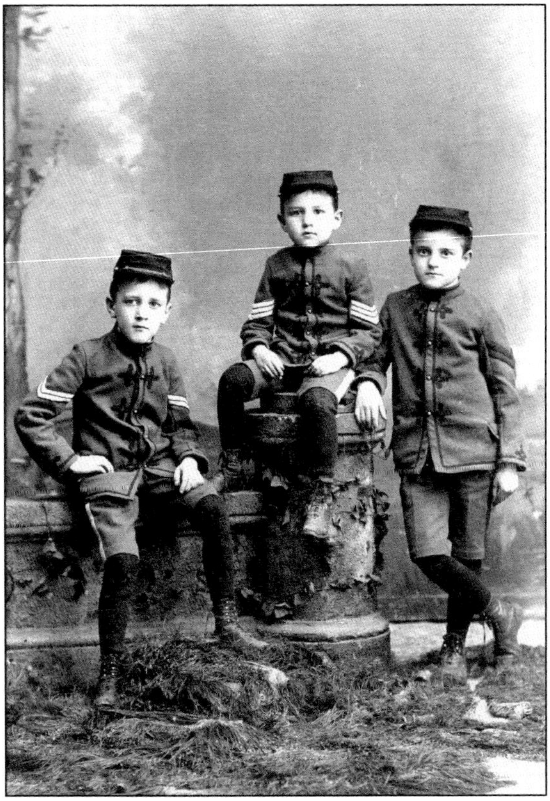

After the Civil War, military-themed studio portraits were popular to celebrate the Union's victory. Studios had military uniforms on hand for patrons to dress up in to show their patriotism, to show their loyalty to a father who had survived the war, or to pay homage to a father who did not. This photograph appears to be three brothers; the fate of their father is unknown.

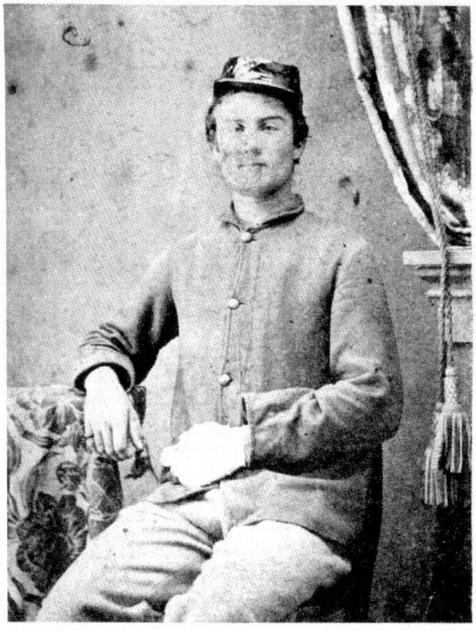

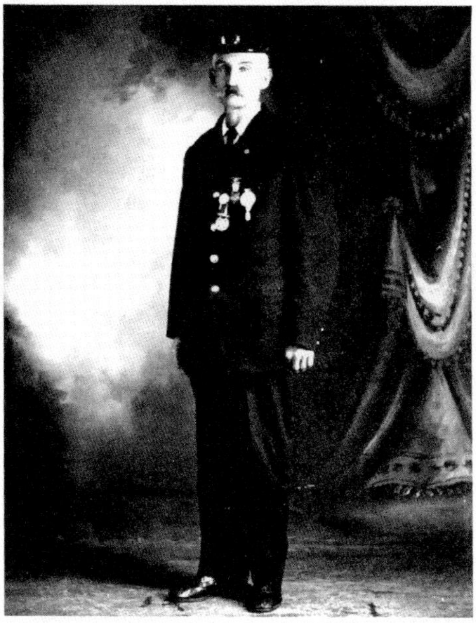

Elk County has furnished soldiers for all the nation's wars, and the county has lists of honored dead from each war. Some veterans survived to live long, productive lives. On the left is St. Marys resident Peter W. Struble shortly after he was wounded in the left hand on April 2, 1865. On the right, he is shown in his later years in his veterans' organization uniform.

In years past, infant mortality was high and cameras scarce. Often when a child died without having a photograph taken, a portrait was taken at the wake to remember the loved one. These coffin photographs were cherished as valuable keepsakes to remember the family member gone too soon but never to be forgotten.

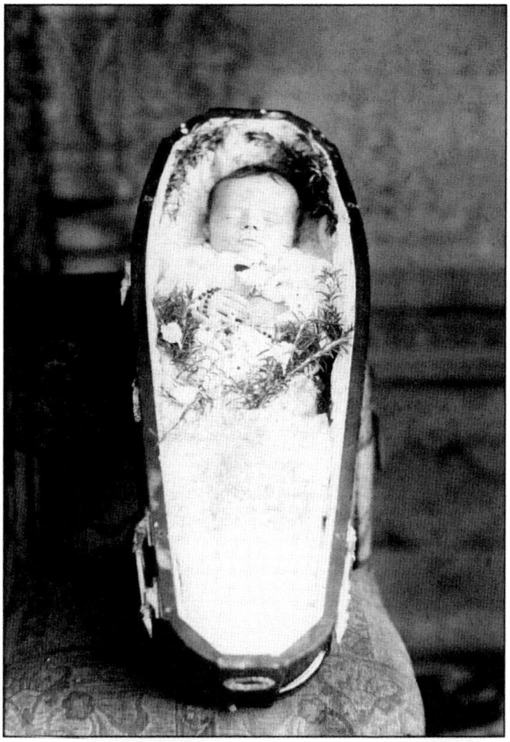

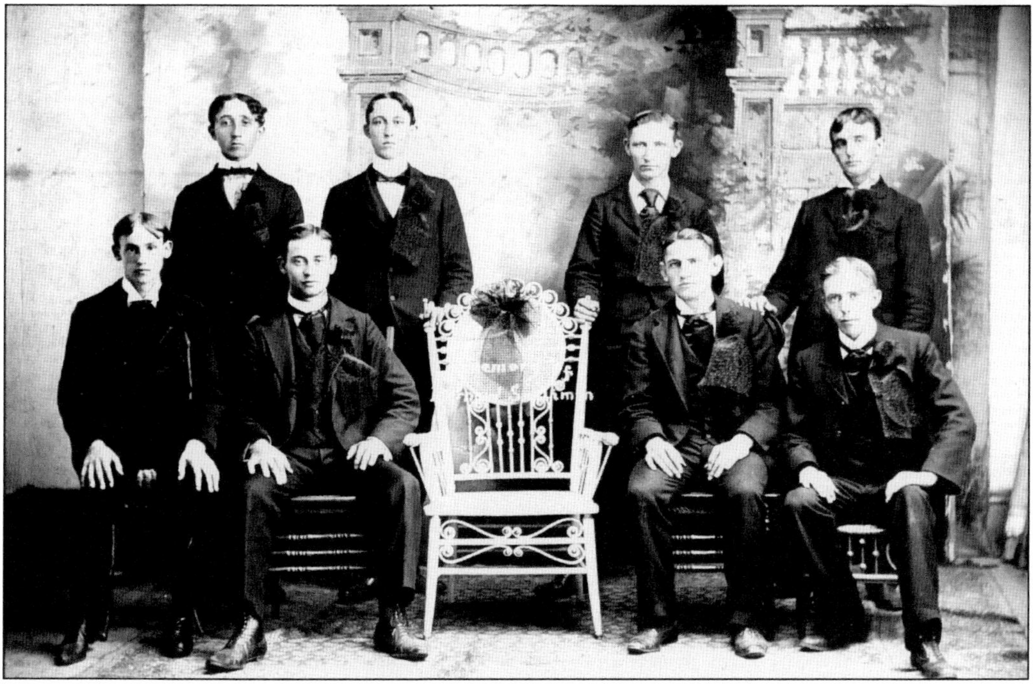

This is a photograph of an empty chair. The chair is empty as a memorial to Bernard Schlimm, who was killed in 1899 while jumping from a moving passenger train. His friends remember him. They are, from left to right, (first row) Lawrie Weidenboerner, Joseph Forster, Frank Geeck, and Joseph Sporner; (second row) "Russie" ?, Fred Weis, Joseph Eckl, and Frank Simbeck.

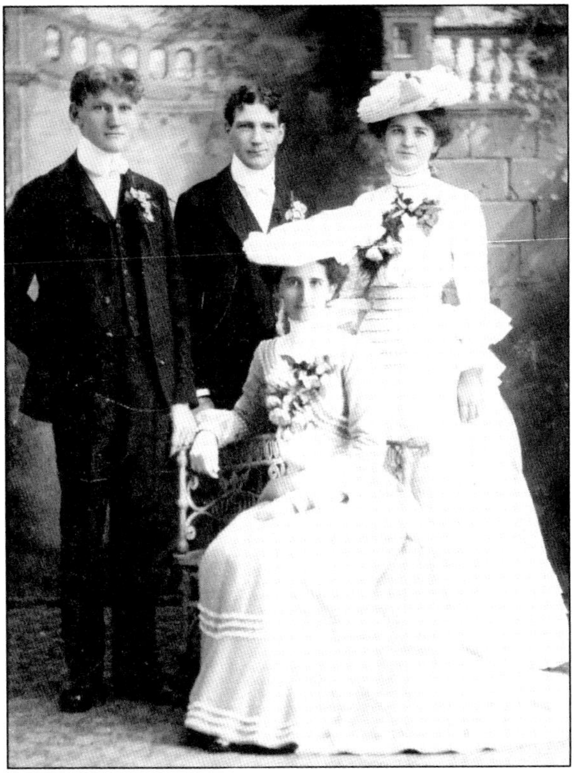

Weddings bring out all the happy couple's friends and relatives. Today the photographer goes to the wedding reception and takes numerous photographs, but in times past, couples went to a studio for a formal portrait. The stiff, white collars and fancy hats make an impressive showing here at the wedding of Benjamin J. and Anna Rose Kronenwetter with their attendants.

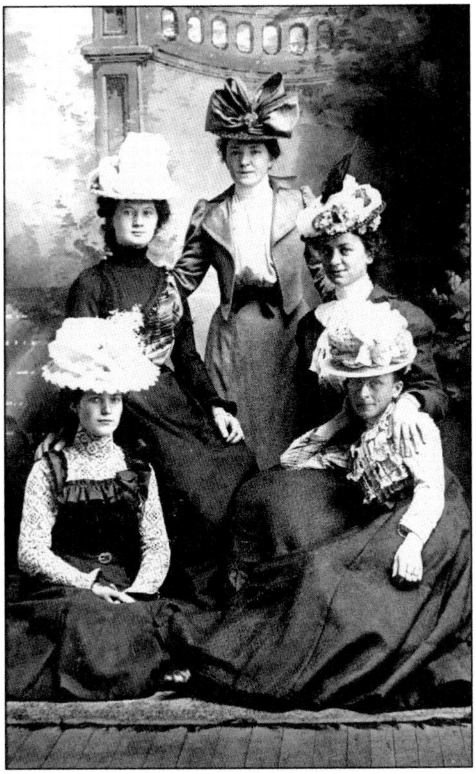

Why this portrait was taken is unknown. Perhaps it was Easter and they were showing off their bonnets. Perhaps they were all sisters. One thing that is known is that the photographer was very popular in St. Marys. The background from this studio is seen over and over again in many photographs. It appears in the previous photograph also.

This photograph is certainly an enigma. The "bearded lady" was a popular sideshow attraction at many carnivals and traveling shows. When the carnival came to town, everyone crowded in to see curiosities that could not be seen locally. Not much is known about this figure except that "she" received a certain degree of fame and was from Elk County. (Mark Wendel.)

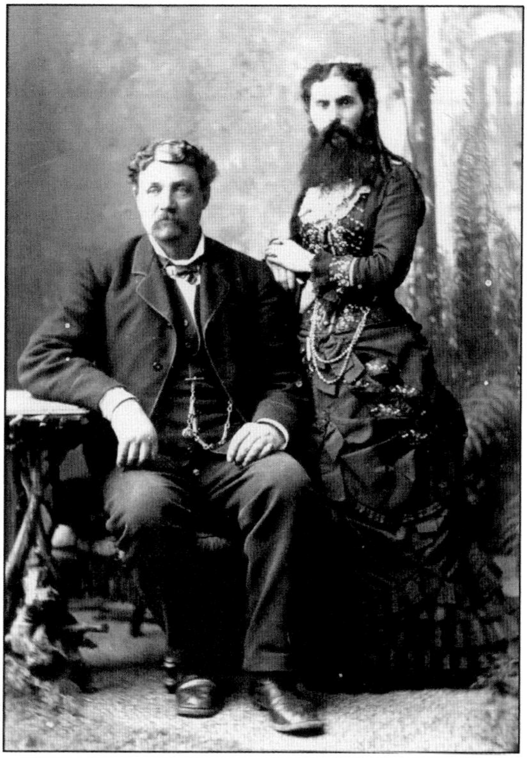

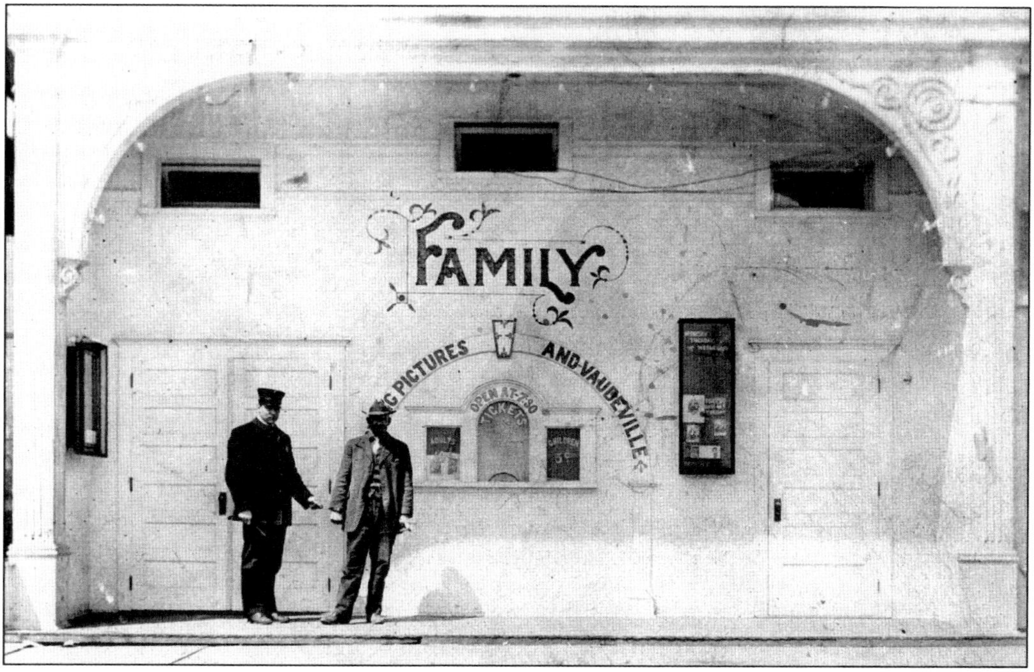

The "Family Theater, Moving Pictures and Vaudeville, Adults 10¢, Children 5¢," reads the front of this well-remembered building on Erie Avenue in St. Marys. Many recall visiting exotic locales, high adventure, or the Wild West through Saturday double features. Many live acts also performed there. Note the uniformed policeman outside the theater.

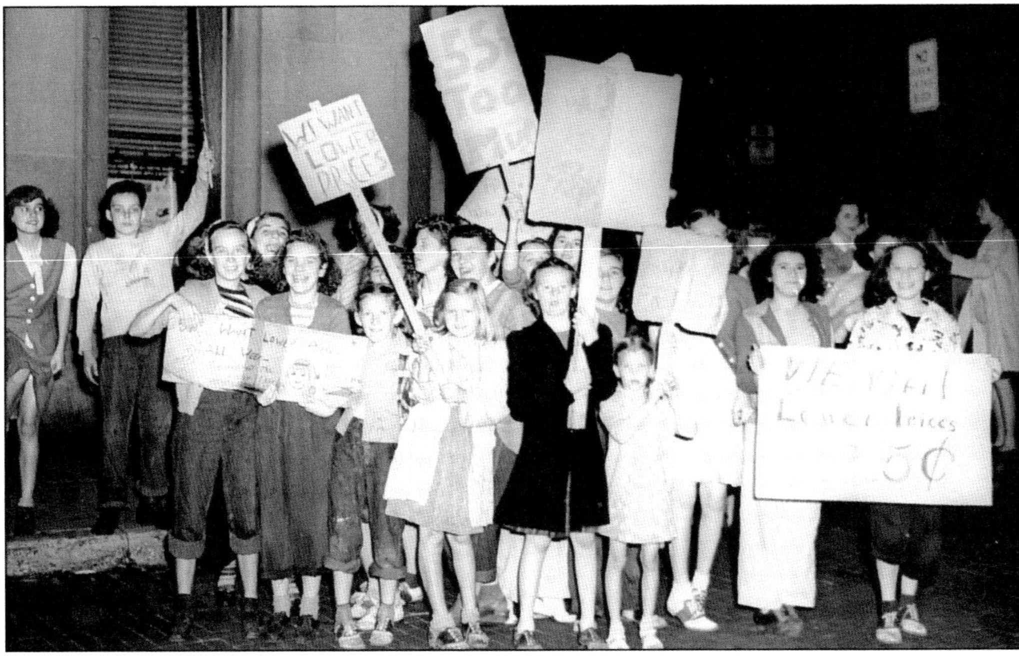

When the St. Marys Movie Theater raised ticket prices from 25¢ to 55¢, it had a strike on its hands. Many young people showed up to voice their displeasure. The price of a movie may seem quaint today, but the young moviegoers believed in their cause, and many came with signs reading, "My father is no banker" and "What do you think we are, millionaires?"

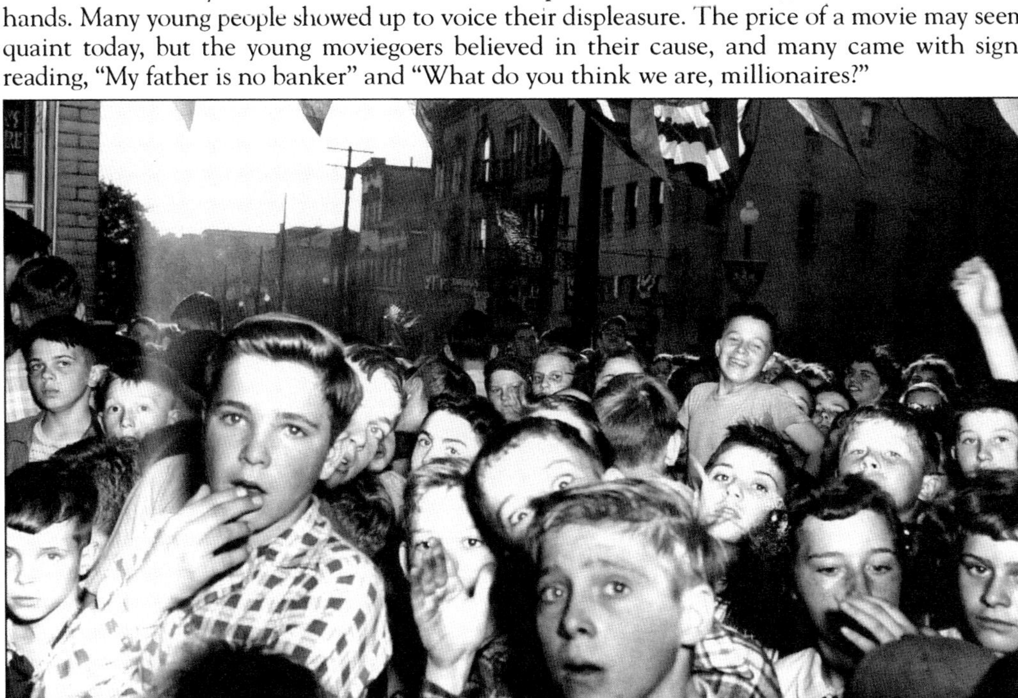

The St. Marys Movie Theater strike did not last long and ticket prices were not affected. When the doors opened, the theater was still a crowded popular place. Looking out from the movie theater in this photograph, the west side of the diamond in St. Marys is visible, including the old Hall and Kaul Department Store, which would eventually become the Boys and Girls Club.

Charles Houston is pictured overseeing young volunteers at the St. Marys Youth Center. The youth center was located in the St. Marys Municipal Building. This building had originally been the Novelty Incandescent Light Company. The company became the Sylvania Corporation. Sylvania donated the building to the Borough of St. Marys with the stipulation that the second floor be a youth center. Many St. Marys youths learned to dance here.

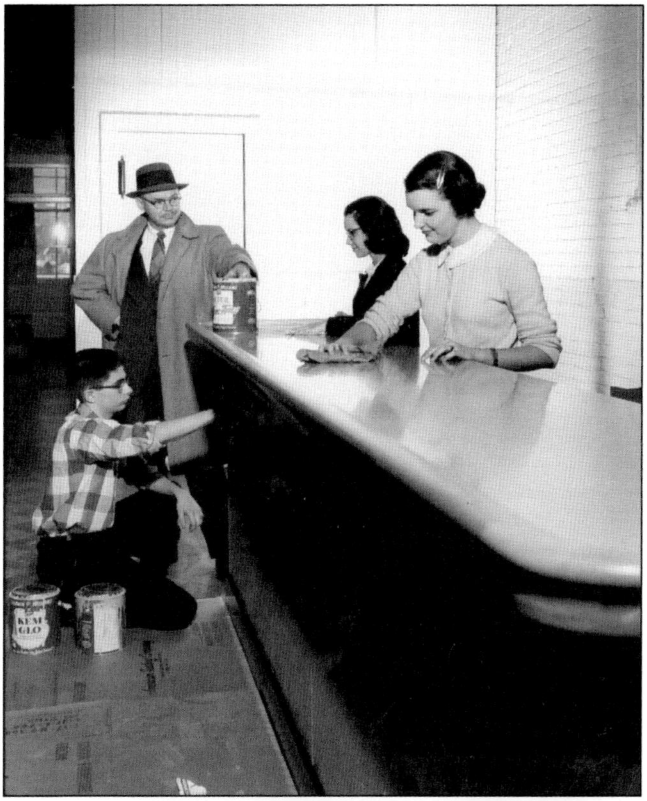

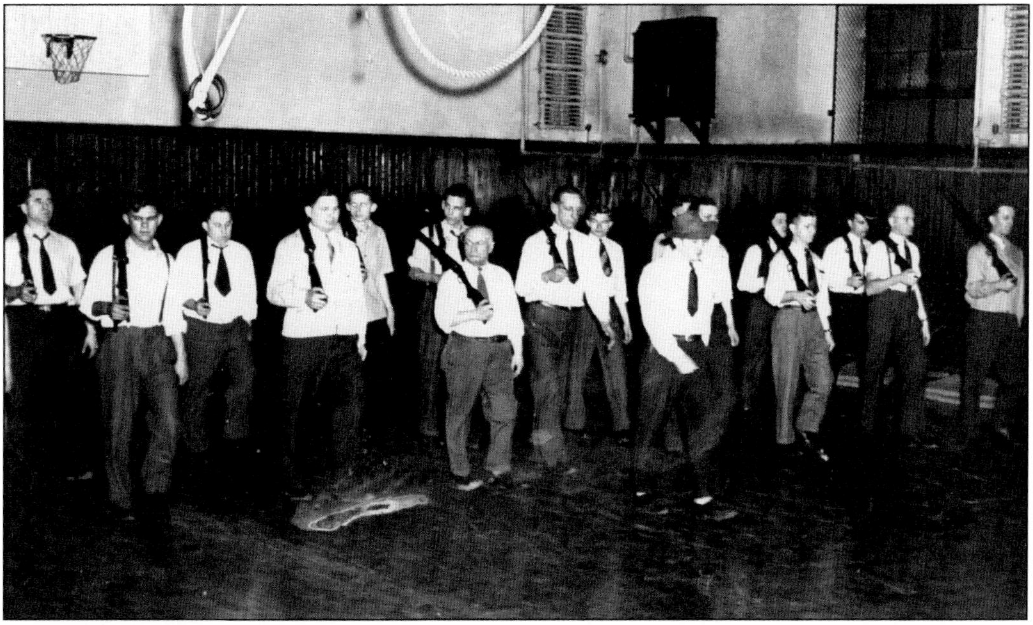

During World War II, the Reserve Defense Corps of St. Marys took its training seriously. It is shown here drilling in a gymnasium with an assortment of different weapons. Its leader was Frank Lambert. In small towns and large cities across America, reservists, young and old, were mobilizing to meet the crisis.

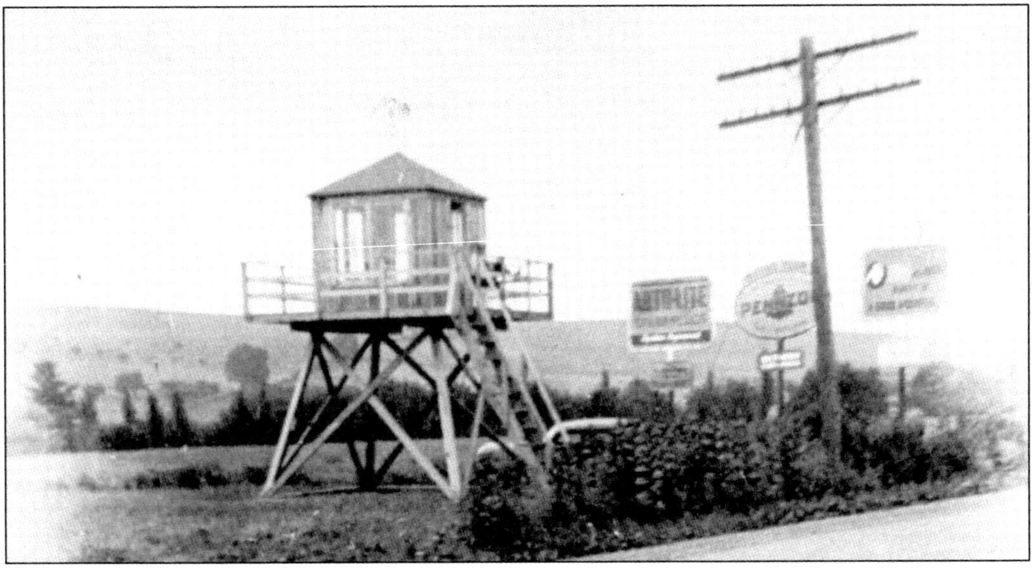

This is a photograph of an air defense watch tower during World War II. The carbon industries of St. Marys were essential to the war effort and considered so important that it was necessary to be vigilant for enemy airplanes. Schoolchildren learned to recognize the silhouettes of possible enemy planes.

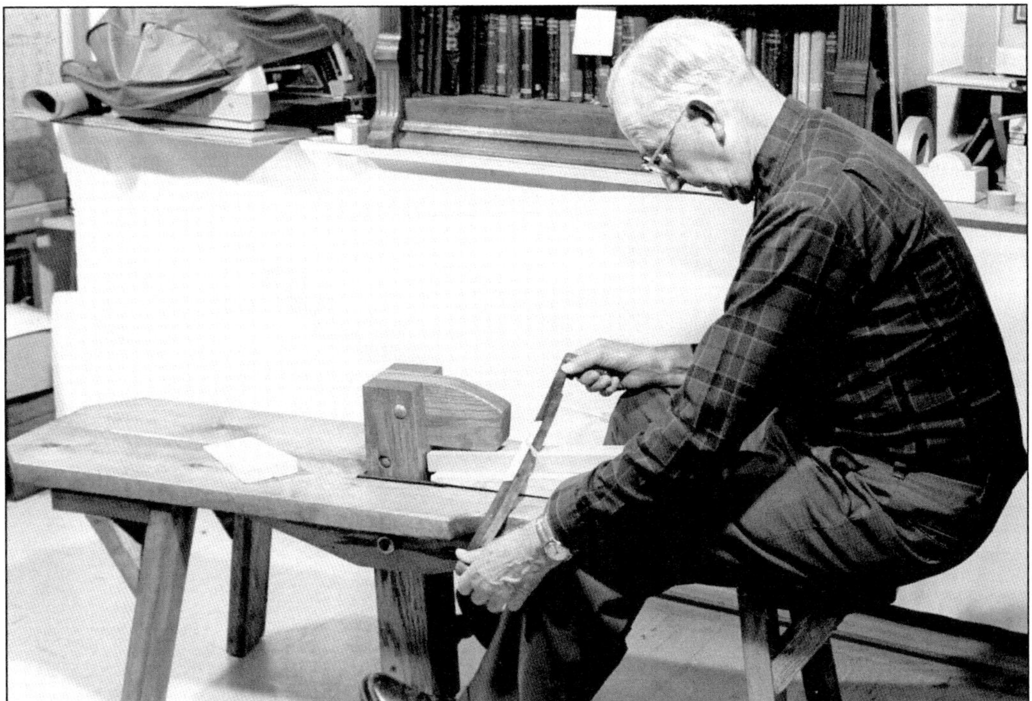

Charles J. Schaut is shown hard at work using a *schnitzelbank*, a workbench of German Bavarian origin. This type of tool was one that the early settlers of St. Marys would have been familiar with. Schaut was the founder of the St. Marys and Benzinger Township Historical Society and built this workbench, which became one of the artifacts in the museum. (Ray Beimel.)

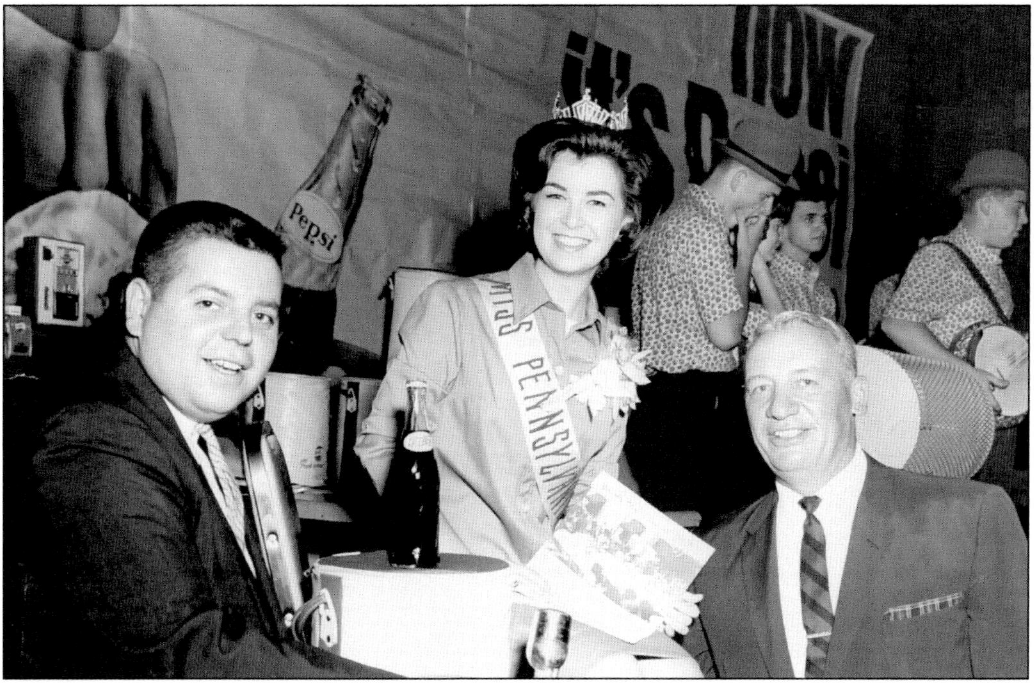

WKBI Radio personalities Johnny Knorr and Gilbert "Gibby" Hoffman interview Miss Pennsylvania at the grand opening of the Pepsi-Cola bottling plant in St. Marys in 1964. Knorr was a disc jockey at the station, and Hoffman was a sports announcer for the station. His program *Straub's Sports Parade* was a staple for many years for area listeners.

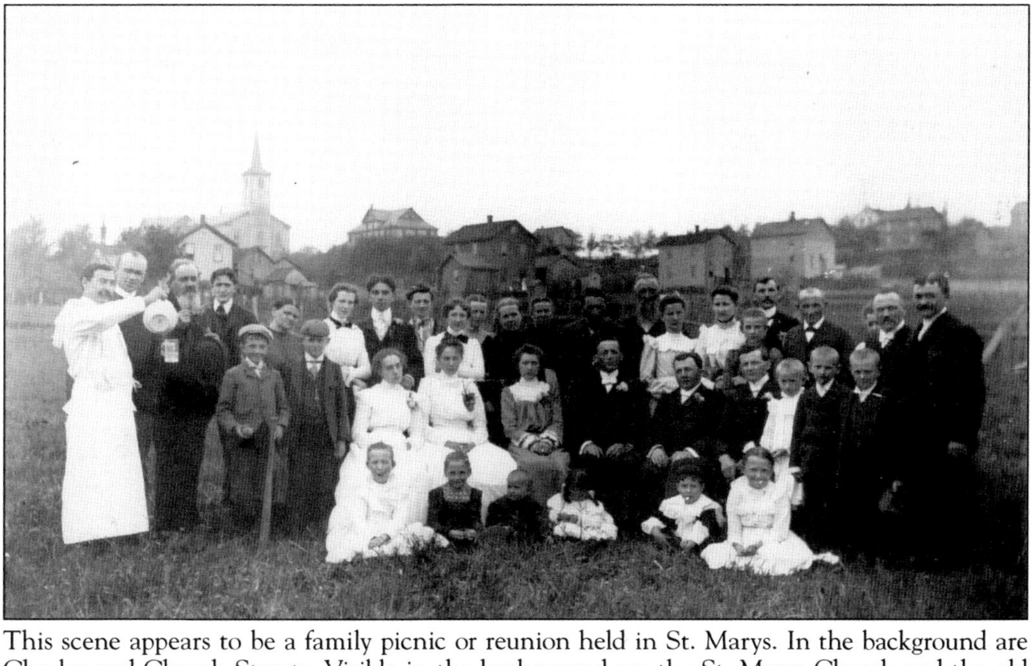

This scene appears to be a family picnic or reunion held in St. Marys. In the background are Charles and Church Streets. Visible in the background are the St. Marys Church and the old wooden grade school. The man on the left appears to be the cook for the affair, and he is shown serving a drink to one of the guests.

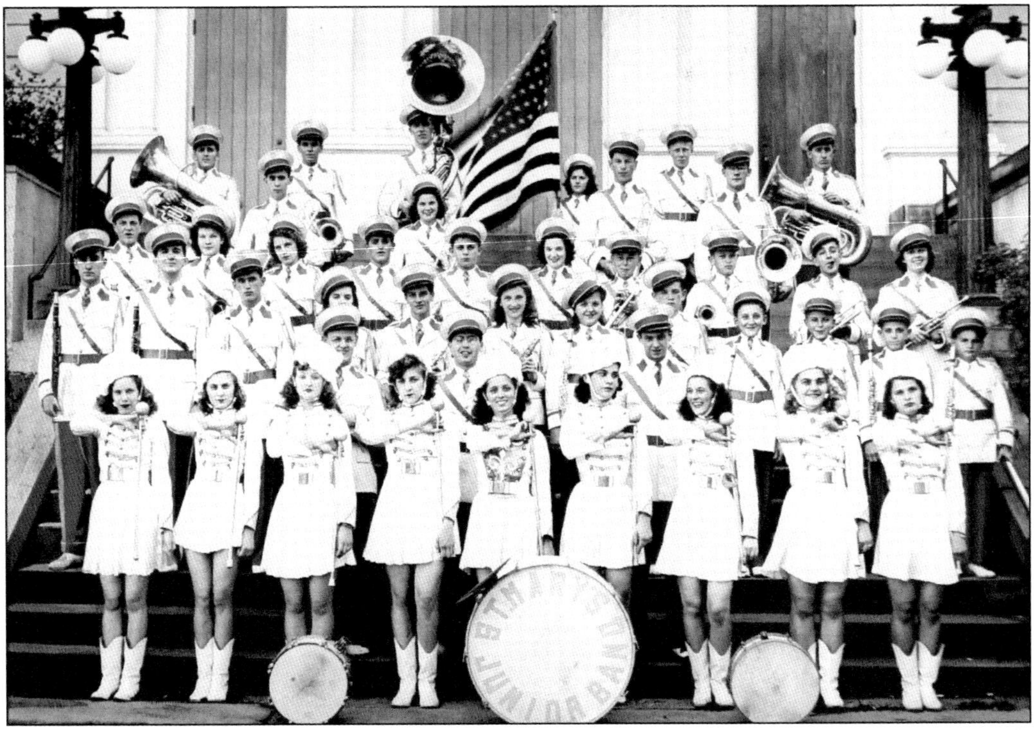

The St. Marys Junior Band poses in front of the St. Marys Church. Elk County had many bands throughout the years to play at area festivities, parades, and on holidays. Snappy uniforms dress up the band and make quite an impression. Hal Fritz, a well-known music maker for many years, is the tuba player in the back row.

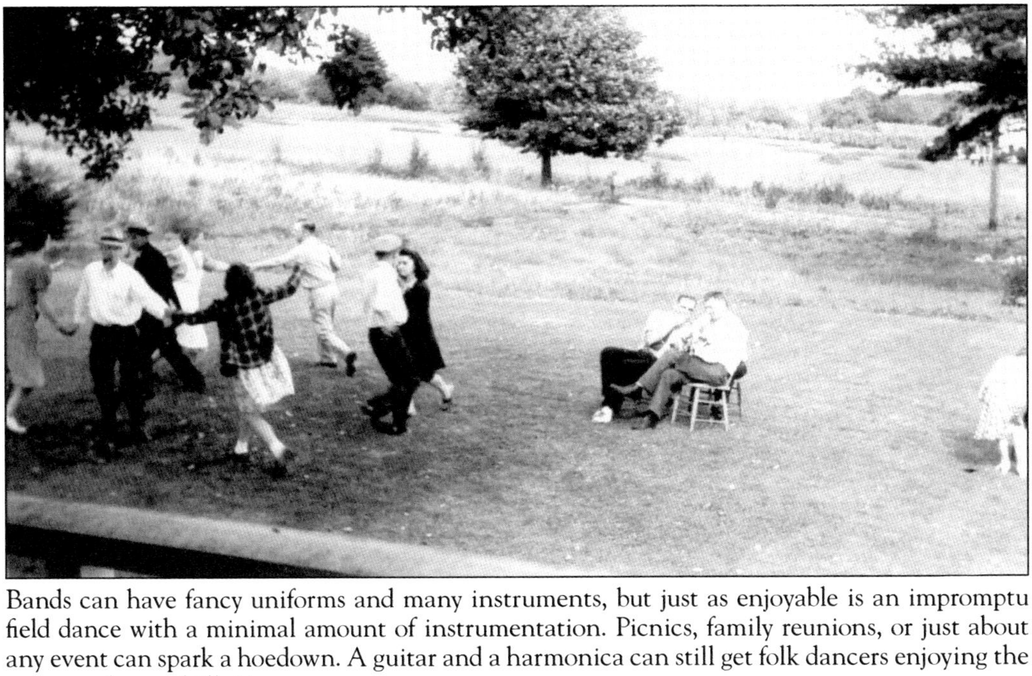

Bands can have fancy uniforms and many instruments, but just as enjoyable is an impromptu field dance with a minimal amount of instrumentation. Picnics, family reunions, or just about any event can spark a hoedown. A guitar and a harmonica can still get folk dancers enjoying the great outdoors of Elk County.

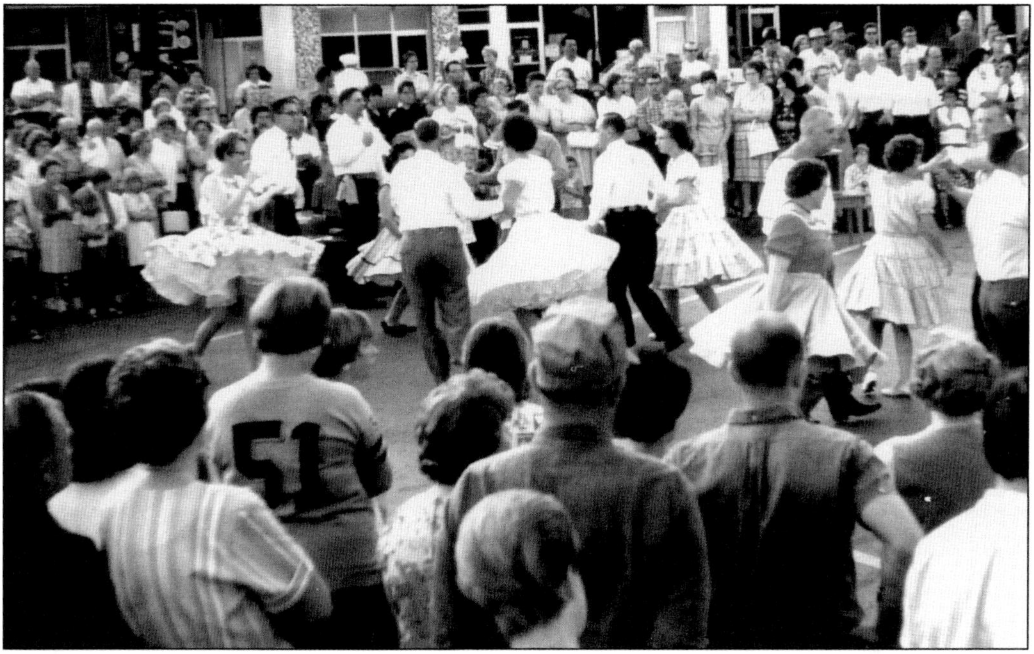

St. Marys had a dedicated group that kept the pastime of square dancing alive. The dancers are shown swinging their partners with skirts swirling. The St. Marys Square Dance Club is seen performing in the municipal parking lot in St. Marys. The event is the celebration in 1967, commemorating the founding of St. Marys.

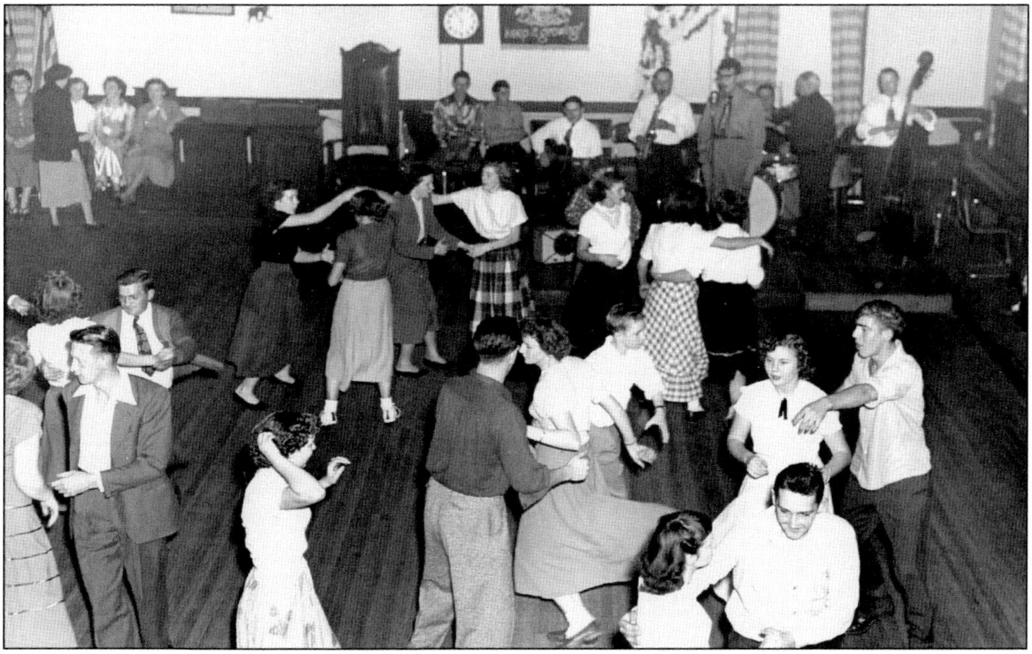

A six-piece band performs at the Elks Club in St. Marys for a group of young and young-at-heart jitterbuggers. Elk Countians have a long tradition of displaying their love for music and dance. Area clubs and bars have always featured live music performed by local talent. New music styles and dances swept Elk County according to the pop culture of the times.

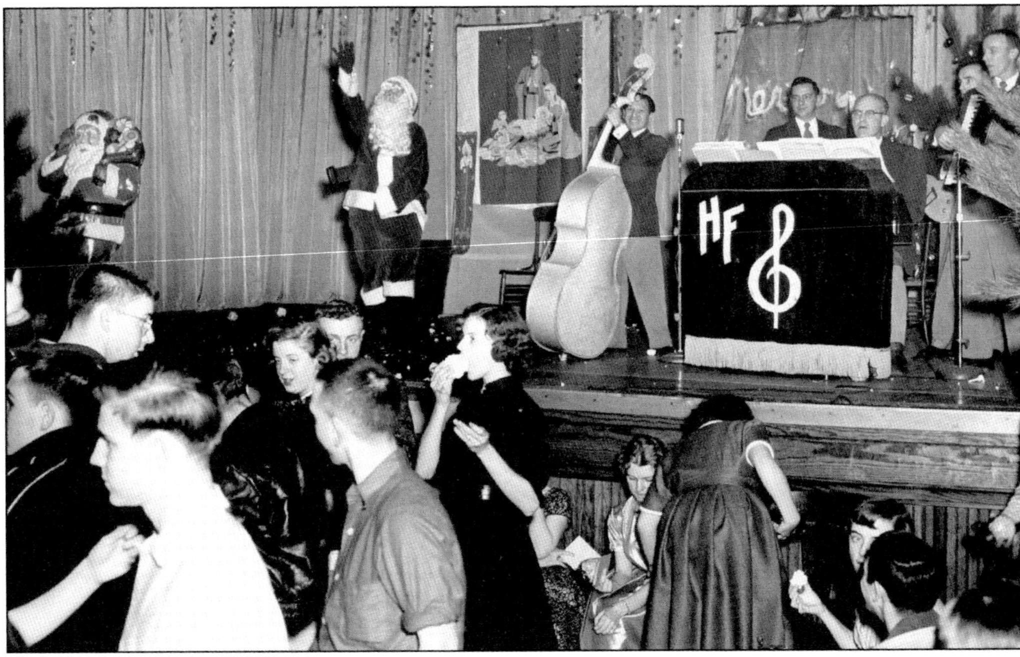

If music keeps one young at heart, the one person who could understand this is Santa Claus. Santa makes an appearance here at one of the Christmas season dances in the area. Winter is the best time to escape the cold and warm up by dancing. The band performing here is the Hal Fritz orchestra. (Grotzinger Collection, St. Marys and Benzinger Township Historical Society.)

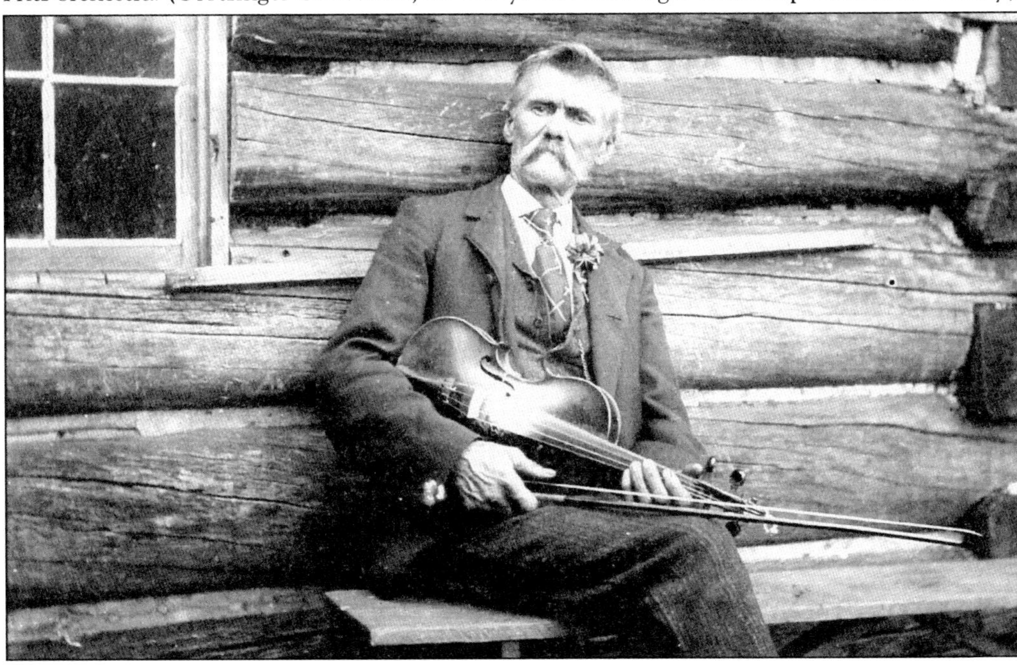

John Salter was an inventor from St. Marys. He was a practical man and enjoyed many interests. During his lifetime, he developed improvements to the repeating rifle and mine-car brakes among other achievements. He was also an accomplished fiddler and was popular at weddings and dances. He is shown here taking a break from his musical pastime. (Bill Krellner.)

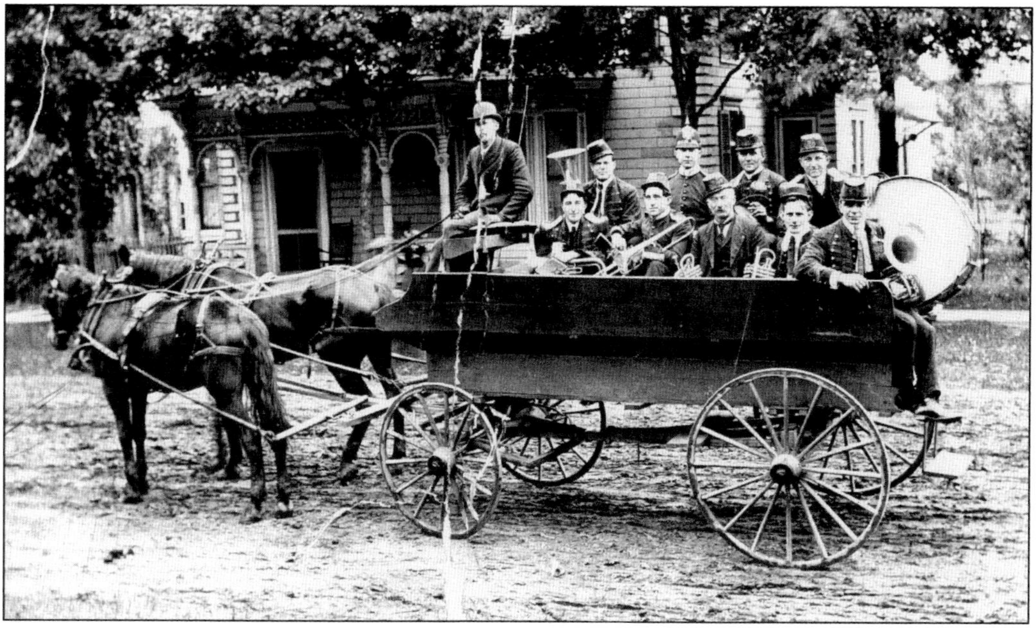

In the summer months, music is portable and parades are very popular, especially on the Fourth of July. Here is the St. Marys band in 1902 celebrating the Fourth of July. Band members are, from left to right, (first row) Al Brunner, J. Cotter, ? Kreuger, Ed Dippold, and Joe Glatt; (second row) "Blinky" Morgan, Harry Wittman, Jake Rupp, and George Zelt. The driver is unidentified.

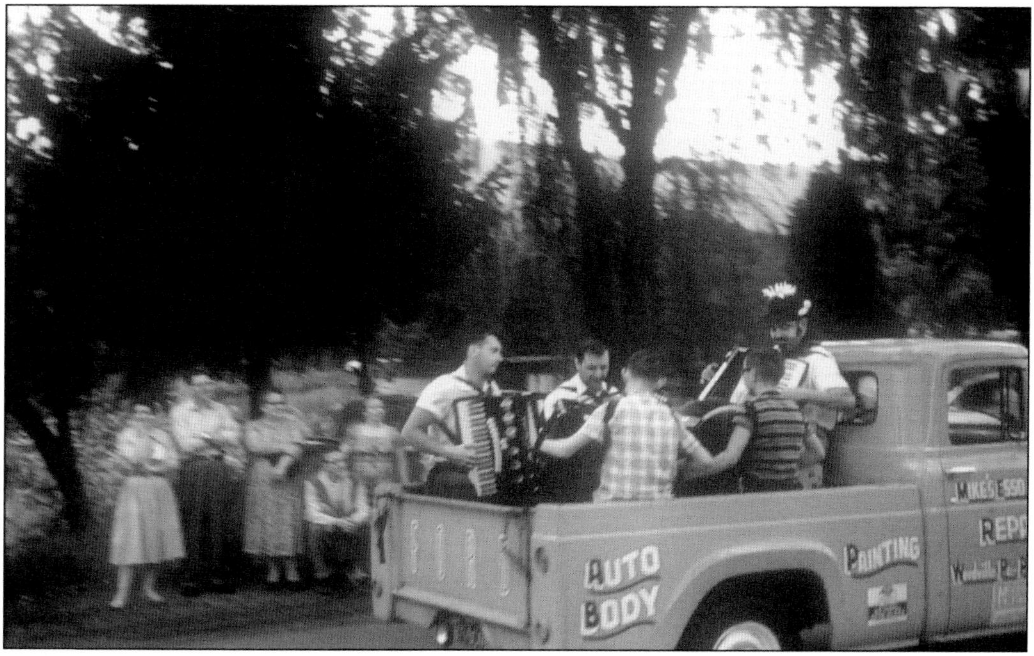

Times may change but music is still a favorite at holiday parades and festivals. Musical styles may come and go also, but polka music is always a local favorite. Here an accordion ensemble entertains from the back of a pickup truck during the annual Labor Day parade in Bennetts Valley. This scene is in Weedville. (Christopher Dill.)

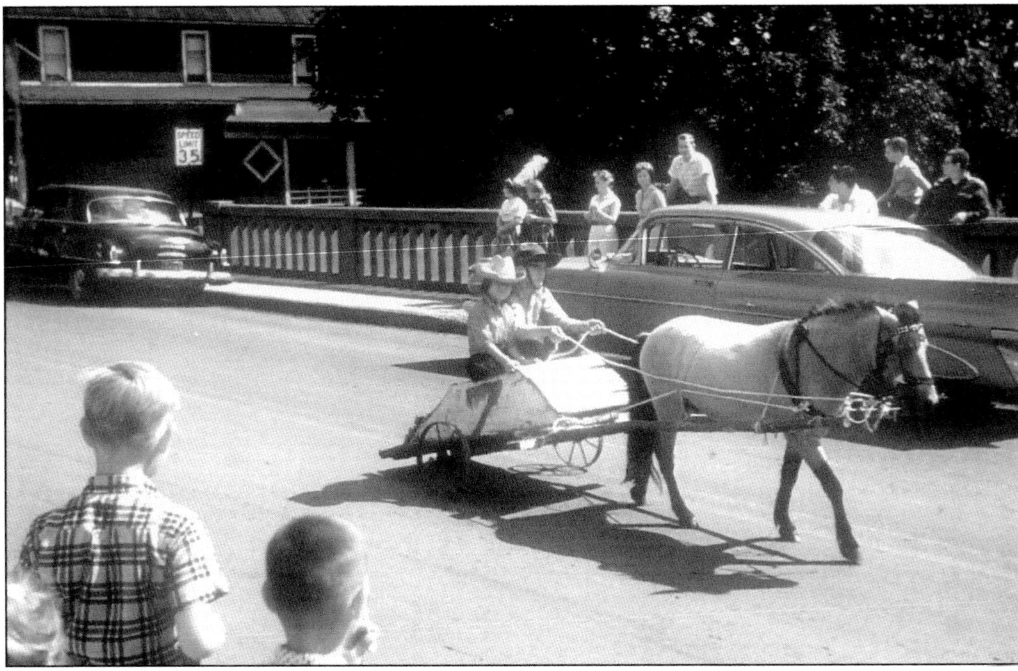

Here is another scene from the Labor Day parade in Weedville, Bennetts Valley. The charm of small local parades is that many of the floats are homemade and not very elaborate. The pet pony hauling a crude box on wheels is all that is needed. Spray paint a number seven on the side of the vehicle and don a cowboy hat and one is ready to go. (Christopher Dill.)

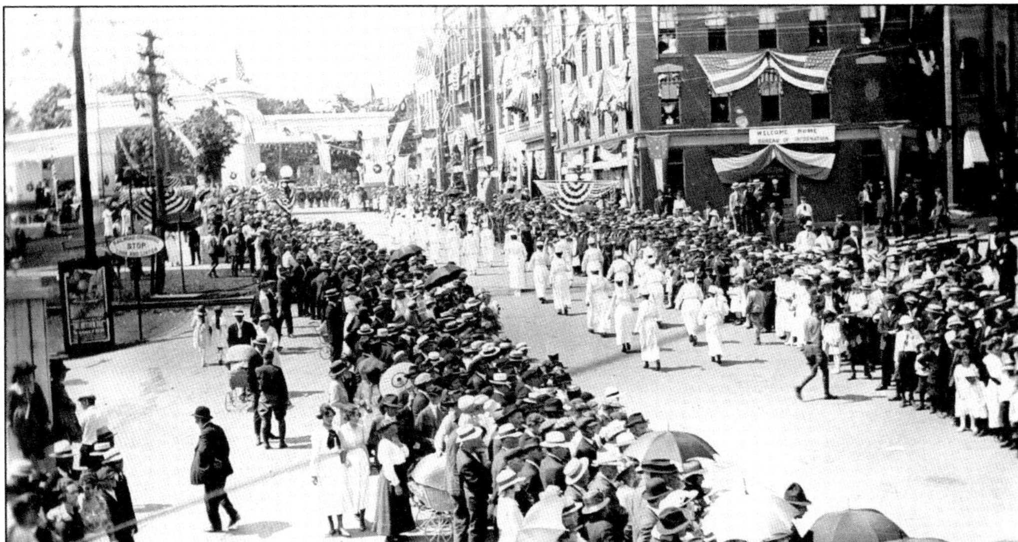

Here is a scene from the 1919 welcome home celebration in St. Marys at the end of World War I. The parade is seen passing the bank corner on the diamond. Note the grand victory arch at the top of the photograph. The diamond was also the scene of musical concerts, speeches, and award ceremonies.

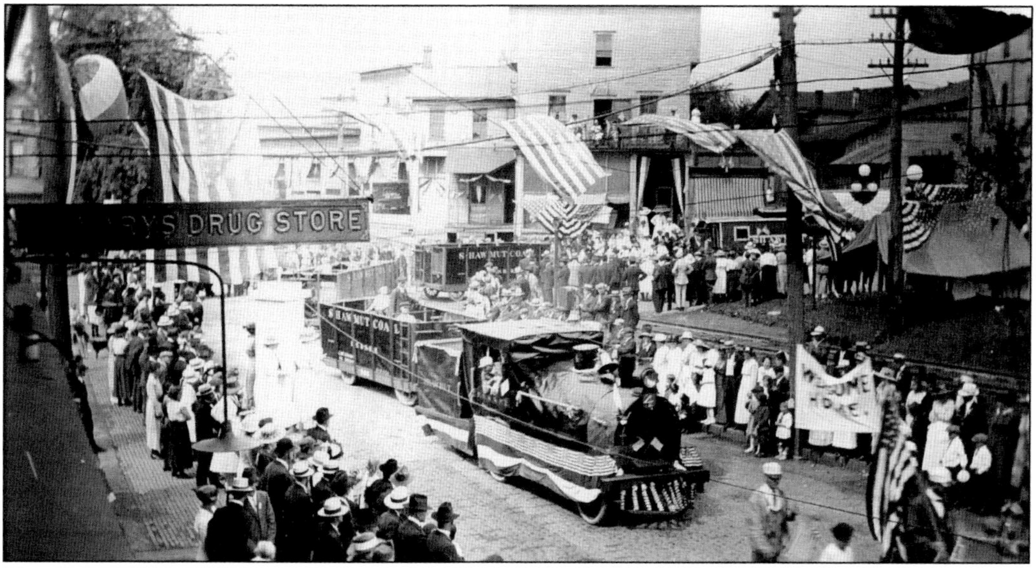

Here is another scene from the 1919 welcome home celebration in St. Marys at the end of World War I. Some of the floats in the parade were very elaborate as this locomotive pulling several Shawmut coal cars illustrates. In the background is the west side of the diamond, including the Hall and Kaul Department Store (later the Boys Club).

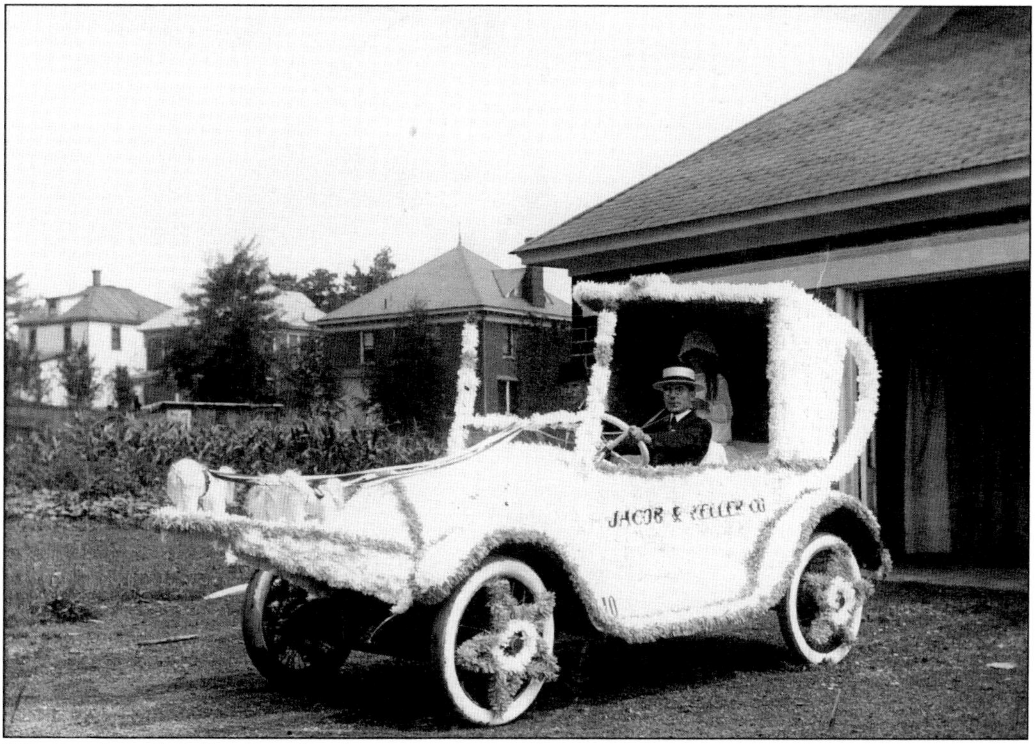

The Jacob and Keller float for the 1919 welcome home celebration in St. Marys is shown. This event marked the end of World War I and featured many events, including the large parade for which this float was constructed. This unique float features a team of dogs mounted on the front of this decorated automobile.

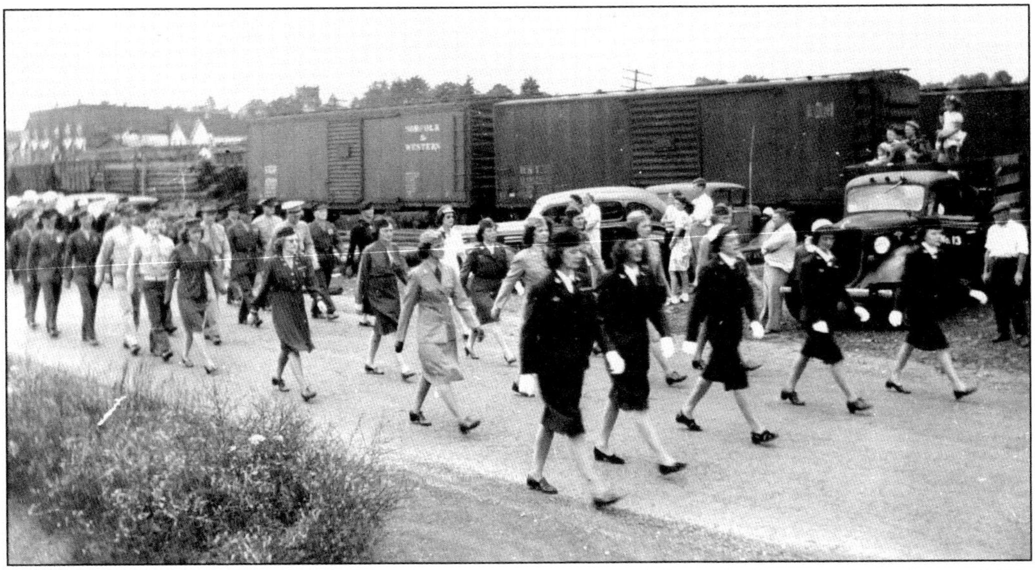

At the end of World War II, welcome home parades were celebrated all across America, and Elk County was no exception. Commemorative photographs, speeches, and ceremonies preceded the parade. In this scene, St. Marys servicewomen march on Depot Street. In the left rear of the photograph, the St. Marys Municipal Building is visible.

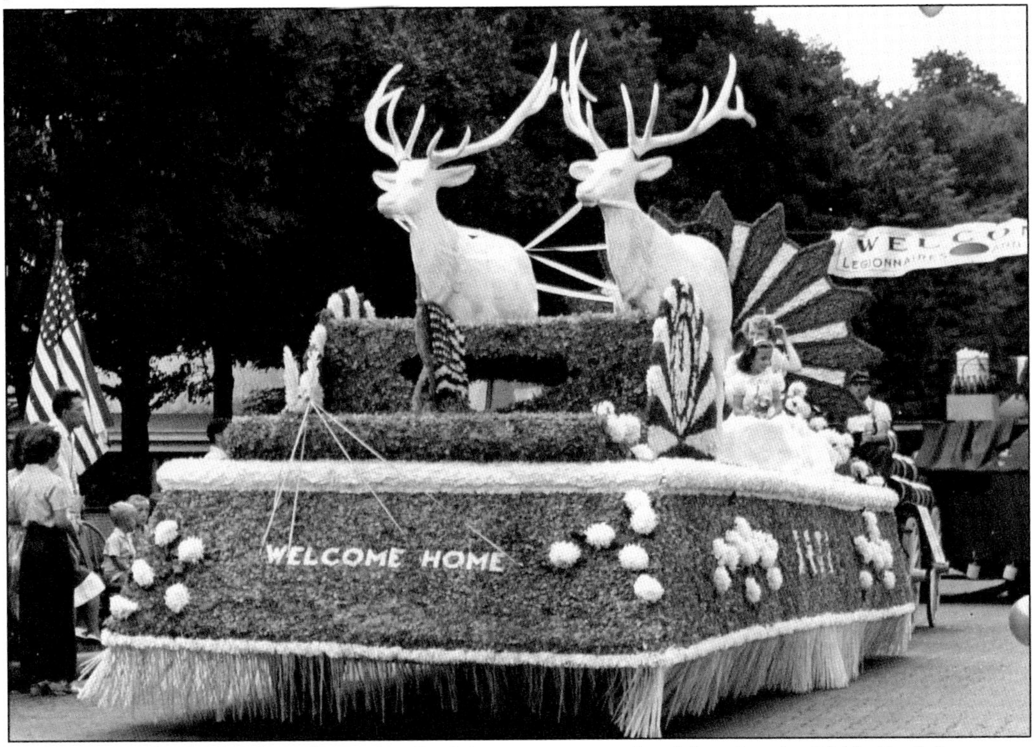

This is the Elks lodge float from the St. Marys centennial celebration in 1946. St. Marys was founded in 1842, and the actual centennial date fell during World War II, so the celebration was held in August 1946. Since the elk is the namesake of the county, the local Elks lodge took great pride in its float.

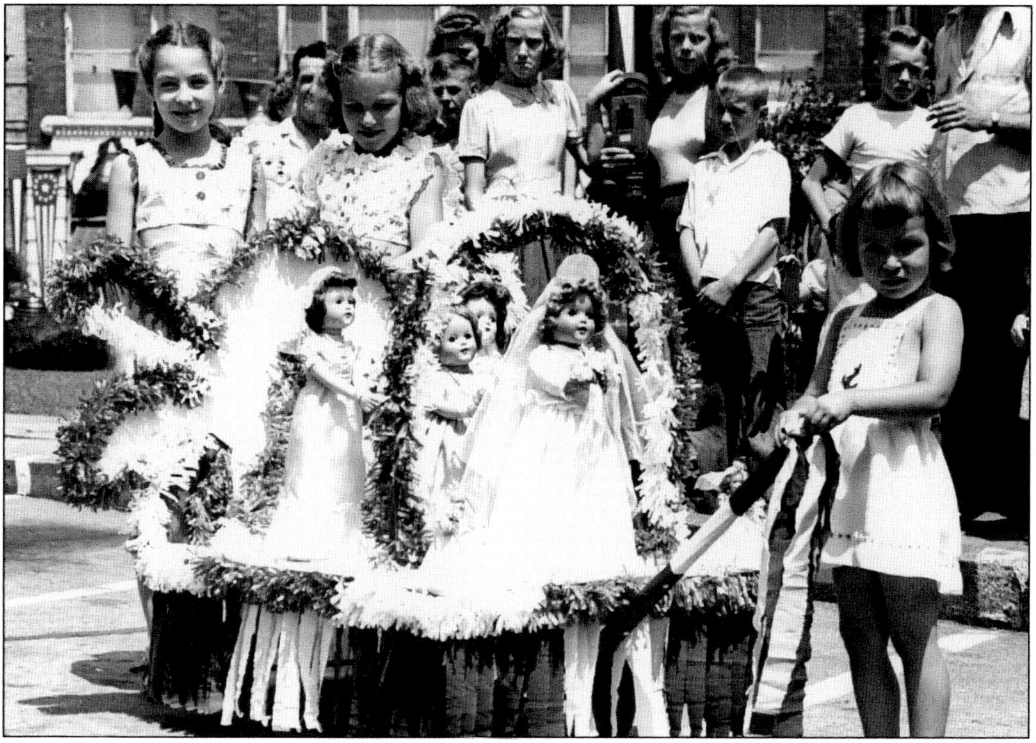

Here is another float from the St. Marys centennial celebration in 1946. This is the Women's Club entry. A group of little girls is pulling what looks like a homemade float displaying its dolls. St. Marys was all decked out with lots of flags and bunting, and a parade wound its way around the diamond and adjoining streets.

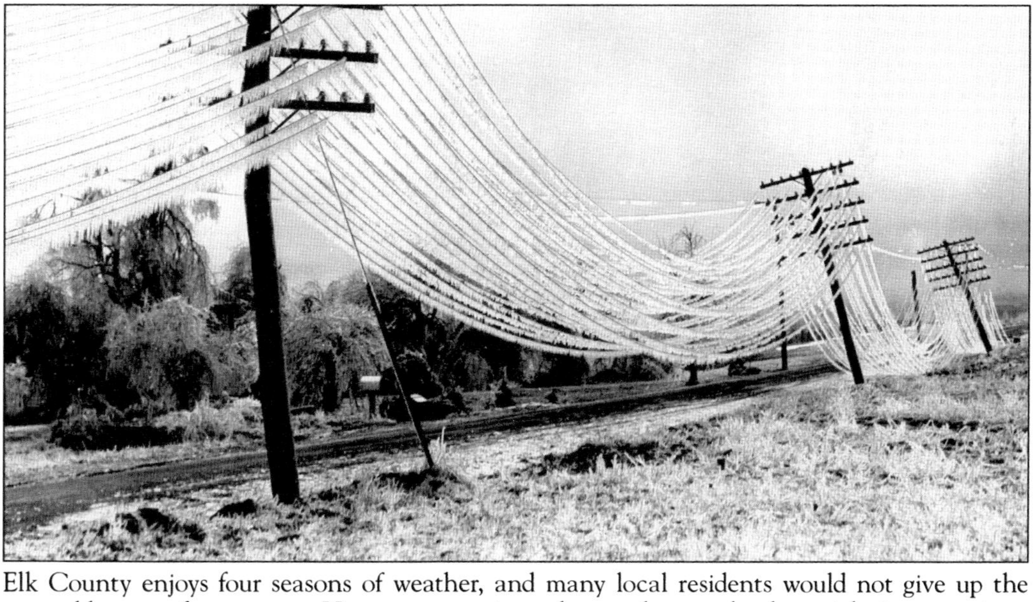

Elk County enjoys four seasons of weather, and many local residents would not give up the natural beauty of any season. However, sometimes the weather can be downright inconvenient. The severe ice storm of March 17, 1936, and the ensuing St. Patrick's Day floods devastated much of western Pennsylvania, including Elk County.

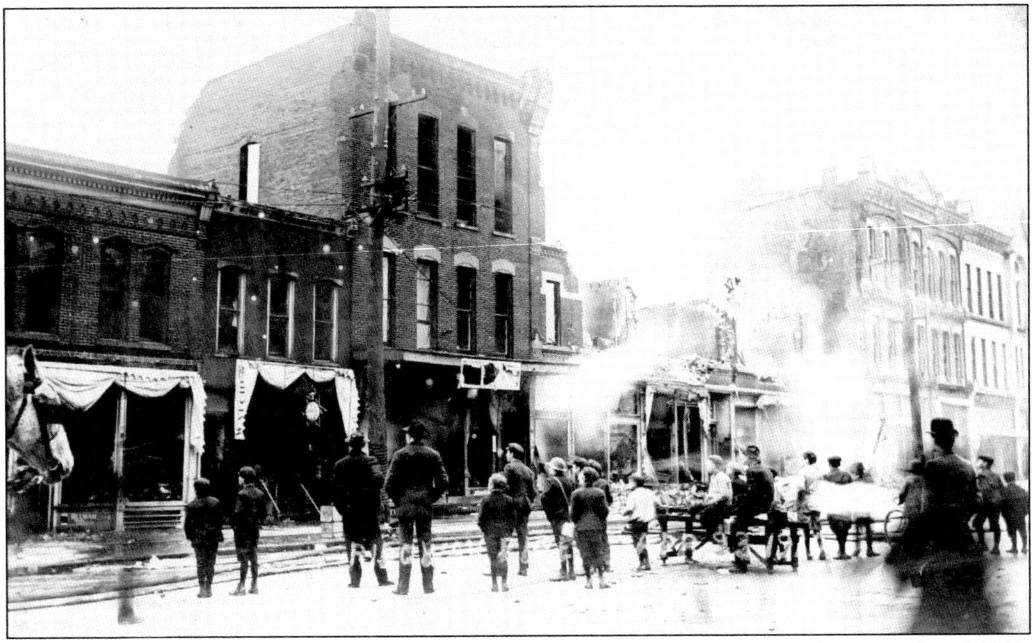

Onlookers view the remains of the Hyde-Murphy fire on Main Street in Ridgway in April 1910. Ridgway has had many spectacular fires over the years and has responded by creating a very fine and active volunteer fire department. The Ridgway Fire Department's annual weeklong celebration, with parade, carnival, and fireworks, is one of the high points of the Elk County calendar. (Mark Wendel.)

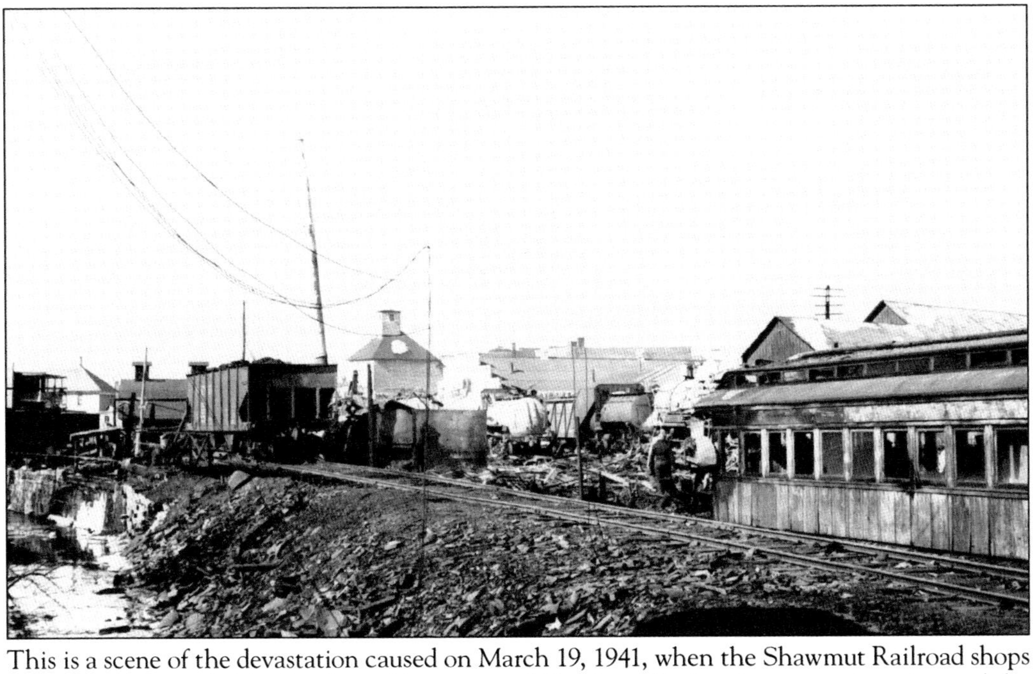

This is a scene of the devastation caused on March 19, 1941, when the Shawmut Railroad shops in St. Marys burned. The Pittsburg, Shawmut and Northern Railroad was a coal carrier, and the shops in St. Marys rebuilt locomotives. The tall structure in the background is the Lewis and Bauer grain silo.

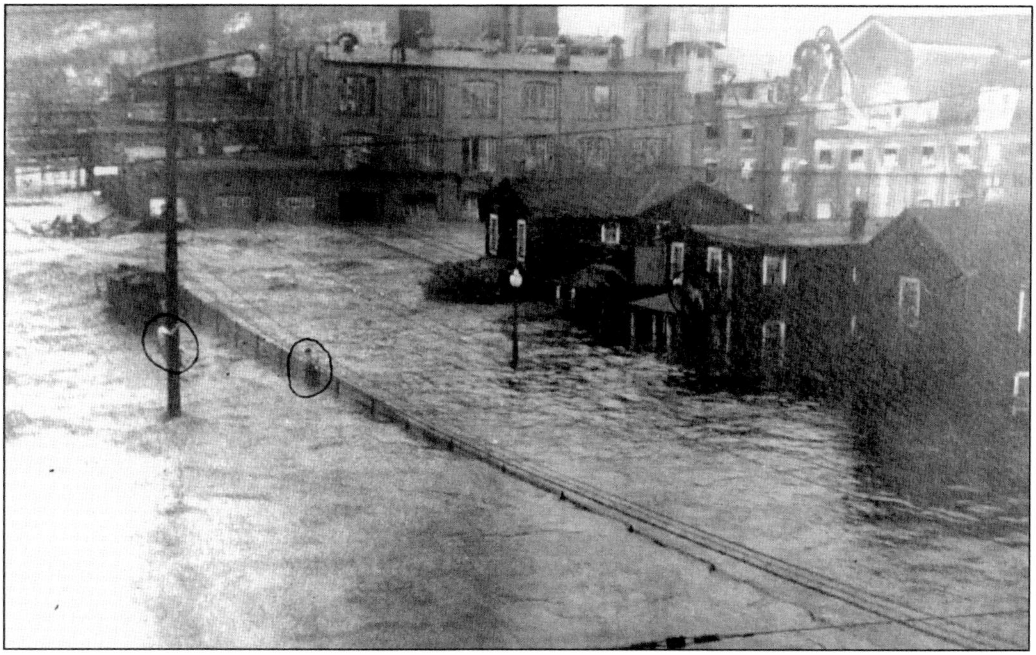

Johnsonburg, located at the juncture of the East and West Branches of the Clarion River, has often suffered damaging floods. In this scene from 1942, Bill Leathers (on the telephone pole) and an unidentified man are trying to rescue Harry Dixon and his wife, who are trapped on their porch roof. The men are trying to get a rope to the stranded couple.

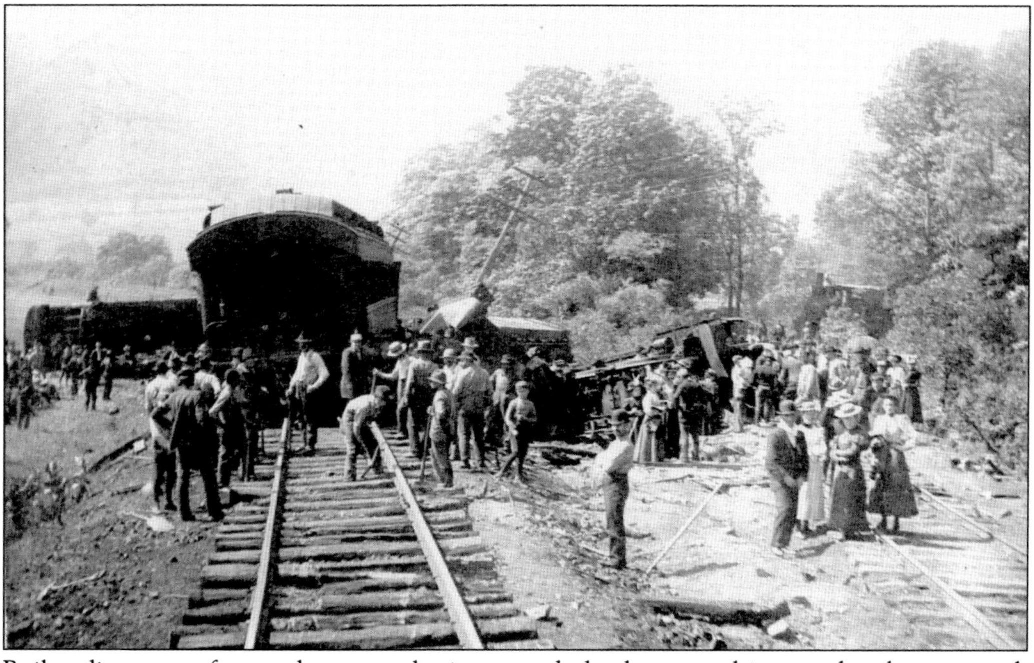

Railroading was often a dangerous business, and the huge machines and unknown track conditions could be unpredictable. Fatalities were not unknown. Here a crowd of onlookers turns out to view an accident and speculate about the cause. Note the fancy dress of some of the spectators as they pose for photographs.

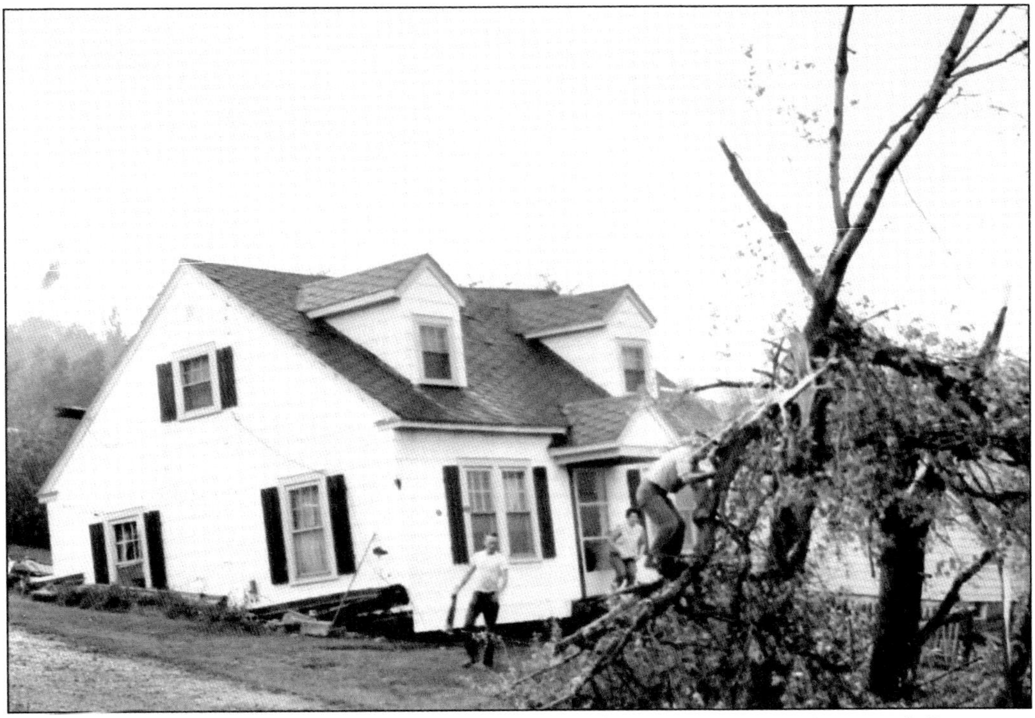

On September 3, 1963, a tornado touched down and tore across St. Marys and Benzinger Township, causing $1 million in damages. The Lynchville area of St. Marys received the most property damage; luckily there was no loss of life. In this photograph, a house has been blown off its foundation, and several men work to remove downed limbs and trees.

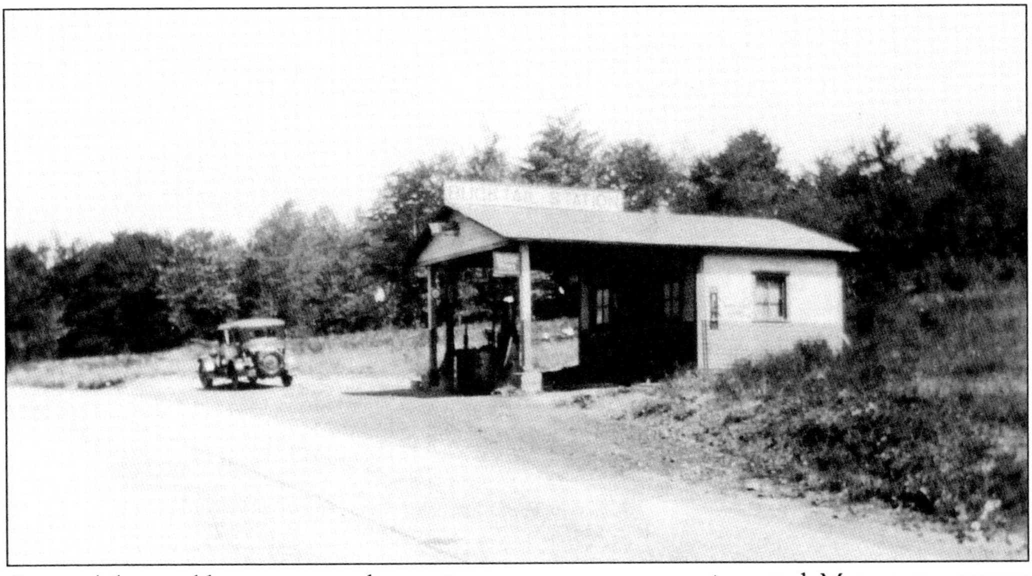

Automobile travel became a popular pastime as soon as cars were invented. Motorcars were not plentiful, and motor touring was considered a sport. Filling stations were primitive by today's standards, but gasoline was comparatively inexpensive. Service stations usually had an attendant who could fix one's vehicle, unlike today. The Bucktail Station, in 1928, was located on the Bucktail Trail between St. Marys and Emporium. (Bill Krellner.)

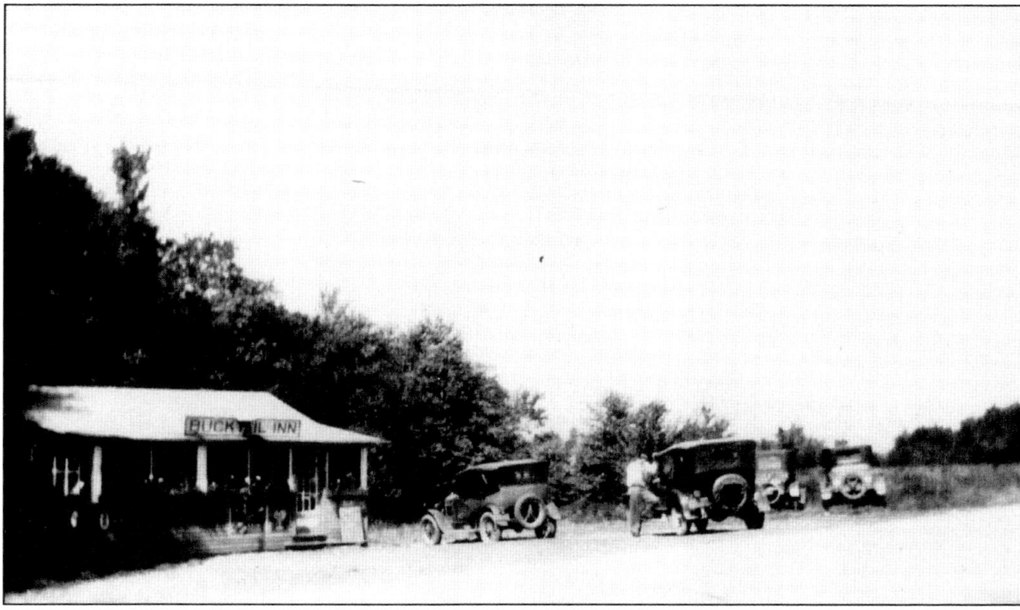

The Bucktail Inn was located across from the Bucktail Station in 1928. The Bucktail Trail was a popular touring route that was eventually designated a scenic highway (Route 120) from St. Marys to Lock Haven. It opened in August 1926. The section between Emporium and Lock Haven is a state park with beautiful mountain scenery following the Sinnemahoning and Susquehanna Rivers. (Bill Krellner.)

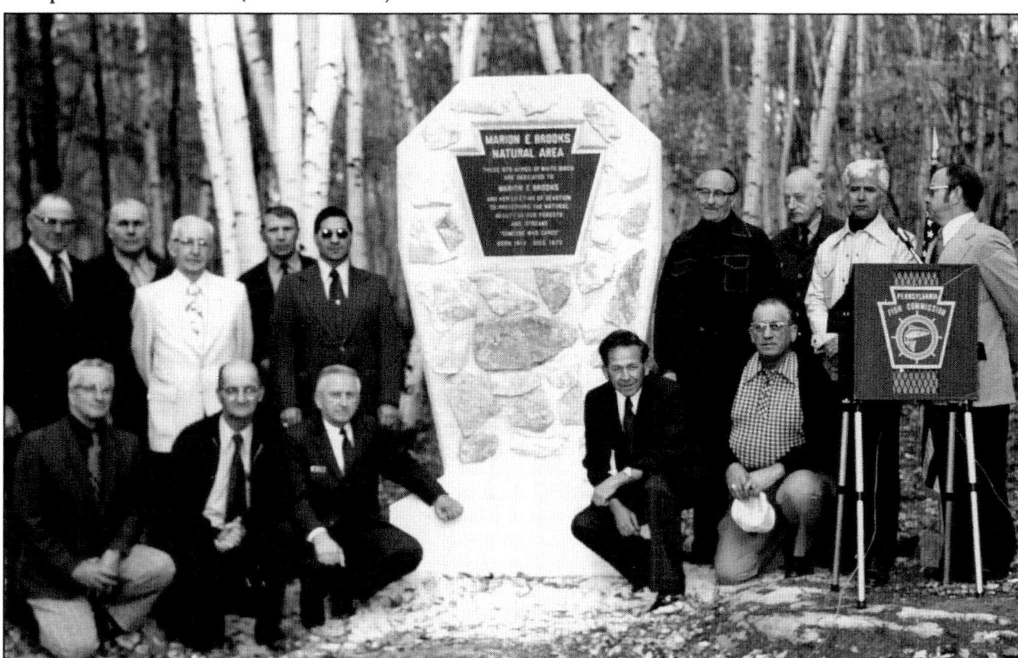

This is a scene from the 1975 dedication of the Marion Brooks Natural Area, a pure stand of white birch trees within the Quehanna Wild Area on the southern edge of Elk County. The Quehanna Wild Area is the largest wilderness area in the state. The 875 acres of white birch trees is one of the most scenic spots in Elk County.

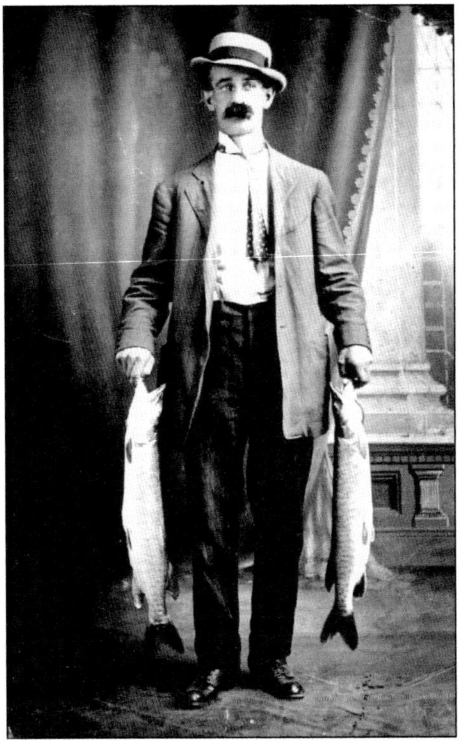

Elk County is noted for its love of the angling sport and its abundance of fine fishing streams. Frank Wegemer was a noted fisherman from the area. It was not unusual for him to walk 30 miles in a day to visit one of his favored fishing streams. Here he is shown with a fine catch.

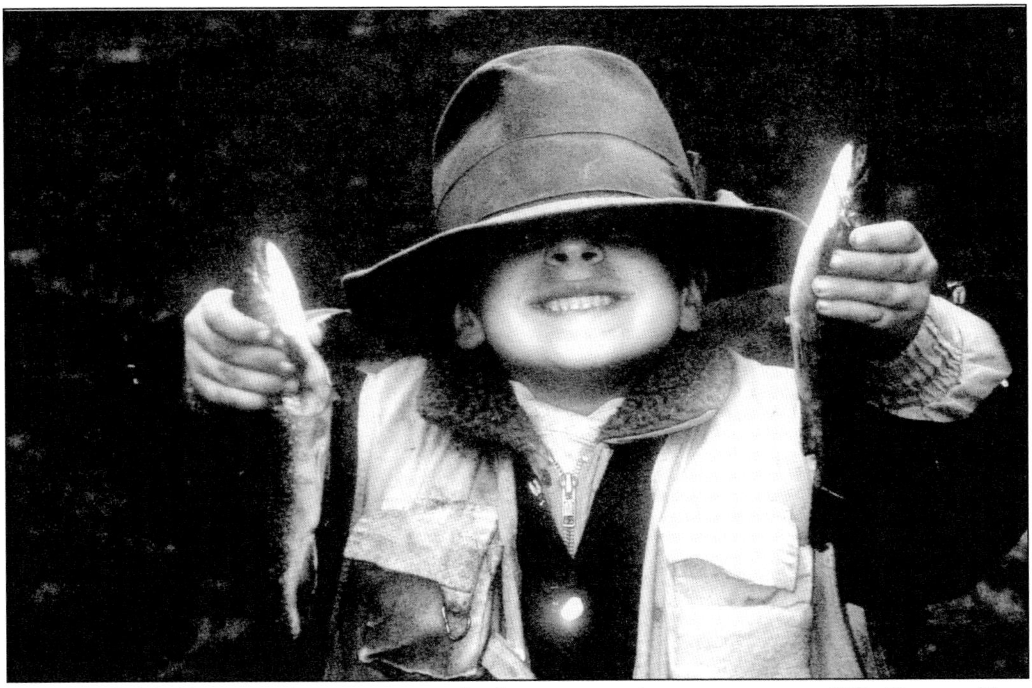

Young and old alike enjoy the excitement of a day spent on the trout streams of Elk County. Here a young angler displays his catch from the Twin Lakes Recreational Area, near Dahoga, part of the Allegheny National Forest. Twin Lakes was constructed by workers in the 1930s as part of the CCC program. The area was one of several CCC camps in Elk County. (Dennis McGeehan.)

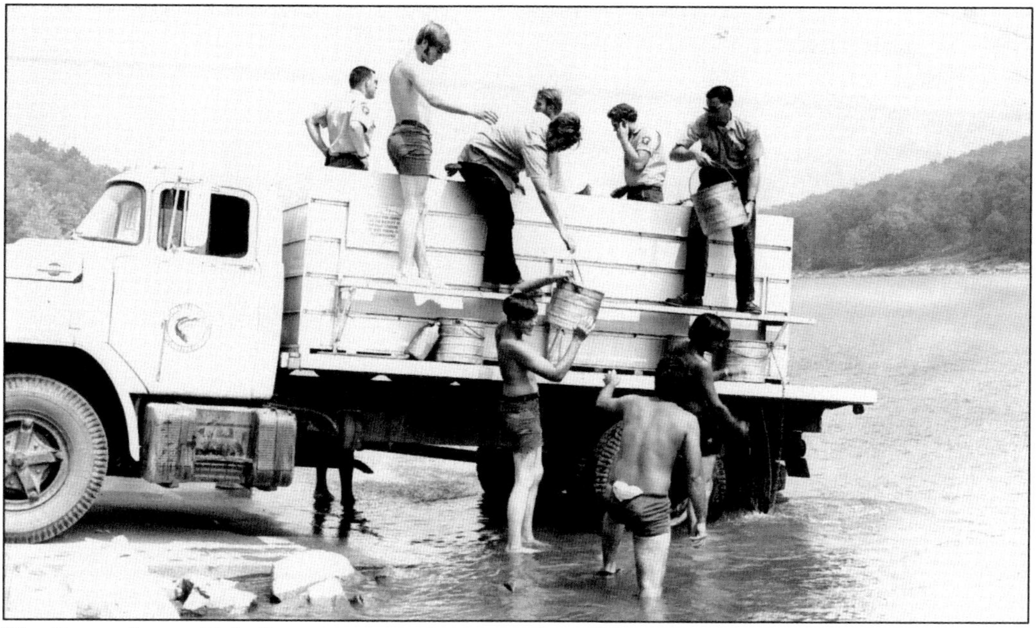

The Pennsylvania Fish Commission is shown stocking fish at East Branch Dam with the help of area volunteers. East Branch Dam is the largest lake in Elk County and attracts many fishermen as well as recreational boaters. Most of the lake's shoreline is undeveloped as it is either state game lands or state forest, and thc lake has the feel of a wilderness paradise.

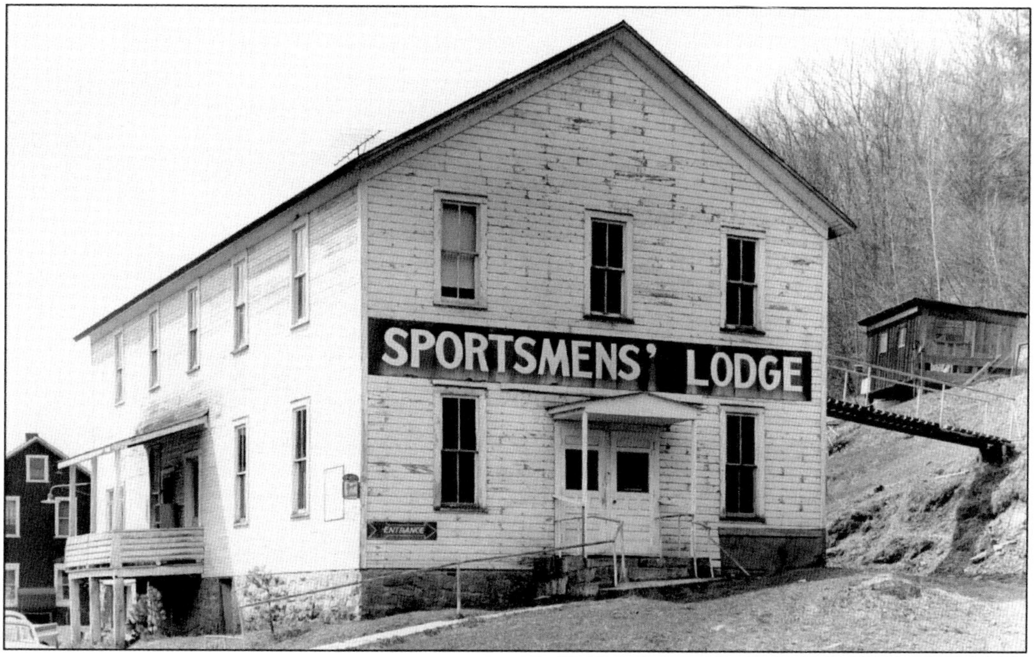

The Sportsmens' Lodge is known as the Hallton Hilton bar today. It is located on the Clarion River within the Allegheny National Forest. The Wild Turkey Federation, the Ruffed Grouse Society, and Ducks Unlimited have all developed projects in the area. Canoeing is very popular on the river from Ridgway to Belltown and into Cook Forest. The Owl's Nest Gas Field is particularly noted for its wildlife.

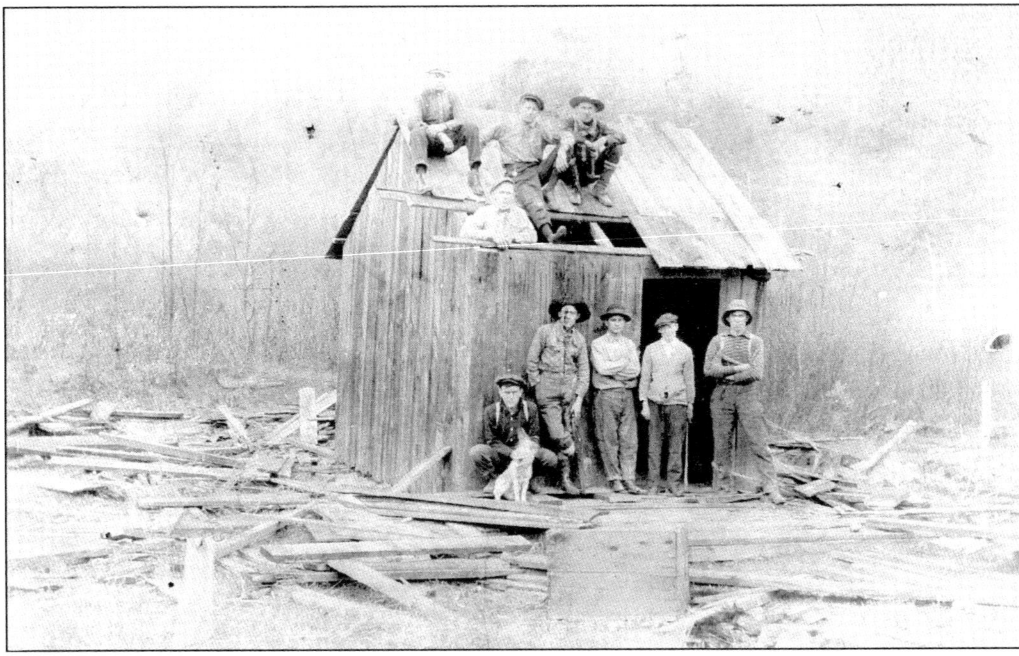

Elk County has many camps, primarily used for hunting or fishing. Many area residents have two houses, in town and "down at camp." Many of the camps are only occupied one or two weeks of the year by city dwellers. Often a group of buddies get together and construct a rough-and-tumble shack just to keep the rain off.

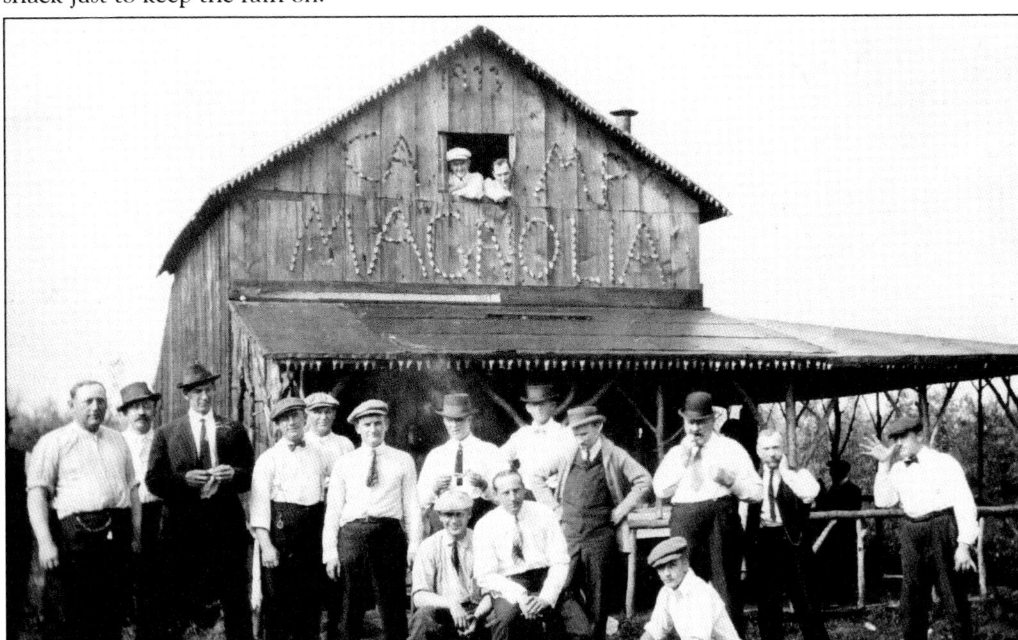

Some Elk County camps are more substantial than others, and some are downright elegant. Here is a scene from the Magnolia Camp in 1913. Not all camps were strictly for hunting or fishing. Social occasions of all kinds were celebrated at camp. This occasion is unknown, but all the men are dressed up and most are wearing ties, including the joker on the right.

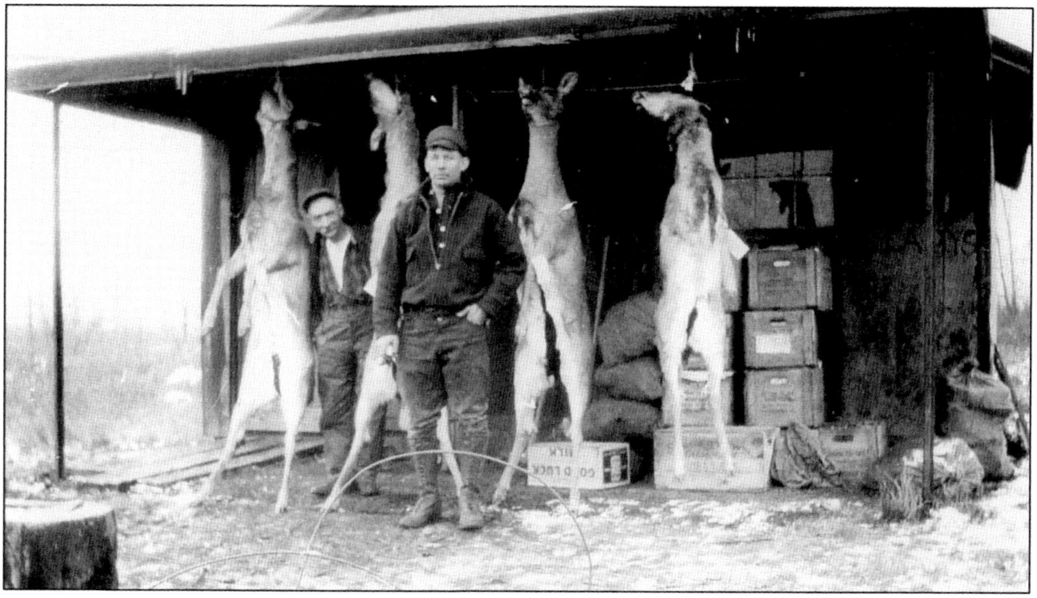

During Pennsylvania's two-week deer season, Elk County camps fill up with hunters from all over, creating a population influx and tourist bonanza. Much of Elk County is still forested wilderness, and the state of the deer population is endlessly debated. Deer camp traditions are solemnly followed and passed down from generation to generation.

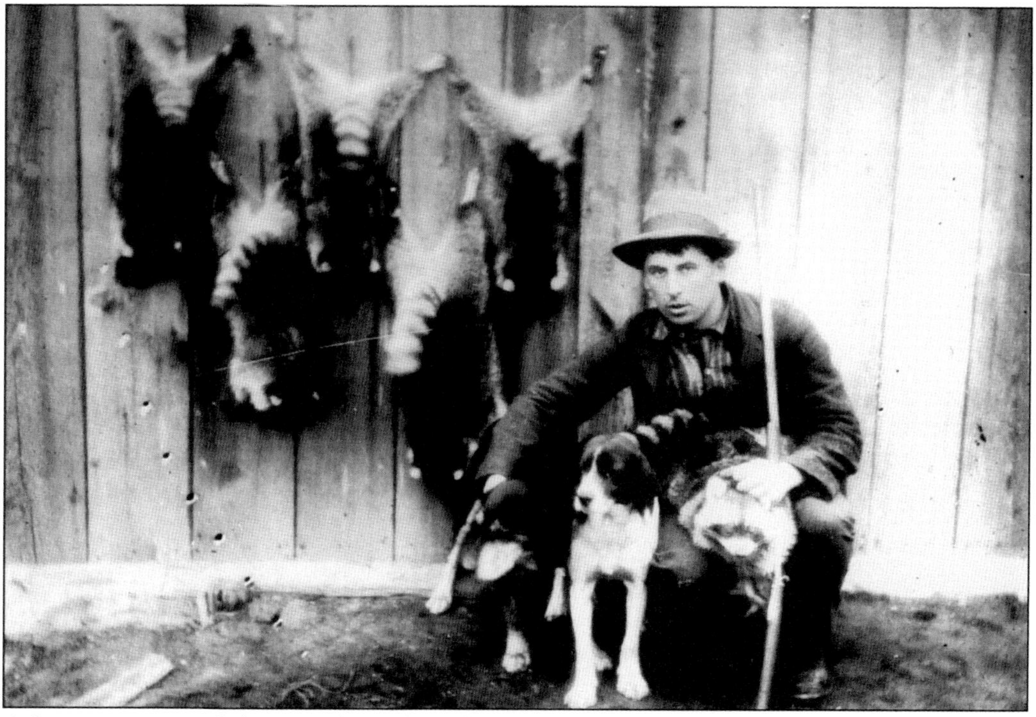

A hunter poses with his coonhounds and a night's take of raccoon hides. Raccoon hunting involves chasing the sound of a hound through the night forest with a flashlight. In the early days of the county, many residents made extra money by trapping and hunting. These ancient sports are still popular with modern hunters.

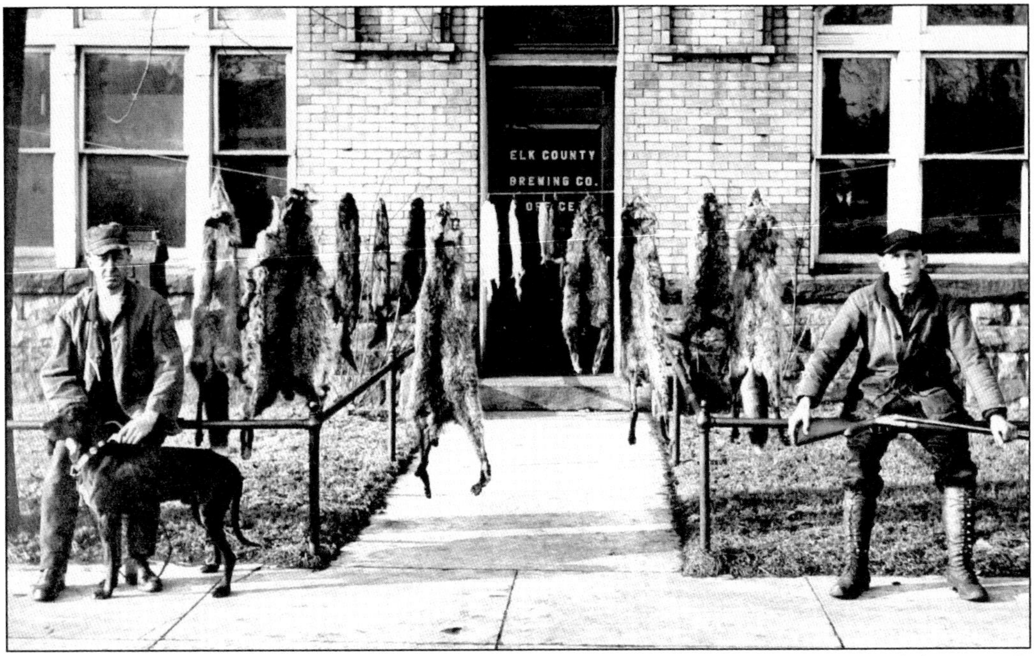

Tony Straub (left) and Fritz Haberberger (right) pose with their hound and a good day's catch of various quarry, including a few ermine, in front of the Elk County Brewing Company office. Wildlife was more plentiful years ago, but this is still an impressive mixed bag. Note the brewery employee looking out the window at right.

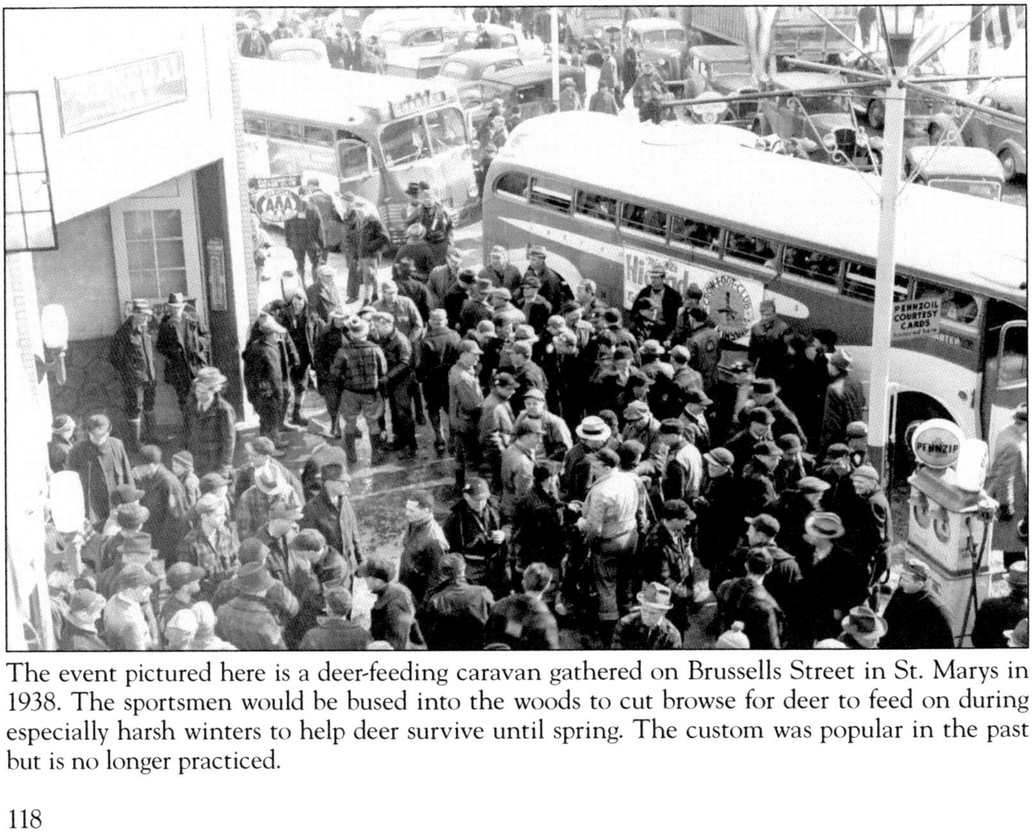

The event pictured here is a deer-feeding caravan gathered on Brussells Street in St. Marys in 1938. The sportsmen would be bused into the woods to cut browse for deer to feed on during especially harsh winters to help deer survive until spring. The custom was popular in the past but is no longer practiced.

Elk County lies in a northerly latitude and enjoys some hearty winter weather. Rather than relocate or complain, many local residents choose to get out and enjoy the seasons all year around. Deep snow is a common occurrence in the county, and hunters must use snowshoes to get around in the backcountry.

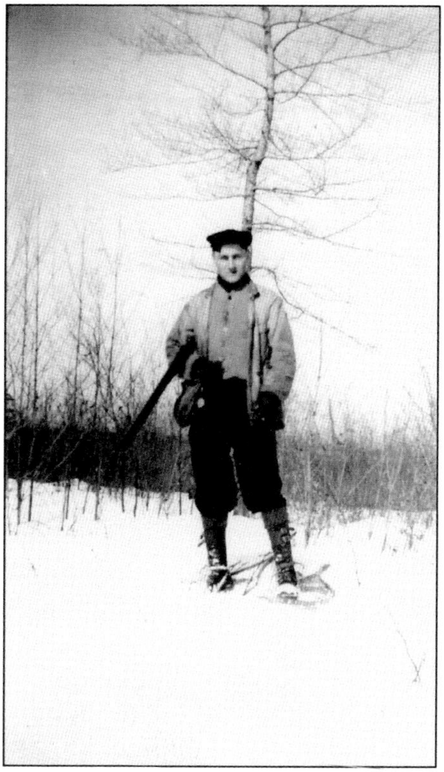

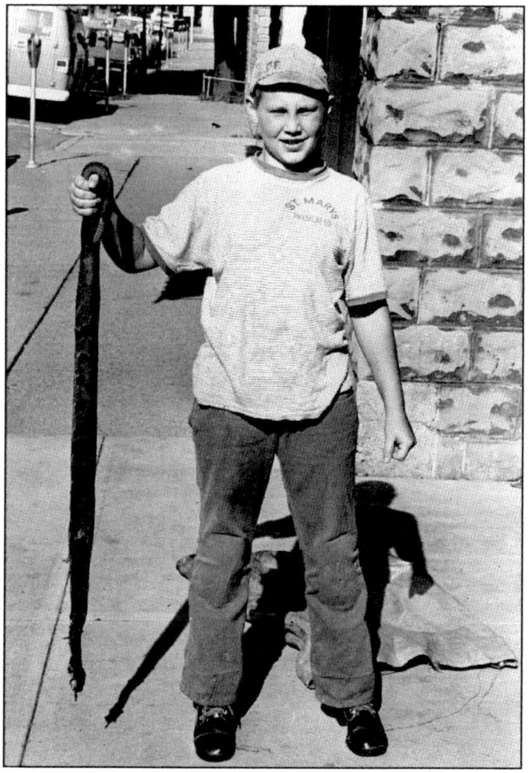

Elk County sits atop the eastern continental divide between the Atlantic Ocean and the Mississippi River and is a mountainous region. Much of the county's terrain is rocky and covered with mountain laurel, which is perfect habitat for timber rattlesnakes. Here a young hiker has brought a rattlesnake into the *St. Marys Daily Press* office for a photograph. Rattlers come in two color phases, yellow and, here, the rarer black phase.

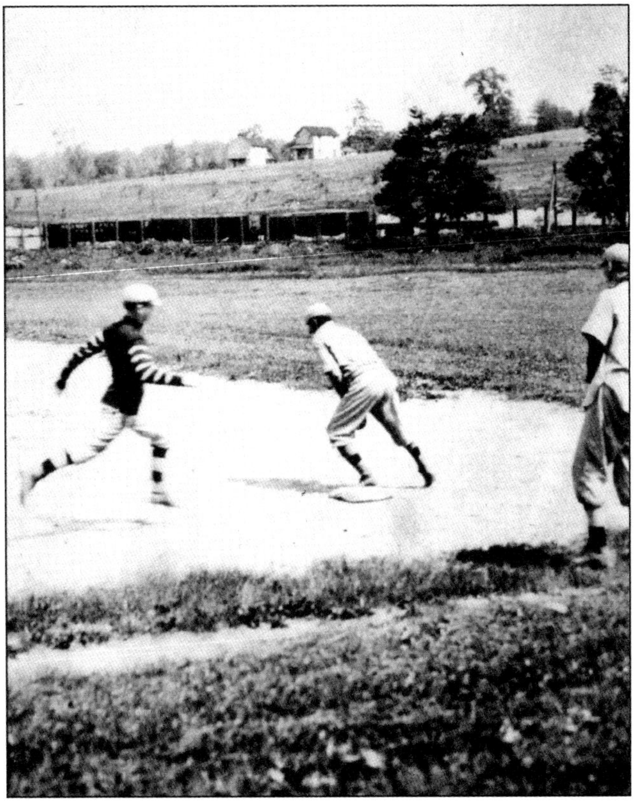

This is a scene from the old fairgrounds baseball park on Theresia Street in St. Marys from around 1895. Baseball was America's pastime, and every town had its own team. America just could not seem to get enough baseball, and for a privileged few, it offered a career. Hall of fame baseball pitcher George "Rube" Waddell was raised in St. Marys. His father operated a store on Theresia Street.

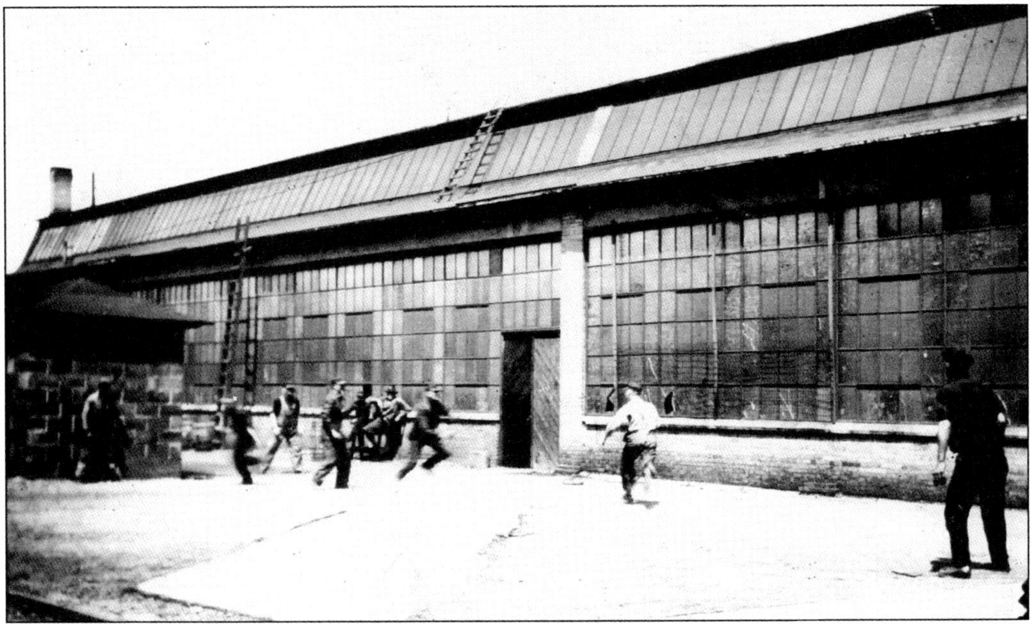

After a morning of hard work, employees of Speer Carbon in St. Marys appear to be using their lunch hour to enjoy a game of touch football. Factory work was rigorous, but the workers always had energy left over to enjoy athletic diversions. Anyone who was present for the end of shift whistle could witness the footrace of employees to enjoy their leisure hours.

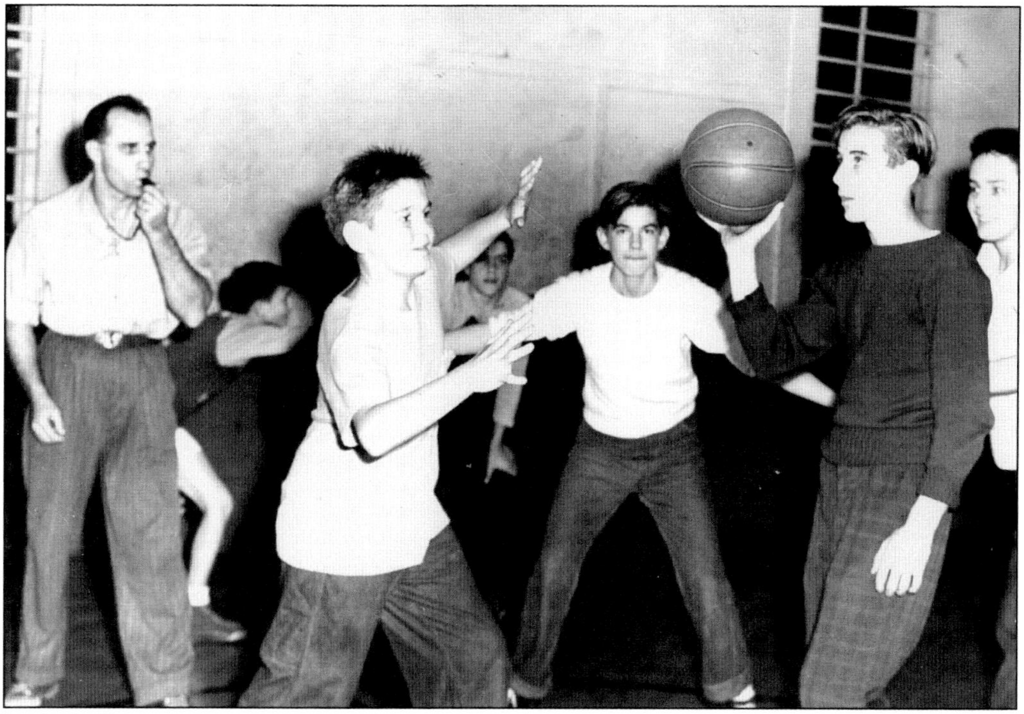

Basketball was a serious sport in the county and extremely competitive whenever the contest pitted area high school teams from Ridgway, Johnsonburg, St. Marys, or Central/Elk County Christian. Pickup basketball was also very popular and occupied many youthful hours in YMCAs, community buildings, Boys Clubs, and playgrounds, as well as schools.

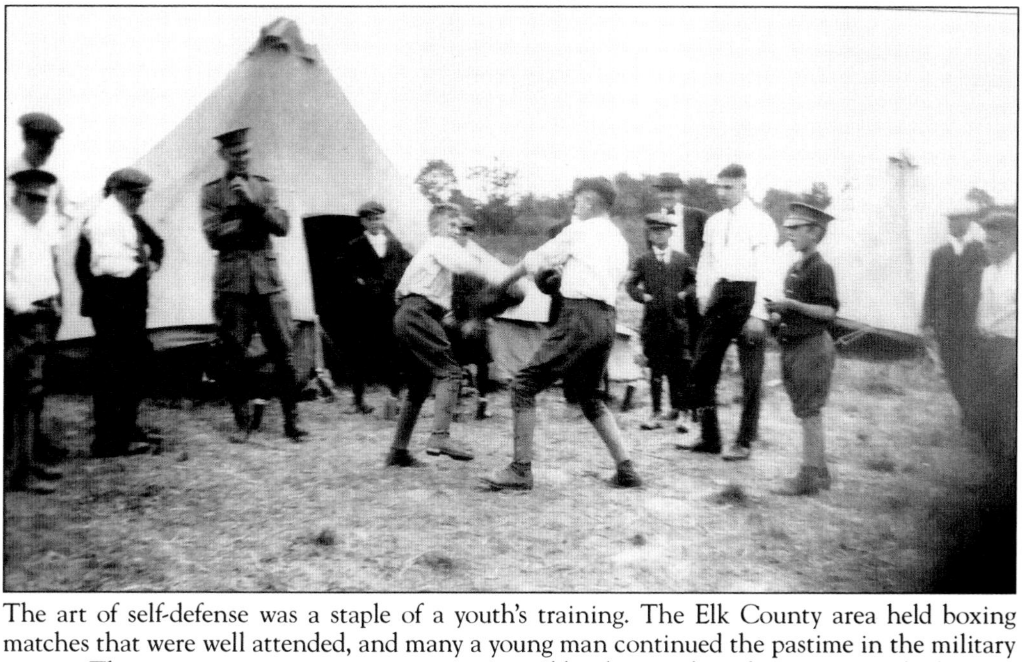

The art of self-defense was a staple of a youth's training. The Elk County area held boxing matches that were well attended, and many a young man continued the pastime in the military service. This event is a camping excursion arranged by the Knights of St. George, which was a church club. The young cadets of the society learn a little boxing at the camping event.

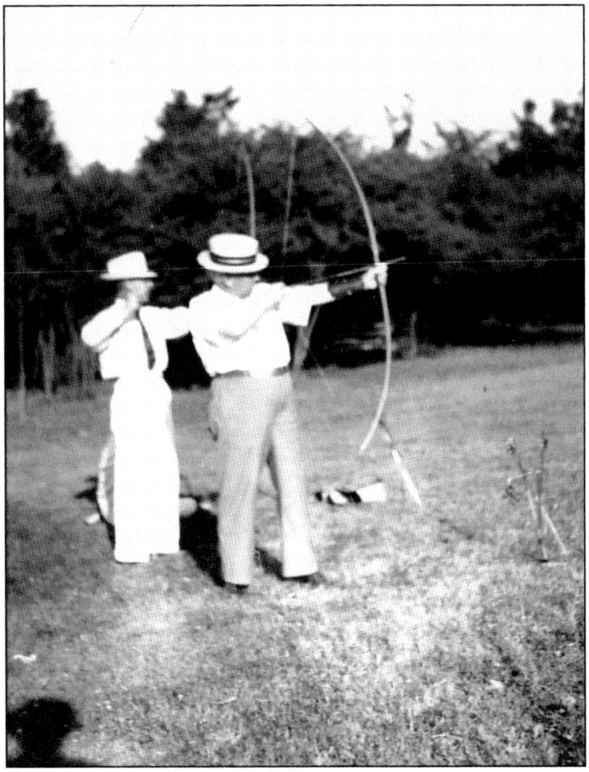

Archery was a popular pastime in the region. The Bucktail Archers is a local club dedicated to the sport, and today there is high-tech, indoor electronic archery available in the county. Part of the appeal of archery is the state's archery season for deer hunting, which draws a lot of sportsmen to Elk County. However, not all archers are hunters. This photograph is from a picnic at Glen Hazel.

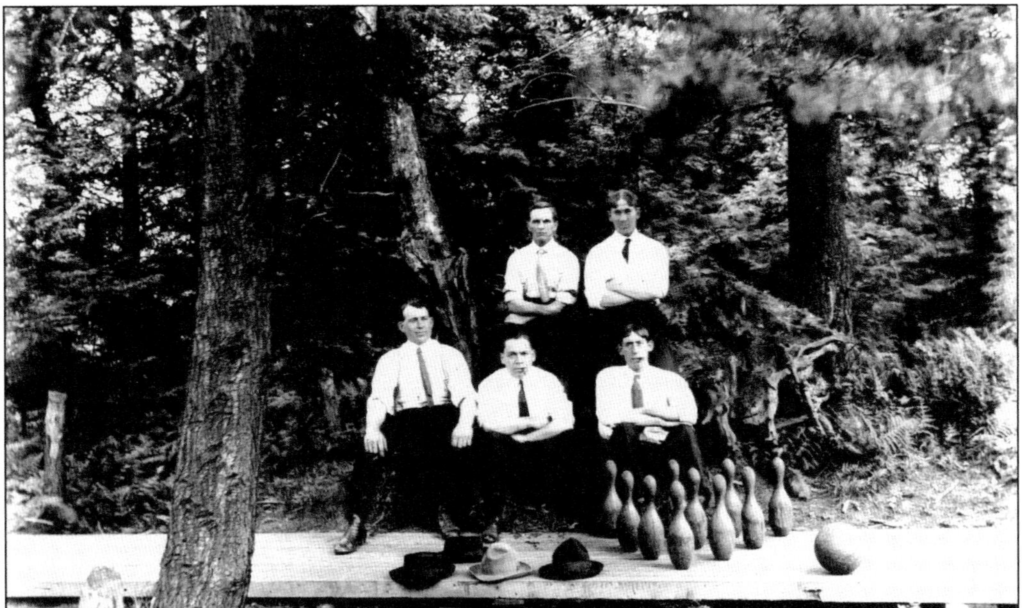

Here is a scene of early bowling in the county taken in Kersey. Note the unpainted wooden pins and bowling ball. Also notice that the single-lane "alley" is open to the elements, and the gutter is as big as all outdoors. The men are all dressed in white shirts and ties, so it is possibly a Sunday afternoon frame.

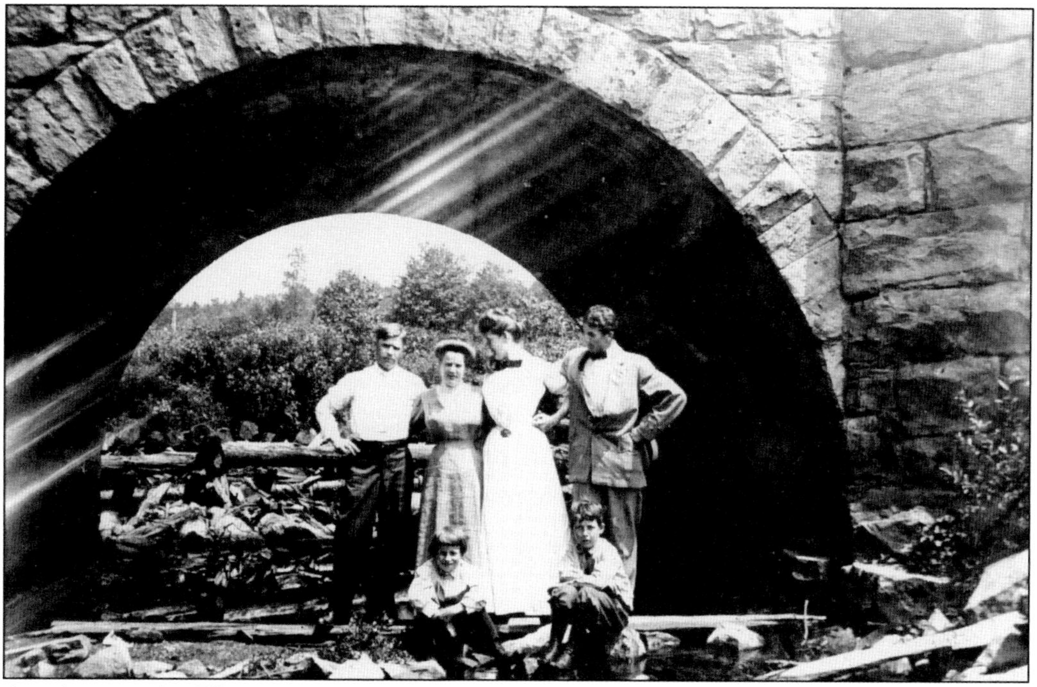

Another popular Elk County recreational activity was hiking excursions. Before everyone had automobiles, people used to enjoy walking, especially on Sundays after church. People thought nothing of covering a dozen miles in a day. This group of hikers has arrived at the Silver Creek Bridge near St. Marys that carried the Pennsylvania Railroad over the creek.

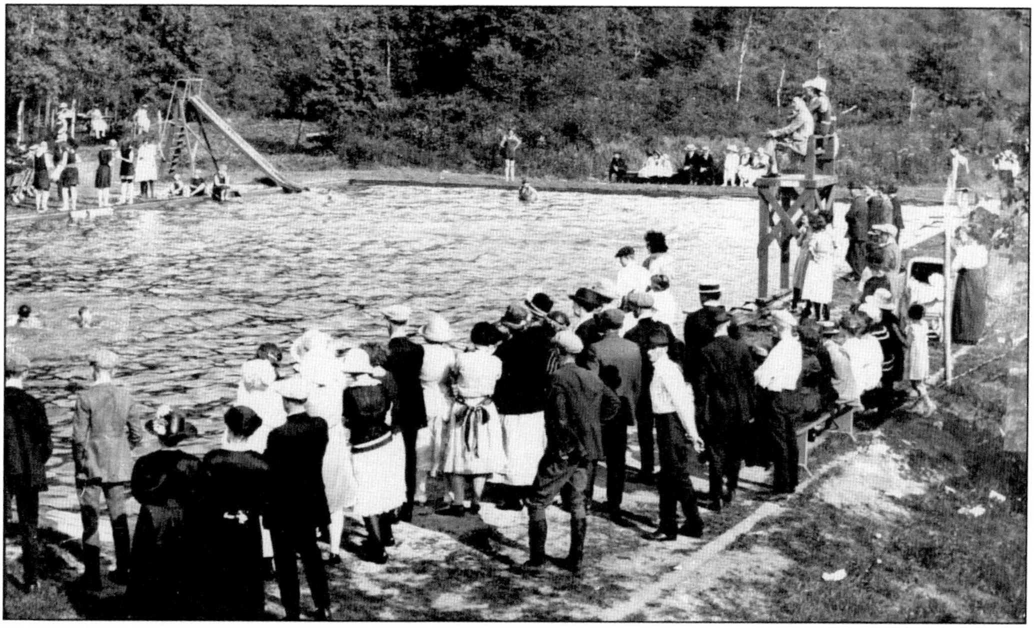

Marshall's Swimming Pool was located in Daguscahonda between Ridgway and St. Marys. This event from 1922 is an organizational picnic. Note the large number of fully dressed spectators. Anyone who ever swam in Marshall's pool remembers the extreme cold water that the mountain stream fed into the pool. Buses from St. Marys and Ridgway ran to the facility all summer.

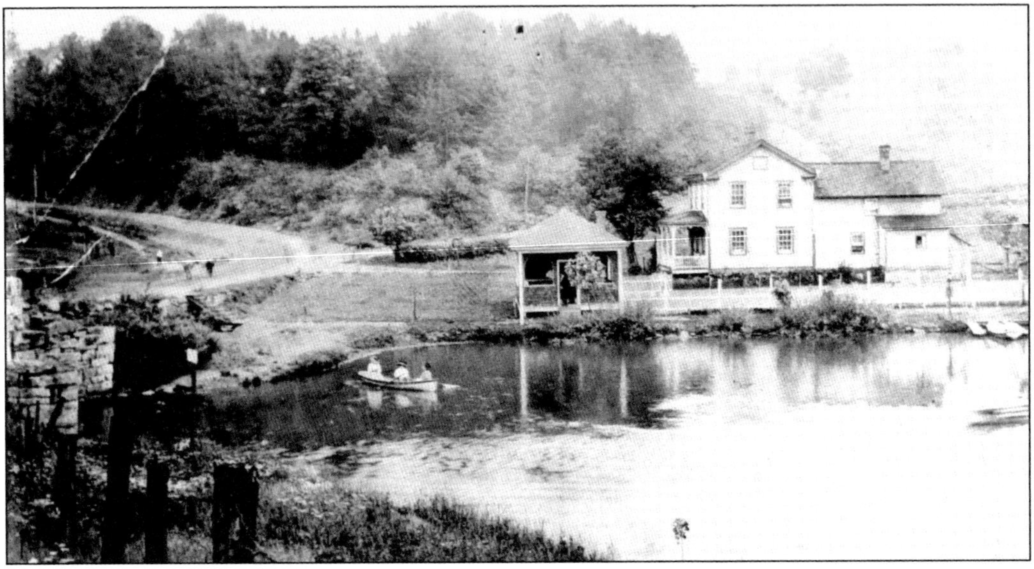

Zwack's Picnic Grove was a popular recreational facility just outside St. Marys on Iron Run. Boats were available for hire, and there were picnic pavilions and a baseball field. When the Million Dollar Highway was built, it buried the beautiful stone arch bridge seen in the left of the photograph.

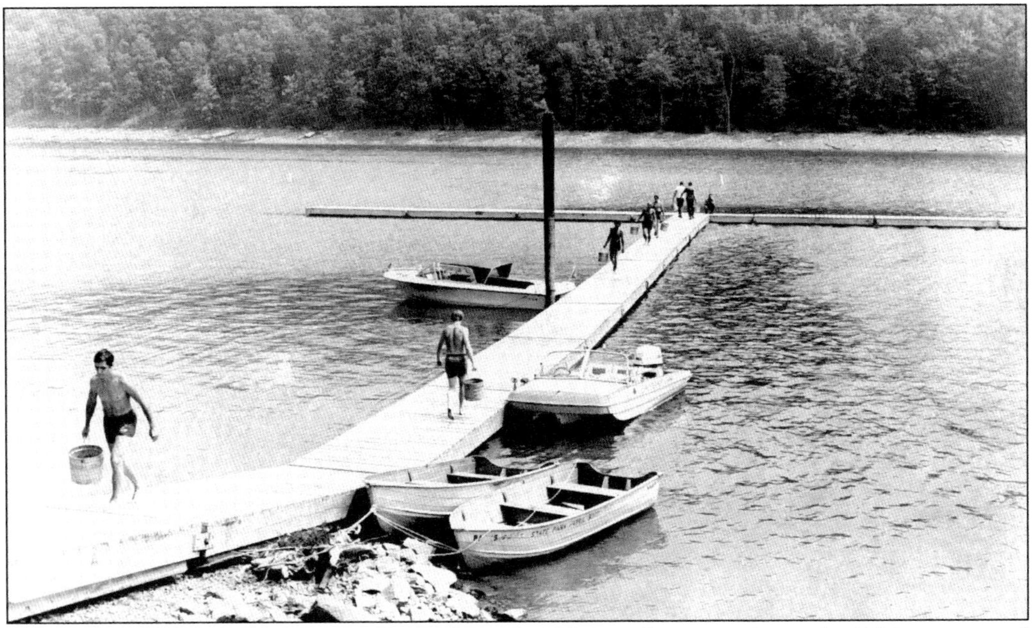

When East Branch Dam was constructed on the Clarion River in the early 1950s, it opened up a whole new era of recreation in Elk County. Boating, water-skiing, fishing, and picnicking attracted residents to the northern edge of the county. This is a scene of fish-stocking at Elk State Park. Just downstream, Bendigo State Park offers bathing in its swimming pool in a beautiful wooded setting.

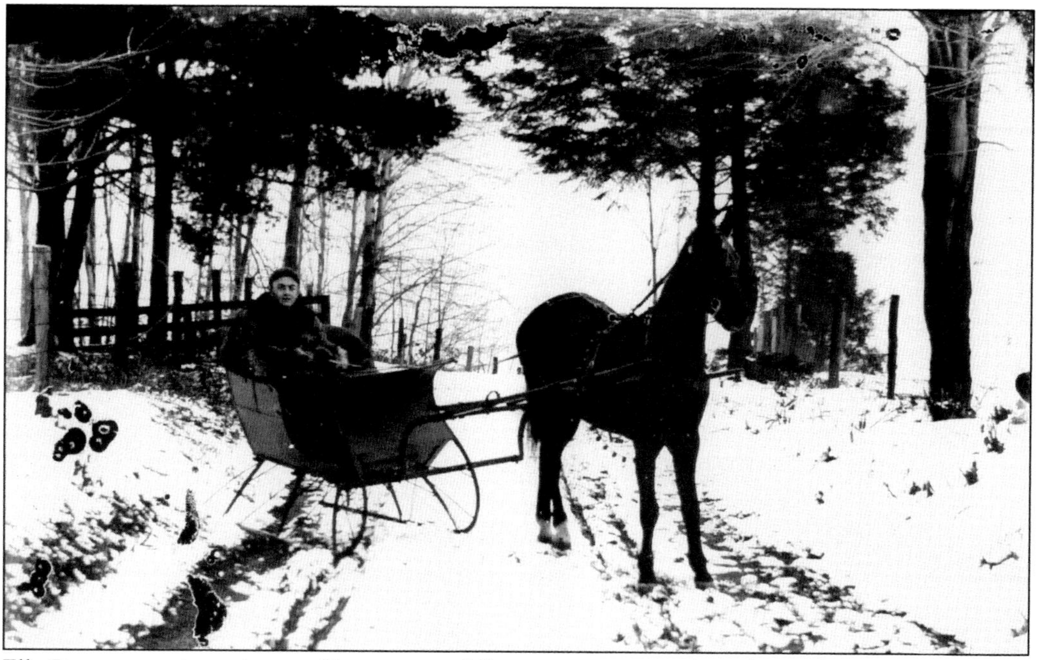

Elk County receives plenty of heavy snowfalls every winter, and roads can become impassable. Today modern snow-removal equipment clears the roads quickly, but in the past, life moved at a slower pace. A horse-drawn sled was practical, efficient, and a very enjoyable way to experience the beauty of the season as this scene from Kersey illustrates.

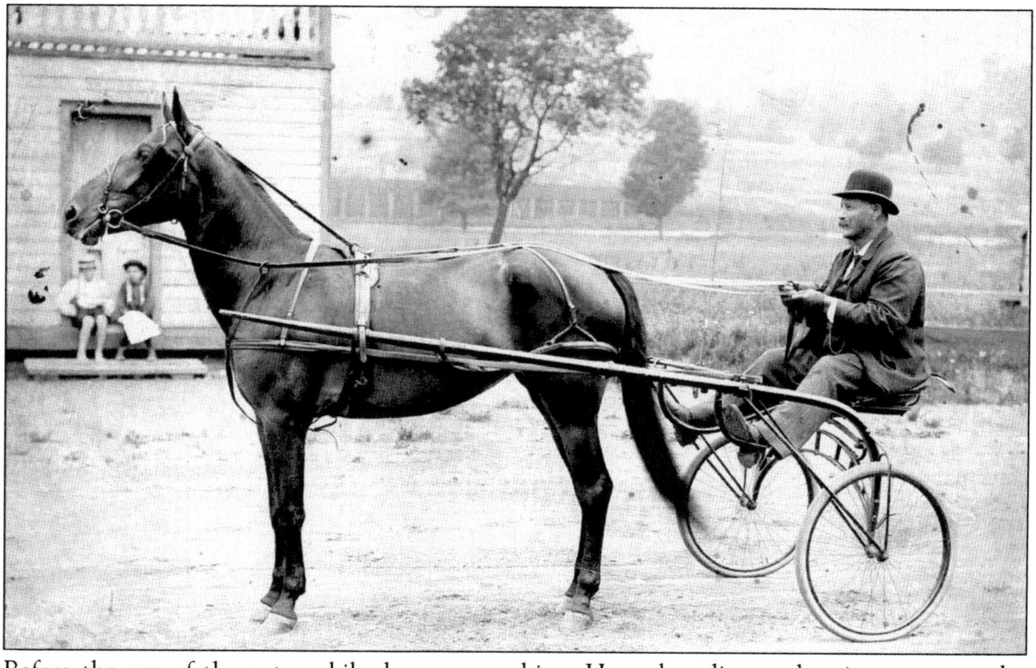

Before the age of the automobile, horses were king. Horse breeding and racing were popular pastimes. People from miles around would bring their horses to the fairgrounds on Theresia Street in St. Marys to test their speed against all competitors. Joseph Hanes is shown in his racing sulky, as two barefoot youths admire the horseflesh.

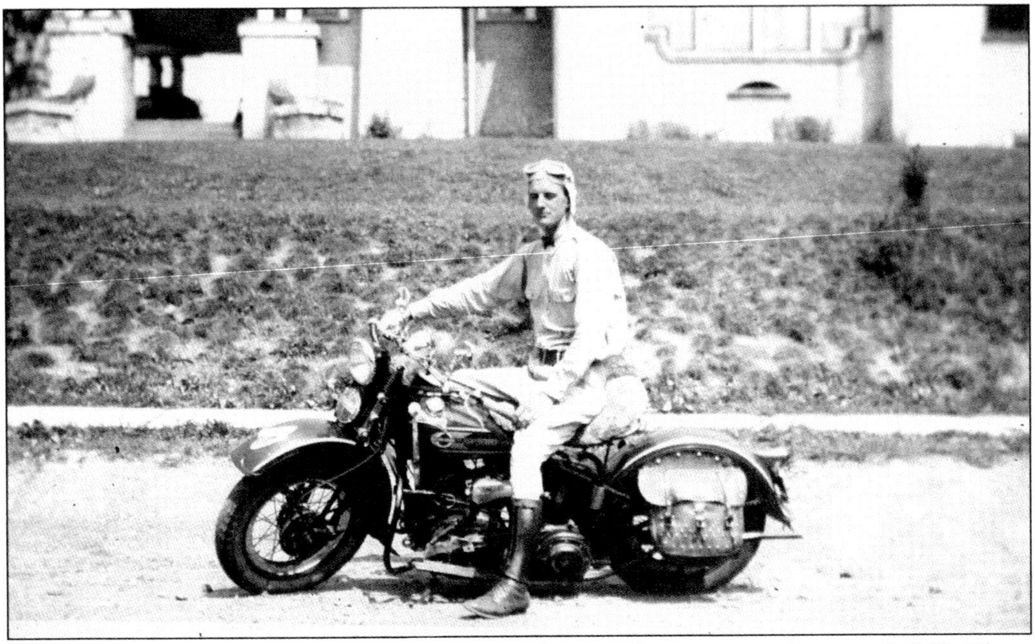

Ted "Tiny" Challingsworth is shown on his Harley-Davidson motorcycle around 1939. There were several motorcycle clubs and racetracks in the Elk County area. Motorcycle enthusiasts would often tour to more distant racetracks to test their skills or simply to see the country in the wind. Several two-wheeled tourists saw the country from coast to coast.

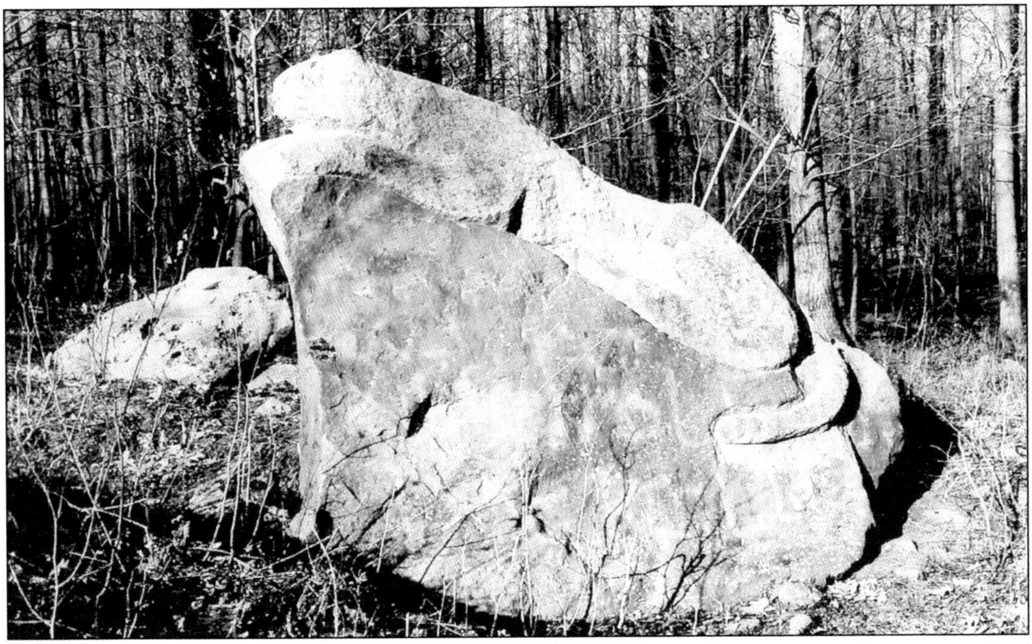

Mountain lions used to roam high on the ridges of Pennsylvania's mountains. Pioneer settlers' accounts are filled with mountain lion lore. Locals still occasionally insist on recent sightings, but the mountain lions are mostly gone. One mountain lion remains. This stone lion on Gardner Hill was carved by local resident Andrew Shutters. Penn State Nittany Lion and Pitt Panther fans both claim it as their own. The lion itself is silent. (Dennis McGeehan.)

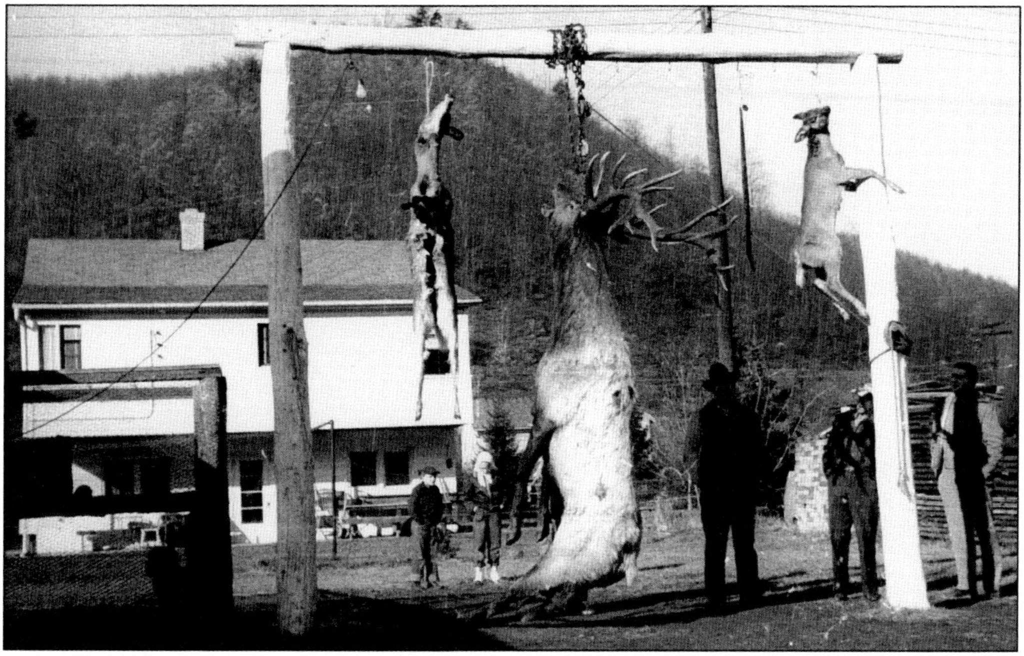

The rugged terrain south and east of St. Marys is the home range of one of the only elk herds east of the Rocky Mountains. It was illegal to shoot elk but occasionally someone shot one mistaking it for a deer. This scene is from Benezette, and the animals were shot in Trout Run. As this photograph illustrates, it is hard to make that mistake.

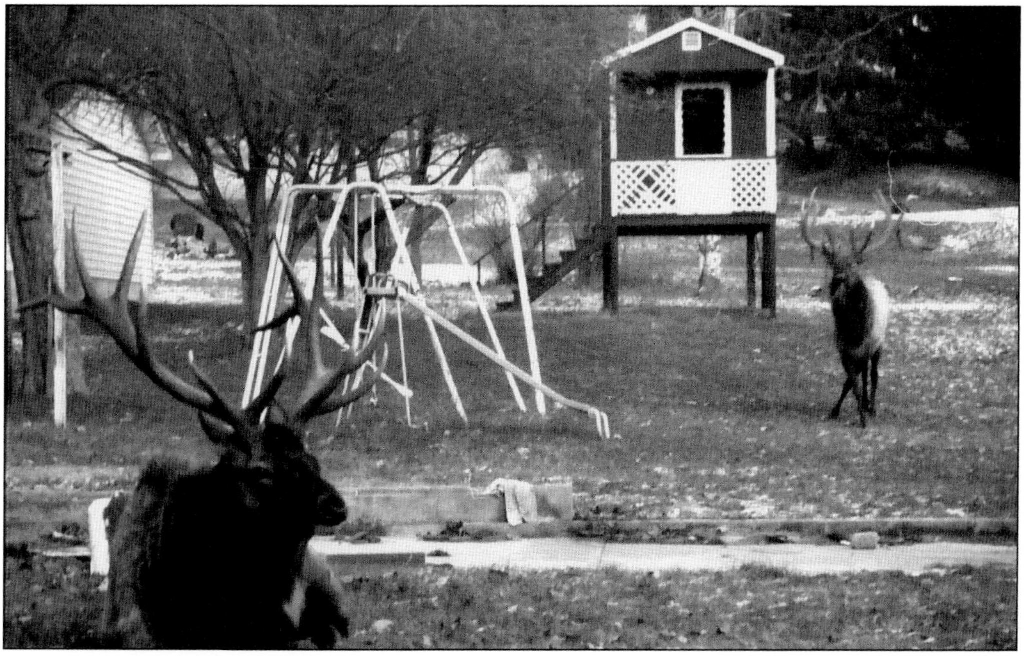

The elk herd has been a blessing and a curse to the county. It brings in wildlife tourists and hunters, but it also tramples farmers' fields and becomes a nuisance to homeowners' privacy. This scene from Benezette shows how tame the animals have become. The elk have often become a traffic hazard when sightseers block the highways. (Dennis McGeehan Wildlife Photography.)